STECK-VAUGHN

PreGED
Language Arts, Writing

REVIEWERS

Robert Christensen
Principal
Handlon Correctional Facility
Michigan Department
of Corrections
Ionia, MI

Arnoldo Hinojosa
Senior Director
Community Initiatives
Harris County Department
of Education
Houston, TX

Linda Correnti
GED Staff Developer
Alternative Schools & Programs
New York City Department
of Education
New York, NY

Nancy Lawrence
E-teacher
KC Distance Learning, Inc.
Butler, PA

Dr. Gary A. Eyre
Consultant
GED Testing Service
Advance Associates
and Consultants
Phoenix, AZ

Charan Lee
Director
Adult Education
Anderson School Districts 1 & 2
Williamston, SC

STECK-VAUGHN
Harcourt Supplemental Publishers

www.steck-vaughn.com

ACKNOWLEDGMENTS

Executive Editor: Ellen Northcutt

Senior Editor: Donna Townsend

Associate Design Director: Joyce Spicer

Senior Designer: Jim Cauthron

Senior Photo Researcher: Alyx Kellington

Editorial Development: Learning Unlimited, Oak Park, IL

Photography Credits: p. 12 © Workbook Stock; p. 148 © José Luis Pelaez, Inc./CORBIS. Additional photography by Getty Royalty Free and Picture Quest.

Literary Credits

p. 14   Reprinted with the permission of Simon & Schuster Books for Young Readers, an imprint of Simon & Schuster Children's Publishing Division from *My Grandmother's Journey* by John Cech. Text copyright © 1991 John Cech.

p. 26   "The Voice from the Wall," from *The Joy Luck Club* by Amy Tan, copyright © 1989 by Amy Tan. Used by permission of G. P. Putnam's Sons, a division of Penguin Putnam Inc.

p. 40   Excerpt from "On Becoming A Scientist" by Dr. Mae C. Jemison as appeared in *Odyssey,* January 1996.

pp. 121, 129   © 1994–1998 Federal Express Corporation. All Rights Reserved. Reprinted by permission.

ISBN 0-7398-6696-6

11 12 13 14 15 16   1421   14 13 12 11

4500276479

CONTENTS

UNIT 1 CREATIVE AND ESSAY WRITING 12

• Elements of Narrative Writing • Time Order • Supporting Details • *Language Links:* Subjects and Predicates • Complete Sentences and Fragments • Pronouns • Point of View • *GED Essay Link:* Using Your Personal Experiences • Apply Your Writing Skills

• Elements of Descriptive Writing • Descriptive Details • Precise Words • Sensory Details • Figurative Language • *Language Links:* Adjectives and Adverbs • Compound Sentences • Complex Sentences • Words in Series • *GED Essay Link:* Using Description • Apply Your Writing Skills

• Elements of Expository Writing • Connecting Words and Phrases • Connecting Words for Style • Expanding Your Vocabulary with Synonyms • Choosing the Best Synonym • Point of View • Polishing Your Work • *Language Links:* Active and Passive Voice • Changing Voice • Sentence Revision • Style and Word Choice • Slang and Word Choice • *GED Essay Link:* Using Examples • Apply Your Writing Skills

• Elements of Persuasive Writing • Using Connecting Words • Writing Compare and Contrast Sentences • Using Specific and Fresh Language • Supporting the Main Idea • *Language Links:* Subject-Verb Agreement • Compound Subjects • Singular and Plural Words • *GED Essay Link:* Using Cause-and-Effect Relationships • Apply Your Writing Skills

• The Writing Process • Step 1: Prewriting— Define Your Topic, Generate Ideas, Organize Your Ideas • Step 2: Writing the First Draft— Writing an Opening Sentence, Developing Supporting Details, Organizing Details, Writing the Conclusion • Step 3: Revising and Editing— Revising, Editing • Step 4: Writing the Final Draft • Step 5: Publishing (Sharing the Final Draft)

UNIT 2 PERSONAL AND WORKPLACE WRITING 88

• Personal Correspondence • Business Correspondence • Writing Style • Personal Letter Format • Business Letter Format • Organizing Business Correspondence • *Language Links:* Capitalization • Punctuation • Apply Your Writing Skills

• Resumes • Personal Data Sheet • Job Application Forms • *Language Link:* Action Verbs and Phrases • Apply Your Writing Skills

• Forms • Order Forms • Invoices • Shipping Forms • Messages • Fax Messages • Email Messages • Memos • *Language Links:* Plurals • Possessives • Contractions • Apply Your Writing Skills

• Time-order Transition Words • Transition Words in "How-to" Writing • Precise Words and Specific Details • Completeness • Clear Presentation • *Language Links:* Verb Tenses • Misplaced and Dangling Modifiers • Parallel Structure • Apply Your Writing Skills

How to Use This Book

The purpose of this book is to help you develop the foundation you need to pass the *GED Language Arts, Writing* Test. In this book, you will be introduced to many different kinds of writing, from creative and essay writing to writing you use in the workplace. You will also learn language skills to improve your usage and sentence structure as well as punctuation, capitalization, and spelling.

Pretest and Posttest

The Pretest is a self-check to see which skills you already know. When you complete all the items in the Pretest, check your work in the Answers and Explanations section in the back of the book. Then fill out the Pretest Evaluation Chart. This chart tells you where each skill is taught in this book. When you complete this book, you will take a Posttest. Compare your Posttest score to your Pretest score to see that your skills have improved.

The Writing Process

Writing is a process, a series of steps. A five-step writing process is presented at the end of Unit 1 in the Essay Writing lesson. The first step of this process will help you generate ideas and organize them before you begin writing. Then you will follow additional steps to write, edit, revise, polish, and publish—or share—your work.

Lessons

Each lesson in Unit 1: Creative and Essay Writing and Unit 2: Personal and Workplace Writing covers one type of writing. You will learn the skills and elements that are unique to that type of writing. As you work through each lesson, you will practice these skills by doing several writing activities. There are three main kinds of writing activities in the lessons.

Practice. Practice activities are short writing exercises that you can usually complete in this book. You will write on the lines provided. Then you can check your answers in the **Answers and Explanations** on pages 228–257.

Write. These are longer writing activities that give you a chance to use the skills you've worked on in the practice activities. Then you can compare your writing to sample answers given in the Answers and Explanations.

Apply Your Writing Skills. This is the last activity in each lesson. Here you will use all the skills you learned in the lesson to produce a piece of writing. These pages guide you through each step of the writing process for a given topic. At the end of the activity, you can add your work to your **Writing**

Portfolio, a special folder or notebook where you collect your best pieces of writing.

Language Links

In addition to Unit 3, language skills are also presented throughout Units 1 and 2 on pages titled Language Link. These language skills are the ones most often used with the types of writing covered in the lessons. Exercises allow you to practice the language skills and, if you need further practice with a particular skill, the colored box next to the Language Exercise directs you to a specific lesson in Unit 3.

GED Essay Links

In the first four lessons you will find a feature entitled GED Essay Link. This section will help you apply the writing skills you have learned to the type of essay you will write on the GED. Each GED Essay Link has a sample topic similar to the one that will appear on the GED. This topic is followed by a sample response. Using this example as a model, you will plan your own response to the topic and write an essay.

Checklist

There is a Revising and Editing Checklist at the end of Unit 3 (pages 216–217). This checklist will help you check your writing and edit it for any errors in grammar, mechanics, or organization. This checklist is a good reference to consult any time you are working on your writing.

Writing at Work

Writing at Work is a two-page feature included in each unit. Each Writing at Work introduces a specific job, describes the writing skills the job requires, and includes comprehension and writing activities related to it. It also gives information about other jobs in the same career area.

Unit Reviews and Mini-Tests

Unit Reviews let you see how well you have learned the language and writing skills covered in each unit. Each Unit Review also includes an **Extension** activity that provides an opportunity for further practice with the writing skills in the unit.

Mini-Tests follow each Unit Review. These timed practice tests allow you to practice your skills with the kinds of questions that you will see on the actual GED Test.

Setting Goals

A goal is something that you aim for, something you want to achieve. What is your long-term goal for using this book? You may want to get your GED or you may just want to learn more about writing. These are large goals that may take you some time to accomplish.

Write your long-term goal for writing.

_____

_____

_____

This section of the book will help you to think about how you already use writing and then to set some goals for what you would like to learn in this book. These short-term goals will be stepping stones to the long-term goal you wrote.

Check each activity that you do. Add more activities.

I use writing in my everyday life to

_____ communicate with friends via email or letters

_____ write memos at my job

_____ fill out applications or forms

_____ keep track of daily events in a journal

_____ other _____

_____

_____

List your experiences with using writing skills

What I've Liked	What I Haven't Liked
_____	_____
_____	_____
_____	_____
_____	_____
_____	_____

Think about your writing goals.

1. I decided to improve my writing skills when I _____

    _____

    _____

2. My writing goals include (check as many as you like)

    ☐   writing a resume and filling out a job application

    ☐   being able to write an effective cover letter

    ☐   using correct spelling when I write

    ☐   using proper grammar when I write

    ☐   communicating with family and friends through writing

    ☐   using writing as a means of communication at work

    ☐   using details to make my writing more interesting

    ☐   writing to persuade others

    ☐   explaining a process through writing

    ☐   writing about events that are important to me

    ☐   other _____

    _____

    _____

3. I will meet my long-term goal for writing when I am able to

    _____

    _____

    _____

Keep track of your goals.

As you work through this book, turn back often to this page. Add more goals at any time you wish. Check each goal that you complete.

Learn about the skills you have.

Complete the Pretest that begins on the next page. It will help you learn more about you strengths and weaknesses in writing. You may wish to change some items in your list of goals after you have taken the Pretest and completed the Pretest Evaluation Chart on page 11.

Use this Pretest before you begin Unit 1. Don't worry if you cannot easily answer all the questions. The Pretest will help you determine which writing skills you are already strong in and which skills you need to practice further. Read and answer the items that follow. Check your answers on pages 228–230. Then use the chart on page 11 to plan your course of study.

Capitalization and Punctuation

Write *C* if the underlined part is correct. Write *E* if there is an error in capitalization or punctuation.

_____ 1. Who do you consider to be a hero these <u>days.</u>

_____ 2. Many people think of <u>actors athletes, or singers</u> as heroes.

_____ 3. My husband, for example, thinks that former <u>Dallas Cowboys</u> running back Emmitt Smith is the greatest.

_____ 4. If you don't already know, Smith holds the all-time rushing record in the <u>National Football league.</u>

_____ 5. He set the record on <u>October 27 2002.</u>

_____ 6. Some people think football players are <u>heroes but</u> I think my Aunt Ann is just as much a hero as Emmitt Smith or any other athlete.

_____ 7. Aunt Ann lives and works in <u>Chicago, Illinois.</u>

_____ 8. She goes to school during the <u>day, and</u> works as a nurse's aide at night.

_____ 9. Next <u>march</u> she will graduate and become a licensed physician's assistant.

_____ 10. She'll work in the office of <u>Dr. Jonah Scott.</u>

_____ 11. My <u>Aunt</u> is a hero to me because she helps people selflessly and tirelessly.

_____ 12. In fact, both Emmitt <u>Smith, and</u> Aunt Ann are heroes because they inspire people to work hard and do their best.

Nouns, Plurals, and Possessives

Write the correct word to complete each sentence.

13. Sometimes _____ cannot get their children to behave.

    parents   **parents'**   **parent's**

14. They appreciate getting an _____ advice.

    experts   **experts'**   **expert's**

15. Experts say it is wise to show _____ an example of good behavior.

    childrens   **children's**   **children**

16. Mothers and fathers are the most important role models in their children's _____ .

    lifes   **lives**   **life's**

17. Also, be consistent, and make sure your _____ rules do not change.

    familys   **family's**   **families**

18. Remind children to show good manners when they go to a _____ house to play.

    friends   **friends'**   **friend's**

Spelling, Homonyms, and Contractions

Write the correct word to complete each sentence.

Did you _____ that diamonds are the hardest
   (19) no   know

substance on Earth? You can only _____ a diamond with
                                   (20) break   brake

a sharp blow in a certain spot. The diamond will then split, producing

_____ with flat, even surfaces. A diamond's value is
(21) pieces   peaces

based on its clarity, color, and _____ . Diamonds are
                                 (22) weight   wait

used in jewelry, but they can also be used to drill a _____
                                                      (23) hole   whole

through metal because _____ so very hard. In fact,
                       (24) their   they're

_____ difficult to think of anything that a diamond
(25) its   it's

_____ cut _____ .
(26) ca'nt   can't   (27) threw   through

Pronouns

If the underlined part is correct, write *C* in the blank. If it is wrong, write it correctly in the blank.

_____ 28. How does your family feel about <u>you</u> working at this restaurant?

_____ 29. When your application form is complete, give it to Mary or <u>I</u>.

_____ 30. If you need another copy, just ask for <u>it</u>.

_____ 31. Every woman who wants a job here must think about <u>their</u> ability to work nights and weekends.

_____ 32. The owner and <u>him</u> want to hire only qualified people.

_____ 33. Jean and Paula are waitresses here, so ask <u>her</u> what the job is like.

Adjectives and Adverbs

Write the correct word to complete each sentence.

34. It is a fact that widows and widowers do not live as

_____ as married people.

well   good   best

35. Their illnesses are _____ than those of married people.

worse   worst   bad

36. They often recover from illnesses more _____.

slow   slowly   slower

37. They are also likely to die _____.

soon   sooner   soonest

38. Perhaps a lonely life is the _____ life of all.

difficult   difficultest   most difficult

Verb Tenses

Write the correct verb form to complete each sentence.

39. In the past, recovery from surgery _____ slow.

    is   was

40. No one _____ home quickly after an operation.

    goed   went

41. Until recently, many doctors _____ with them from medical school some old-fashioned ideas of what the human body could do.

    bringed   brang   brought

42. Today, medical students _____ that patients should resume activity as soon as possible following surgery.

    learn   learned

43. Scientists expect that in the future many surgeries

    _____ necessary because of new healing technologies.

    were not   will not be   are not

Subject-Verb Agreement

Write the correct verb form to complete each sentence.

44. All the supervisors on this floor _____ that too many employees are arriving late.

    agrees   agree

45. We understand that there _____ several reasons for this situation.

    is   are

46. Ms. Gomez and her staff _____ come up with some possible solutions.

    has   have

47. Although each one of us _____ we have a good excuse for tardiness, there is usually no good reason.

    believes   believe

Sentences, Fragments, and Run-Ons

Write *S* next to each correctly written sentence (complete thought), *F* next to each fragment (incomplete thought), and *RO* next to each run-on (two or more complete thoughts that run together without correct punctuation and/or a connecting word).

_____ 48. One good way to save money.

_____ 49. You should take some time to learn basic car repair.

_____ 50. One cost-saving measure is fixing your own flat tire any able-bodied person can do it.

_____ 51. Can also buy basic auto supplies at a discount store.

_____ 52. You can change your own oil you can rotate your own tires.

_____ 53. If you are willing to invest time up front.

Compound and Complex Sentences

Combine each pair of sentences with the connecting word given in parentheses. Use correct punctuation.

54. **(and)** The sun dries out your skin. It affects the growth of skin cells.

_____

_____

55. **(but)** The sun feels good. It's not good for you.

_____

_____

56. **(if)** You should see a doctor. A mole changes shape or color.

_____

_____

57. **(because)** Moles can be cancerous. It is a good idea to pay attention to changes.

_____

_____

Parallelism, Modifiers, and Clarity

Underline the word or phrase that best completes each sentence.

58. Some of the best ways to reduce stress are to cut back on obligations, to have clear priorities, and (**understanding, to understand**) what makes you anxious.

59. Knowing your stressors, (**it is easier to, you can more easily**) control your environment to avoid anxiety.

60. In (**today's world, the current world of the present day**), reducing stress is a challenge.

Paragraph Organization

Read the following paragraphs. Circle the number of the best answer to each question.

(A)

(1) Choosing whom to vote for in an election can be a tough task. (2) Before you even consider the candidates, you need to have some idea of what your own opinions are on domestic issues such as the economy, education, and healthcare. (3) To develop your own opinions, you need to read newspapers, listen to people you respect, and do some soul searching. (4) You also need to think about your opinions on world affairs such as the environment, peace vs. war, and third-world development.

(B)

(5) Again, reading a variety of newspapers and perhaps listening to the candidates' debate are useful ways to find out their views on issues. (6) The cost of many newspapers is rising due to fewer advertisers. (7) Most often, public television and radio are the best ways to get unbiased reporting of candidates' viewpoints.

61. Where is the best place to move sentence 4 in paragraph A?

    (1) before sentence 2   (2) after sentence 2

62. Which of the following would be the best sentence to insert at the beginning of paragraph B?

    (1) Once you have developed your own opinions, it's time to identify a candidate who most closely represents your point of view.

    (2) Casting a vote in an election is an obligation for all citizens.

63. Which sentence should be removed from paragraph B?

    (1) sentence 6   (2) sentence 7

Writing Assignment

This part of the Pretest will help you determine how well you write. You will write about something that happened to you. To write clearly, follow these steps.

1. Read the topic carefully.

2. Get your thoughts flowing. On a separate sheet of paper, write down all your ideas that relate to the topic.

3. Plan what you will say before you start to write. Choose the details of your story that will be the most interesting. Decide the order in which you will tell them.

4. Write your first draft on a separate sheet of paper.

5. Review what you have written, and make any changes that will improve your work.

6. Read over your writing for correct sentence structure, spelling, punctuation, capitalization, and usage.

7. Copy your final draft on a separate sheet of paper.

TOPIC

Write about a decision that changed your life. Tell about the events leading up to the decision, how you eventually decided, and the consequences of your choice. Try to write at least three paragraphs.

When you have finished your writing assignment, give it to your instructor or a person you know with good writing skills. You may also give the person the checklist on page 10 to help him or her evaluate your essay.

Writing Assignment Evaluation Guide

Put a check mark in the YES or NO box for each question.

	YES	NO

Content

For Content, if an area is checked NO, see pages 16–17, 27–28, 40–41, 62–63, 70–81

	YES	NO
Does the content achieve its purpose—that is, does it respond to the assignment topic?	☐	☐
Is the content right for its audience?	☐	☐
Is the main idea stated clearly?	☐	☐
Does each paragraph have a topic sentence?	☐	☐
Are topic sentences supported by details?	☐	☐
Are details written in a logical order?	☐	☐
Is the right amount of information included—that is, are any details missing? Are any details unnecessary?	☐	☐
Does the writing hold your interest?	☐	☐

Style and Word Choice

For Style and Word Choice, see pages 42–44, 47–51, 60–61

	YES	NO
Are thoughts and ideas expressed clearly?	☐	☐
Are any ideas repeated?	☐	☐
Are some words used too many times?	☐	☐
Are precise words and fresh language used?	☐	☐
Are slang and informal expressions used appropriately, if at all?	☐	☐

Sentence Structure

For Sentence Structure, Usage, and Mechanics, see pages 150–167, 168–183, 184–207.

	YES	NO
Are all sentences complete sentences?	☐	☐
Are any sentences too long and hard to understand?	☐	☐
Are any sentences too short and choppy?	☐	☐

Usage

	YES	NO
Are nouns and pronouns used correctly?	☐	☐
Are verbs used correctly?	☐	☐
Are adjectives and adverbs used correctly?	☐	☐

Mechanics

See also the Evaluation Chart on page 11 for pages to practice specific topics.

	YES	NO
Are all words spelled correctly?	☐	☐
Is punctuation used correctly?	☐	☐
Are words capitalized correctly?	☐	☐

Overall, on a scale of 1–4, how would you rate

this piece of writing? _____

10

Pretest Evaluation Chart

The chart below will help you determine your strengths and weaknesses in language skills.

Directions

Check your answers on pages 228–230. On the chart below, circle the number of each question you answered correctly on the Pretest. Count the number of questions you answered correctly in each row. Write the number in the Total Correct space in each row. (For example, in the Usage row, write the number correct in the blank before *out of 20*.) Complete this process for the remaining rows. Then add the four totals to get your total correct for the Pretest.

Skill Area	Questions	Total Correct	Pages
Usage			
Pronouns	28, 29, 30, 31, 32, 33	_____ out of 20	20, 152–156
Adjectives and Adverbs	34, 35, 36, 37, 38		30–31, 157–160
Verb Tenses	39, 40, 41, 42, 43		161–164
Subject-Verb Agreement	44, 45, 46, 47		64–65, 165–167
Sentence Structure			
Sentences, Fragments, and Run-ons	48, 49, 50, 51, 52, 53	_____ out of 13	19, 168–171
Compound and Complex Sentences	54, 55, 56, 57		32–34, 172–173, 176–177
Parallelism, Modifiers, and Clarity	58, 59, 60		49, 138–139, 174–175, 178–179, 180, 182–183
Mechanics			
Capitalization and Punctuation	1, 2, 3, 4, 5, 6, 7, 8, 9, 10, 11, 12	_____ out of 27	97–99, 184–189
Nouns, Plurals, and Possessives	13, 14, 15, 16, 17, 18		125–126, 150–151, 190–191
Spelling, Homonyms, and Contractions	19, 20, 21, 22, 23, 24, 25, 26, 27		125–127, 154, 191–196
Paragraph Organization	61, 62, 63	_____ out of 3	198–207

Total Correct for Pretest _____ out of 63

If you answered fewer than 56 questions correctly, look at the skill areas listed above. In which areas do you need more practice? Page numbers to refer to for practice are given in the right-hand column above.

UNIT 1

Creative and Essay Writing

Creative and Essay Writing

Creative and Essay Writing

Through **creative and essay writing,** you can express yourself. You can write stories about your own life or invent stories about other people and places. You can write your ideas in essays and tell about the experiences you've had.

Have you ever written a story or an essay? What was it about?

_____

_____

Thinking About Creative and Essay Writing

You may not realize how familiar you already are with creative and essay writing. Think about what you have written recently.

Check the box for each activity you did.

☐ Did you write a letter?

☐ Did you send an email message?

☐ Did you write in a diary or journal?

☐ Did you write a note to explain something to someone?

☐ Did you take a message from someone who telephoned?

☐ Did you write a fictional story?

☐ Did you write a true story?

Write some other activities where you have used writing skills.

_____

_____

_____

Previewing the Unit

In this unit, you will learn:

● how to write a story that comes alive for your reader

● how to write good descriptions

● how to inform or explain about events or ideas

● how to get across your own point of view

● how to write a GED-type essay with more than one paragraph

Lesson 1	**Narrative Writing**
Lesson 2	**Descriptive Writing**
Lesson 3	**Expository Writing**
Lesson 4	**Persuasive Writing**
Lesson 5	**Essay Writing**

LESSON 1

Narrative Writing

Elements of Narrative Writing

Narrative writing is a form of writing in which you tell a story about yourself or someone else. If you are writing about yourself, the piece is called a **personal narrative.** This might be an anecdote, a brief story about something that happened to you. Or it could be an autobiography, the story of your life.

Writing a personal narrative in a diary or journal is a good way to think about things that you have done or that have happened to you. It is also a good way to consider what you might do differently. A personal narrative in a letter can connect you with a family member or friend.

A narrative essay is a way for you to tell a story about real people—yourself or someone you know. A fictional story is a kind of narrative writing, too. In a fictional story, you make up the people and the events that happen to them.

EXAMPLE Below is an example of a personal narrative. The narrator is the Russian grandmother of writer John Cech, to whom she is telling her story. She survived wars and troubles in Eastern Europe before she came to the United States.

Then came World War II. The enemy marched through our country and took everything—our animals, our crops, our young people. Again we tried to escape to somewhere safe, but soldiers were everywhere, ours and theirs. Both would shoot you if they caught you—they thought you might be a spy.

We hid in a forest while the fighting raged around us. That's where your mother was born, by the banks of a river on a cold March day. When she slept in my arms, I remember thinking that there must still be angels.

WRITE In the example, John Cech's grandmother realized something. She learned that there is hope and goodness even in times of war and fear.

On a separate piece of paper, write a personal narrative paragraph about an event in your life that taught you something important.

You might choose the birth or death of a loved one. You might write about your wedding day or a day that was ordinary until something unusual happened. Describe the events that led up to the moment when you learned an important lesson.

Time Order

When you write a narrative, you can tell about the events in the order in which they happened. This is called **time order.** Time order is a good way to organize a narrative. It makes the story easy to understand.

EXAMPLE Below is an example of a narrative written in time order.

When Sam moved to a new apartment, he had to make lots of arrangements. First, he had to call the water and electric company to turn on the utilities. Then he had to get his cousin Vincent to help him move his furniture. Finally, when he moved into the apartment and found that the stove was broken, he had to call the building manager to get the stove fixed.

Some words you can use to show time order are *first, then,* and *finally.*

Put each list of events in time order. Number the first event 1, the second event 2, and so on. The first list has been started for you.

1. _____ a. Griffin swatted wildly at the wasp.

   _____ b. The car jumped the curb and knocked over a hot dog cart.

   _____ c. Fortunately, no one was hurt.

   ___1___ d. Griffin carefully backed his car out of the driveway.

   _____ e. As Griffin backed out, a large wasp flew into the car.

2. _____ a. A week later she called the company to follow up on her letter.

   _____ b. Rosa looked in the Help Wanted section of the newspaper.

   _____ c. Next, she wrote a letter of application and mailed it with her resume.

   _____ d. Then she went to the library to research the company.

   _____ e. She saw an ad for a job opening at Blakely Insurance.

WRITE On a separate piece of paper, write a paragraph about a recent experience. Use time order to tell the story.

Prewrite: List the events of the experience. Number them in the order in which they occurred.

Write: Write sentences about the events. Use time order words.

Narrative Writing

Supporting Details

A piece of narrative writing has one or more paragraphs. Each paragraph has a **topic sentence** that states the main idea. Other sentences in the paragraph contain **supporting details** that relate to the main idea.

Good supporting details make your narrative clearer and more interesting. They can help your reader picture what happened. They can also help your reader understand why things happened and how you feel about them. Supporting details do this by answering the questions *Who? What happened? Where? When? Why?* and *How?*

EXAMPLE This personal narrative has a topic sentence followed by several detail sentences. Notice how the detail sentences relate to the main idea and answer *Who? What happened? Where? When? Why?* or *How?*

My hockey team gets together every Saturday morning before practice. We meet at 8 A.M. at a local coffee shop. Gino, Bo, and Paul eat a big breakfast. The rest of us eat donuts and drink coffee. We like to talk about sports, especially professional hockey. This weekly breakfast is a great time for us to socialize before we head off to the rink.

PRACTICE

Match each detail with the question it answers. Write the letter.

Topic Sentence: Going camping was a humbling experience.

_____ 1. I went as one of the parent leaders for my son's school camping trip.

_____ 2. We left the city at noon on Friday.

_____ 3. The campground near the lake was called Whispering Pines.

_____ 4. That night I could not sleep. The sounds of trees "whispering" kept me awake all night.

_____ 5. I was so tired the next day that all the boys made fun of me.

a. *Where did you go?*

b. *Why was this a humbling experience?*

c. *Why did you go camping?*

d. *What happened on the camping trip?*

e. *When did you go camping?*

Narrative Writing

WRITE A Use your imagination to write narratives. Complete each paragraph below by writing 3 or 4 sentences with details that support the topic sentence. Remember, your details should tell the reader *Who? What happened? Where? When? Why?* and *How?*

1. Topic Sentence: Carlos came to the United States to improve his life, but he never dreamed he would become such a success.

   _____

   _____

   _____

   _____

   _____

   _____

   _____

   _____

2. Topic Sentence: Patricia has learned that hard times can make you stronger.

   _____

   _____

   _____

   _____

   _____

   _____

   _____

   _____

WRITE B On a separate piece of paper, write a personal narrative about one of these topics.

a childhood memory   an unforgettable experience   a hard decision

Prewrite: List as many ideas about your topic as you can. Then underline the most important ideas.

Write: Write one or more paragraphs about your topic. Remember to support your topic sentence(s) with details that add interest and answer questions such as *Where?* and *What happened?*

Language Link
Subjects and Predicates

When you write a narrative, you tell the story in sentences. A **sentence** is a group of words that expresses a complete thought. It contains a **subject,** which is the person or thing that the sentence is about. It also contains a **predicate,** which tells what the subject does or is, or what is being done to the subject.

The simple subject is a noun or a pronoun. The simple predicate is a verb.

> simple   simple
> subject   predicate
>
> **EXAMPLE** Shelly started her own business.
>
> noun verb

The **complete subject** may be one word or several words. The **complete predicate** may also be one or more words.

EXAMPLES

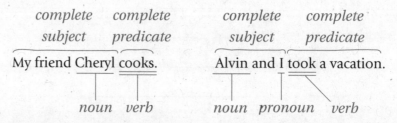

Language Exercise

Draw <u>one line</u> under the complete subject and <u>two lines</u> under the complete predicate in each sentence.

1. My niece Alicia plans to be a track star.

2. She runs and exercises every day.

3. Her father trains and coaches her for track meets.

4. My sister and I attend and give our support.

5. Alicia runs for the high school track team.

6. The team won a meet against the state champs last week.

7. My niece competed in three events.

8. She got first place in two events.

For more work with subjects and predicates, turn to pages 165–166.

Complete Sentences and Fragments

Remember that a sentence expresses a complete thought in addition to having a subject and predicate. To make your narrative essays—and all your writing—clear, you will generally want to write in complete sentences and avoid sentence fragments. A **sentence fragment** is a group of words that does not express a complete thought. It may *look* like a sentence—it may begin with a capital letter and end with a punctuation mark; it may even have a subject and a predicate. But if it does not express a complete thought, it is a sentence fragment.

EXAMPLES

Sentence: The A-1 Software Company on 6th Street hired me today.
Fragment: The A-1 Software Company on 6th Street. (needs a predicate)

Sentence: I will have two weeks of vacation each year.
Fragment: Will have two weeks of vacation each year. (needs a subject)

Sentence: If I want to start right away, I can.
Fragment: If I want to start right away. (incomplete thought)

Language Exercise A

Write *S* by each complete sentence and *F* by each fragment.

_____ 1. Judy plays practical jokes all the time.

_____ 2. Was not so funny.

_____ 3. After Al told us the wrong place to meet.

_____ 4. For two hours before leaving.

_____ 5. She was sorry and embarrassed.

Language Exercise B

Circle what each fragment needs to become a sentence—a subject, a predicate, or both.

1. As I arrived at the surprise   subject   predicate
    party last night.

2. The host and hostess.   subject   predicate

3. At seven o'clock, Li Ling.   subject   predicate

4. Was the funniest thing ever.   subject   predicate

On a separate piece of paper, rewrite fragments 2–4 above to make each one a complete sentence.

EXAMPLE 1. As I arrived at the surprise party last night, I was told to hide behind the sofa.

For more work with writing complete sentences, turn to pages 168–169.

Check your answers on pages 230–231.

Language Link
Pronouns

The personal narrative by John Cech's grandmother on page 14 used **pronouns** such as *we, us,* and *our.* Pronouns are words that can replace nouns in a sentence. We use pronouns in our writing to keep from repeating the same noun over and over again.

EXAMPLES

<u>Janice</u> is getting a new job.   <u>She</u> starts training next week.
noun   *pronoun*

A pronoun can be used as a subject, as an object, or to show possession.

EXAMPLES

He bought <u>me</u> a wallet for <u>my</u> birthday.   <u>She</u> drove <u>him</u> to <u>his</u> job every day.
subject   object   possessive   *subject   object possessive*

Language Exercise A

Write pronouns to replace the underlined words. The first one has been done for you.

1. On New Year's Day, <u>Sam</u> will marry <u>Alice</u>.   *he* _____
        he   him   her   them

2. <u>Paolo</u> will be going to <u>Sam and Alice's</u> wedding.   _____ _____
        he   they   their   my

3. Invitations should go to <u>Sally, Keisha, and Corinne</u>.   _____
        him   them   they   her

4. The bills for the wedding will be sent to <u>Diego</u>.   _____
        them   he   him   his

5. <u>Sam and Alice</u> are going on a honeymoon.   _____
        Them   They   Their   My

> For more work with pronouns, turn to pages 152–156.

Language Exercise B

Choose the correct pronoun. Write it in the blank.

The apartment belongs to Terri and _____ (**I, me**). _____ (**Us, We**) can
                                 1   2

both save money by sharing the rent. This tiny bedroom is _____ (**my,**
                                                           3

mine). The furniture was loaned to _____ (**we, us**). Last week _____ (**I,**
                                     4   5

me) painted the living room, and tomorrow _____ (**we, us**) will paint the
                                                      6

halls. _____ (**Their, Our**) goal is to paint all the rooms by Friday.
       7

Point of View

You can write a narrative from different **points of view.** When you write a personal narrative, use the **first-person point of view.** This means that you refer to yourself by using the pronouns *I, me, my,* or *mine.*

EXAMPLE Below is a diary entry. The writer uses first-person point of view.

Today was the happiest day of my life. Today, Tina and I got married! When she finally agreed to marry me, I could not believe my luck. I thought it might never happen—especially when I dropped her ring! Now Tina is mine and I am hers.

When you write a narrative about someone else, use the **third-person point of view.** This means that you refer to people by using the pronouns *she, her,* and *hers; he, him,* and *his;* and *they, them,* and *theirs.*

EXAMPLE Below is a brief story. The writer uses third-person point of view.

Hal and Tina were married today. They stood in front of family and friends and exchanged vows. He was nervous and dropped her ring as he put it on her finger. She, on the other hand, was very confident and had no trouble with his ring. They were obviously in love. The crowd cheered for them when the ceremony ended.

PRACTICE

A. **Write the correct pronouns for first-person point of view.**

_____ **(I, He)** left in September for overseas duty knowing that _____
1   2
(his, my) wife was going to have twins. Imagine _____ **(my, their)** surprise
3
when the telegram came telling _____ **(him, me)** that _____ **(he, I)** was
4   5
the proud father of triplets!

B. **Now rewrite the paragraph above on a separate piece of paper. Begin the first sentence with, "Ray left in September . . ." Then write the rest of the paragraph from the third-person point of view.**

WRITE Write a paragraph about an event that turned out differently or better than you or someone else first thought it might. Use a separate piece of paper.

Prewrite: Think of an event you can write about. Make a list of your ideas. Decide which point of view to use.
Write: Write a narrative of the event. Be sure that your pronouns show the correct point of view.

GED Essay Link

Narrative Writing

Using Your Personal Experiences

On the GED Writing Test, you will write an essay on a topic about which you have some personal knowledge or experience. Read the sample essay topic below. What experiences does this topic make you think of?

SAMPLE TOPIC

> ### TOPIC A
>
> Would you prefer to live in a small town, a suburb, or a city?
>
> In your essay, tell where you prefer to live and why. Use your personal observations, experience, and knowledge to support your essay

To write a strong GED essay on this topic, use strong supporting details and examples. To come up with details and examples, think about your own life. Perhaps you can tell a story about yourself.

In the sample response below, a student writer used a personal narrative to help support part of his essay on Topic A. Notice how his details and examples help you picture the experience in your mind.

SAMPLE RESPONSE

> For me, the country is too dull and quiet. When I was twelve, I went to visit my cousins. They live in a small, one-stop-sign town. I arrived at my cousin's house about ten a.m. We talked all morning and swam all afternoon. After dinner, we sat outside on their porch. There was no movie to go to and no store for shopping. Once night fell, I finally heard noise—the chirping of crickets and hooting of owls. I tossed all night. I need city lights and car horns to put me to sleep.

Planning a Response

You know that a good personal narrative has:

- supporting details that answer questions, such as *Who? Where? When? What happened? How?* and *Why?*

- events told in time order

Before you write a personal narrative, you will want to plan the details and events you are going to use.

A. Look at this planner. It shows how the writer of the paragraph on page 22 planned before he wrote.

Who? My cousins and I	Where? in their small town	When? when I was 12
What happened? 1. arrived about 10 a.m. 2. talked all morning 3. swam all afternoon	4. had dinner 5. sat outside on their porch 6. went to bed early	

B. Read Topic A on page 22 again. Think about your personal experience. Is there a story you could use to explain why you would like—or not like—to live in a certain place?

1. **Prewrite:** Write your ideas in the planner below.

Who?	Where?	When?
What happened?		

2. **Write:** On a separate piece of paper, write a paragraph response to Topic A. Use your ideas from the planner.

Apply Your Writing Skills

Write a Narrative Essay

Now you are ready to apply what you have learned by writing a narrative essay.

A narrative essay:

- is a form of writing in which you tell a story about yourself or someone else
- may be told in the order in which events happened, using time-order organization and words
- can be written in first-person or third-person point of view

As you write, follow the steps in the writing process outlined below.

ASSIGNMENT

Write a three-paragraph essay about an important event in your life.

Prewriting

1. List some possible events to write about.

   _____

   _____

   _____

2. Choose one event to write about. List the event and some interesting details about it.

   Event: _____

   Details: _____

   _____

   _____

3. Organize your details. Choose the most interesting and important details. Then list them in time order below.

   1. _____

   2. _____

   3. _____

   4. _____

   5. _____

Writing the First Draft

A **first draft** is the first version of a piece of writing. To write a first draft, you should:

Write an opening sentence that states the main idea of your essay. What is the main point about the event that you want to get across? Try writing the opening sentence several different ways. Write your final version below.

_____

On a separate piece of paper, write your first draft.

Write an introductory paragraph. Use your opening sentence. Then set the scene for the story you are going to tell.

Write a body paragraph. Use the details from your list on page 24 to write an interesting story about the event.
- The body paragraph should support the main idea in your opening sentence.
- Put your details in time order so a reader will be able to follow the story.

Write a concluding paragraph. Write a sentence to signal the end of your story. Add another sentence or two to leave the reader with a final viewpoint, a question, or an idea to think about.

Revising and Editing

Review, revise, and edit. To **review** means to read through your writing again. To **revise** means to improve your writing by making it clearer. To **edit** means to check your word choice, usage, spelling, and punctuation. Read your essay to see if you accomplished what you set out to do. Then use the checklist on page 216 to revise and edit it. Also, pay special attention to these points.

☐ Did you organize the narrative details in logical time order? _See page 15._

☐ Did you use supporting details? _See pages 16–17._

☐ Are your sentences complete? _See pages 18–19._

☐ Did you use pronouns correctly? _See page 20._

Writing the Final Draft

Write a final draft. Then read it one last time. If necessary, recopy or retype it.

Sharing the Final Draft

Publish. Let another person read your final draft. Ask if your message was clear and what else you could do to improve the essay. Make some notes and attach them to a copy of the essay. File the essay in your writing portfolio.

Descriptive Writing

Elements of Descriptive Writing

Descriptive writing describes a person, place, or thing for a reader. When you write a description, you want your reader to see, hear, feel, smell, or taste exactly what you did. You want your reader to experience what you did. To do that, you use all your senses, your memory, and sometimes your imagination to make a picture with your words.

Descriptive writing often includes feelings about the person, place, or thing that is being described. For example, the feeling you have for a grandmother you loved is different from the feeling you experienced at an accident you saw. You will want to create a different feeling when you describe your grandmother than when you describe an accident.

EXAMPLE Below is a descriptive paragraph. The author, Amy Tan, describes smells, sights, and sounds to create a picture of her childhood home.

The apartment building was three stories high, two apartments per floor. It had a renovated facade, a recent layer of white stucco topped with connected rows of metal fire-escape ladders. But inside it was old. The front door with its narrow glass panes opened into a musty lobby that smelled of everybody's life mixed together. Everybody meant the names on the front door next to their little buzzers: Anderson, Giordino, Hayman, Ricci, Sorci, and our name, St. Clair. We lived on the middle floor, stuck between cooking smells that floated up and feet sounds that drifted down. My bedroom faced the street, and at night, in the dark, I could see in my mind another life. Cars struggling to climb the steep, fog-shrouded hill, gunning their deep engines and spinning their wheels. Loud, happy people, laughing, puffing, gasping, "Are we almost there?" A beagle scrambling to his feet to start his yipping yowl, answered a few seconds later by fire truck sirens and an angry woman hissing, "Sammy! Bad dog! Hush now!". . .

WRITE On a separate piece of paper, write a descriptive paragraph about the place where you grew up or where you live now.

Begin with prewriting. List specific details that will help your reader "see" your home. Next, organize the details in an order that will create a picture of your home when you write. You can organize them from the front of the house to the back, from your favorite room to other rooms, or in some other way to make the description interesting. Finally, use your prewriting to write a paragraph.

Descriptive Details

You can create a word picture by including descriptive details when you write. Begin with details you can see, such as shape, color, and size.

EXAMPLE Below is a paragraph about an operating room that includes clear, vivid descriptive details. Picture the operating room as you read.

> As I was wheeled into the operating room, I was still awake. Everything in the room looked clean and professional—the stainless steel table, the gleaming knives, the bright light, the white walls. But there, not quite tucked away under a pile of linen, was a gauze bandage covered with brown, faded blood.

Precise Words

Writers use precise or exact words to draw a word picture. Vague, general words may have different meanings for different readers. As you write, ask yourself if a more precise word could help your reader see exactly what you mean.

EXAMPLES *color*—general   *red*—precise   *scarlet*—even more precise

PRACTICE

A. Use descriptive details to create word pictures. Write a sentence using two details to describe each thing.

1. (a car) _____ A gray Ford Escort was parked near the door. _____

2. (a cake) _____

3. (a tree) _____

4. (a man) _____

B. Find a precise word on the right side that could replace the general word on the left side. Write the letter.

General		Precise	
____ 1. shirt	____ 4. eat	a. devour	d. T-shirt
____ 2. jump	____ 5. doctor	b. leap	e. stare
____ 3. child	____ 6. look	c. six-year-old	f. surgeon

WRITE On a separate piece of paper, write a paragraph about a place that has memories for you.

Prewrite: List as many details as possible. Select those that create a word picture.

Write: Use precise words in your paragraph.

Descriptive Writing

Sensory Details

Another way to create word pictures in descriptive writing is to use words that appeal to the five senses: sight, hearing, smell, taste, and touch. Words that help the reader see, hear, smell, taste, or feel exactly what you did are called **sensory details.** Sensory details make descriptions come alive.

smell
sight
taste
sound
touch

EXAMPLE This morning I ran across a pair of **musty sneakers** in the closet. I wore them the day my grandfather took me to Coney Island. When I look at those **dirt-encrusted, tattered** sneakers, it all comes back to me. I can taste the **salty fries and sweet cotton candy.** My stomach churns at the memory of that **roaring roller coaster,** the Cyclone. I remember grabbing hold of my grandfather's **big, rough hand** so I wouldn't get lost in the crowd.

PRACTICE

A. Write the sense—sight, hearing, smell, taste, or touch—that is affected by the sensory details in the sentence.

_____ 1. The sea shimmered in shades of turquoise.

_____ 2. The waves tickled my toes.

_____ 3. The breeze whispered through the trees.

_____ 4. The sea air carried the scent of salt.

_____ 5. The ice-cold lemonade was delicious.

B. Write a sentence that describes each item. Use specific details that appeal to the sense listed.

1. (**Sight:** sunset) _____

2. (**Hearing:** factory) _____

3. (**Smell:** baby) _____

4. (**Taste:** hamburger) _____

5. (**Touch:** handshake) _____

WRITE On a separate piece of paper, write a paragraph to describe a meal you once had. It could be a holiday dinner, a fast-food meal, or a picnic.

Prewrite: List as many sensory details as you can for each of the five senses.

Write: Use details that let the reader see, hear, smell, taste, and feel the meal.

Descriptive Writing

Figurative Language

When you describe exactly how something looks, tastes, feels, smells, or sounds, you are using **literal language.** Sometimes you may find it useful to describe something by comparing it to another thing that is very different. This type of comparison is called **figurative language.** It can make your writing more interesting. Here are three ways to make figurative comparisons.

1. Use *like* or *as.*
Literal: She was upset.
Figurative: She cried like a baby.

2. Say that something is something else.
Literal: The snow covered the field.
Figurative: The snow was a soft white blanket.

3. Give human qualities to things that are not human.
Literal: The rain fell on my face.
Figurative: The rain caressed my face.

PRACTICE

The following sentences are written in literal language. Rewrite each sentence using figurative language that appeals to the sense listed.

1. (Sight) My apartment is small.
   My apartment is the size of a broom closet.

2. (Touch) Scott has soft hair.
   _____

3. (Hearing) The wind was loud last night.
   _____

4. (Taste) The cold drink was refreshing.
   _____

5. (Smell) I could smell her perfume before she opened the door.
   _____

WRITE On a separate piece of paper, write a descriptive paragraph about one of the topics below.

my favorite holiday   a beautiful (or stormy) day   a strange person

Prewrite: Choose your topic and write the five senses. List sensory details about your topic under each sense.
Write: As you write about the details, use figurative language.

Language Link
Adjectives and Adverbs

In Amy Tan's description on page 26, she included details like "musty lobby" and "drifted down." The words *musty* and *down* helped Ms. Tan paint specific word pictures. *Musty* is an adjective, and *down* is an adverb. Adjectives and adverbs will help you create specific word pictures in your descriptive writing.

- An **adjective** modifies, or helps describe, a noun or a pronoun. Adjectives answer the following questions.

What kind?	This <u>large</u> diner has just opened.
How many?	I'll have <u>two</u> eggs with toast.
Which one?	It is the <u>first</u> item on the menu.

- An **adverb** is a word that modifies a verb, an adjective, or another adverb. Adverbs answer the following questions.

How?	He walked <u>quickly</u>.
When?	He left <u>early</u>.
Where?	He went <u>there</u>.
To what extent?	He went to a <u>very</u> popular restaurant.

Be careful not to use an adjective when an adverb is needed. When adjectives and adverbs are similar, the adverb usually ends in *ly*.

EXAMPLE   **Correct:** Shanna ran to the store <u>quickly</u>.
                Incorrect: Shanna ran to the store <u>quick</u>.
                Correct: Shanna wanted a <u>quick</u> snack.

The first sentence is correct because the adverb *quickly* describes the verb *ran*. The third sentence is correct because the adjective *quick* describes the noun *snack*.

Language Exercise   **Write the correct adjective or adverb to complete each sentence.**

1. Lilly's Kitchen is a _____ restaurant.
   fine (adj.)   **finely** (adv.)

2. The bakery's bread is _____ every day.
   fresh (adj.)   **freshly** (adv.)

3. The dining room is _____ lit.
   bright (adj.)   **brightly** (adv.)

4. The tables are decorated _____.
   beautiful (adj.)   **beautifully** (adv.)

5. I eat at Lilly's Kitchen _____.
   regular (adj.)   **regularly** (adv.)

Descriptive Writing

Comparing with Adjectives and Adverbs

Adjectives and adverbs can show comparison. To compare two things, use the **comparative** form. To compare three or more things, use the **superlative** form.

EXAMPLES

adjective	comparative	superlative
long	longer	longest
careful	more careful	most careful
adverb	**comparative**	**superlative**
fast	faster	fastest
quickly	more quickly	most quickly

Adjective: This is a <u>long</u> movie.
Comparative: This movie is <u>longer</u> than the one I saw last week.
Superlative: This is the <u>longest</u> movie I have ever seen.

Some adjectives and adverbs change completely in the comparative and superlative forms.

EXAMPLES

adjective	comparative	superlative
good	better	best
bad	worse	worst
adverb	**comparative**	**superlative**
well	better	best
badly	worse	worst

Adverb: I bowled <u>badly</u> Friday.
Comparative: I bowled <u>worse</u> on Sunday than on Friday.
Superlative: I bowled <u>worst</u> today.

Language Exercise   **Complete each sentence with the correct form of the adjective or adverb.**

1. hot, hotter, hottest

2. new, newer, newest

3. quickly, more quickly, most quickly

4. important, more important, most important

5. easy, easier, easiest

It was the _____ day of summer, and it was my job to
₁
train the _____ employee in our mailroom. Ramos learned
₂
_____ than the last person. When the _____
₃   ₄
job of the day arrived, he made the work seem _____ .
₅

For more work with adjectives and adverbs, turn to pages 157–160.

Language Link

Good descriptive writing includes a variety of sentences. If all your sentences are short and simple, your writing will also seem simple. If you combine ideas into a variety of sentence structures, your writing will be more interesting. You will also be able to show how your ideas are related by using connecting words. Here are three ways to vary sentence structure by combining ideas.

1. Use compound sentences.

2. Use complex sentences.

3. Combine words and phrases in a series.

Compound Sentences

Remember that a sentence is a complete thought. A **compound sentence** has *two* complete thoughts that are closely related. Each of these thoughts could stand alone as a sentence.

EXAMPLE The job will be hard, but I can do it.

The complete thoughts in a compound sentence can be joined with a **comma** and a connecting word called a **coordinating conjunction.** The most common coordinating conjunctions are *and, but, or,* and *so*. Make sure you use both a comma and a coordinating conjunction. Otherwise, you will have a **run-on sentence,** which is a mistake in sentence structure.

EXAMPLES

1. Rosa takes care of stray animals. Rosa finds new homes for strays.
   Compound Sentence: Rosa takes care of stray animals, or she finds new homes for them.

2. Rosa's favorite pet is a sad-eyed puppy. Rosa also loves the white alley cat she found.
   Compound Sentence: Rosa's favorite pet is a sad-eyed puppy, but she also loves the white alley cat she found.

3. The cat roams all over the house. The parakeet has to be kept in its cage.
   Compound Sentence: The cat roams all over the house, so the parakeet has to be kept in its cage.

4. I help Rosa with the animals. She pays me a small amount for my work.
   Compound Sentence: I help Rosa with the animals, and she pays me a small amount for my work.

For practice with identifying and correcting run-on sentences, turn to pages 170–171.

Descriptive Writing

Language Exercise A

Combine each pair of sentences to make a compound sentence. Use a comma and one of the coordinating conjunctions *and, but, or,* or *so.*

1. The skies opened up. Lightning streaked across the clouds.

   _____

2. Last year we had floods. This year was not as bad.

   _____

3. The storm caused severe damage. Several people were injured.

   _____

4. Windows were shattered by the wind. We went into the basement.

   _____

5. We read books. Sometimes we played cards.

   _____

Language Exercise B

Complete each sentence below by adding a related second thought to make a compound sentence. Use the conjunction listed above the sentence. The first sentence is done for you.

1. **but**

   The steak was tender,

   The steak was tender, but it was too well done.

2. **and**

   The street was deserted, _____.

3. **so**

   The couch was new, _____.

4. **but**

   The soldiers marched bravely, _____.

5. **so**

   The sky looked threatening, _____.

6. **so**

   The fruit was ripe, _____.

7. **or**

   I should get gas soon, _____.

8. **or**

   We could see this movie, _____.

For more work with compound sentences, turn to pages 172–173.

 Check your answers on page 232.

Complex Sentences

Another way to vary your writing is to use complex sentences. A **complex sentence** has two parts: one **independent** (or complete) thought and one **dependent** (or incomplete) thought. Each part is called a **clause.** An independent clause has a subject and a predicate and can stand alone as a sentence. A dependent clause has a subject and a predicate, but it cannot stand alone because it is not a complete thought. It depends on the independent clause to complete the thought.

A dependent clause may come either before or after an independent clause. If the dependent clause comes first in the sentence, place a comma after it.

EXAMPLE <u>Wherever</u> you go, you will see tall buildings.
You will see tall buildings <u>wherever</u> you go.

A dependent clause begins with a connecting word called a **subordinating conjunction.** Here are some common subordinating conjunctions.

after	as soon as	even if	though	when
although	as though	even though	unless	whenever
as	because	if	until	whichever
as if	before	since	whatever	while

Language Exercise

Use a conjunction from the box above to combine each pair of clauses to make a complex sentence. Use a comma if the dependent clause is first in the sentence.

1. the weather is still nice/we will take a drive to the mountains

   If the weather is still nice, we will take a drive to the mountains.

2. you drive on the Blue Ridge Parkway/you can stop at many overlooks

   _____

3. most people stop at Mt. Mitchell/that's the most spectacular view of all

   _____

4. you'll want to take pictures/it's hard to get those mountain ranges on film

   _____

5. stay on the parkway/you reach the city of Asheville

   _____

Words in Series

Still another way to make your writing more interesting is to use a series of adjectives, noun phrases, or verb phrases. If you say the same thing over and over again, you will bore your reader. When you combine words to make a series, you reduce the number of times you repeat an idea.

EXAMPLES

- **Adjectives**   The ballpark was noisy. The ballpark was crowded. The ballpark was hot.

  Series   The ballpark was noisy, crowded, and hot.

- **Nouns**   The living room had a picture window. The living room had wood floors. The living room had a view of the park.

  Series   The living room had a picture window, wood floors, and a view of the park.

- **Verbs**   The car spun around. It hit a tree. The car landed in a ditch.

  Series   The car spun around, hit a tree, and landed in a ditch.

Language Exercise   Combine each group of sentences to make one sentence that uses adjectives, nouns, or verbs in a series. Omit the words that are not needed. Use commas between three or more words or phrases in a series.

1.   The bus driver signaled.
     She turned into the traffic.
     She slowly made her way along the street.

     _____

     _____

2.   Jose's car has a sun roof.
     It has bucket seats.
     It has chrome trim.

     _____

     _____

3.   The sofa cushions were old.
     The sofa cushions were plaid.
     The sofa had worn-out cushions.

     _____

     _____

For more work with words in a series, turn to pages 174–175 and 185.

Descriptive Writing

Using Description

On the GED essay, you may find that you want to describe something. Review the sample topic from Lesson 1 (page 22) below.

SAMPLE TOPIC

> ### TOPIC A
> Would you prefer to live in a small town, a suburb, or a city?
>
> In your essay, tell where you prefer to live and why. Use your personal observations, experience, and knowledge to support your essay

To write a strong GED essay on this topic, you might create a word picture of a small town, a suburb, or a city for the scorer who will read your essay. Remember the passage on page 26 by Amy Tan? Her writing shows how words can create a picture.

Can you think of a scene that shows why you like living in a small town, a suburb, or a city? What are your favorite places there? How do these places make living there special? In the sample response below, a student writer has written about a city scene she loves. Notice how her paragraph helps you *see* that scene.

SAMPLE RESPONSE

> I love to live in the city because of places like Bellingham Fountain. This enormous old fountain is filled with sculptures of amazing creatures. They spit jets of water in all directions. The water jets make patterns against the sky. There is a wide, open plaza around the fountain where adults stroll and children run. The wind blows cold spray from the fountain. It feels great on a blistering hot day. If the wind is strong enough, you feel as if you're standing in a shower!

Planning a Response

You know that good descriptive writing has:

- precise words that will hold the reader's interest—like *creatures* and *stroll*

- words that appeal to the senses—like *enormous* and *blistering hot*

- figurative language—like *as if you're standing in a shower*

As you plan a piece of descriptive writing, try to use these kinds of words to describe your subject.

A. The writer of the paragraph on page 36 listed her ideas before she wrote her paragraph. As she wrote the paragraph based on her list, she added descriptive words to make her writing more interesting. For each item from her list below, find the descriptive detail she actually wrote in the paragraph. The first one has been done for you.

Scene: Bellingham Fountain

Idea List	Descriptive Detail
big fountain	*enormous old fountain*
statues of strange animals	
water comes out of their mouths	
people walk around	
you can get wet from the spray	

B. Read Topic A on page 36 again. Think of a scene that shows why you like living in a small town, a suburb, or a city.

1. **Prewrite:** Make a list of ideas that help describe that scene. Then revise each item on your list into a more descriptive detail. Use precise words, sensory details, and figurative language.

Scene: _____

Idea List	Descriptive Detail

2. **Write:** On a separate piece of paper, write a paragraph response to Topic A in which you describe your scene. Use your descriptive details. You may also want to add more details as you write.

Apply Your Writing Skills

Write a Descriptive Essay

Now you are ready to apply what you have learned by writing a descriptive essay.

A descriptive essay:

- helps create a clear picture in the reader's mind
- comes alive through precise words and sensory details
- may contain figurative language to describe something

As you write, follow the steps in the writing process outlined below.

ASSIGNMENT

Write a three-paragraph essay describing your favorite character in a movie or TV show.

Prewriting

1. On a separate piece of paper, jot down a list of several characters you like from TV or movies. Circle the one you would like to write about.

2. Make a list of descriptive details about this character. Write at least one detail for each of the following questions.

   What does the character look like?

   _____

   _____

   What is the character's personality?

   _____

   _____

   How does the character behave?

   _____

   _____

3. Pick four or five of the most interesting details from your list above. On a separate piece of paper, rewrite them to make them more descriptive. Try to use precise words, sensory details, and figurative language.

4. Number your descriptive details in the order you think they should go in your essay. (Hint: Save the best for last!)

Writing the First Draft

Write an opening sentence that states the main idea of your essay. What is the main point about the character that you want to get across? Try writing the opening sentence several different ways. Write your final version below.

_____

_____

On a separate piece of paper, write your first draft.

Write an introductory paragraph. Use your opening sentence. Then introduce the character to your reader in a general way.

Write a body paragraph. Use the descriptive details from your prewriting list to write an interesting paragraph about the character.

- The body paragraph should support the main idea in your opening sentence.
- Put your details in order according to the plan you made in your prewriting.

Write a concluding paragraph. Write a sentence to signal the end of your description. Add another sentence or two to leave the reader with a final viewpoint, a question, or an idea to think about.

Revising and Editing

Review, revise, and edit. Read your essay to see if you accomplished what you set out to do. Then use the checklist on page 216 to revise and edit it. Also, pay special attention to these points.

- ☐ Did you use visual details? _See page 27._
- ☐ Did you use precise words? _See page 27._
- ☐ Did you use sensory details to appeal to the five senses? _See page 28._
- ☐ Did you use figurative language? _See page 29._
- ☐ Did you use adjectives and adverbs to compare items? _See pages 30–31._
- ☐ Did you vary your sentence structure? _See pages 32–35._

Writing the Final Draft

Write a final draft. Then read it one last time. If necessary, recopy or retype it.

Sharing the Final Draft

Publish. Let another person read your final draft. Ask if your message was clear and what else you could do to improve the essay. Make some notes and attach them to a copy of the essay. File the essay in your writing portfolio.

3 LESSON

Elements of Expository Writing

Expository writing informs or explains. You use expository writing to make an idea or situation easier to understand. It is especially useful when you want to explain a complicated idea. Explaining <u>why</u> you believe in something is an example of expository writing. Here are three ways writers explain an idea in an expository essay.

- **Define the word that names the idea.**
  A *friend* is someone who is attached to another by affection.
- **Illustrate an idea by giving a specific example.**
  Calvin's *friend* John drove him to work every morning for eight years.
- **Classify, or group similar types together.**
  Some people are acquaintances, others are good-time buddies, and then there are *friends*.

EXAMPLE   Below is a piece of expository writing by Mae Jemison, the first African-American woman in space. She explains what a scientist is and how she came to be one.

As I was growing up, I found a strong source of inspiration in my parents. My mother was a schoolteacher and my father a carpenter and roofer. They also were two of the best scientists and science role models I have ever encountered. . . . They studied and analyzed any issue that came up. When I had a question or a problem they asked me what information I had and what I thought might be a solution. Sometimes they would give me small clues or hints. Then they encouraged me to find my own answer. And when I came up with a solution, they would evaluate it with me and suggest ways to improve it. Isn't that exactly what scientists are supposed to do? Don't they explore the world systematically—review the unknown, develop a hypothesis to answer a question, and then test their hypothesis? I was lucky to have such parents.

WRITE   In the example, Mae Jemison's parents taught her how to be a scientist. Think about some of the role models in your life.

On a separate piece of paper, write an expository paragraph about someone who has been an important role model for you.

Tell who the person is and define the role this person modeled for you. Give examples that show how this person has been important to you.

Connecting Words and Phrases

Good expository writing moves from one idea to the next in a way that makes sense. If your writing flows smoothly in this way, readers do not have to go back and reread to figure out what you mean. One of the best ways to make your writing flow is to use **connecting words and phrases.**

after a while	finally	furthermore	next
also	first (second, etc.)	however	still
as a result	for example	in addition	then
besides	for instance	later	therefore

Some of these connecting words are the time-order words you used in narrative writing on page 15. You can also use the coordinating conjunctions *and, but, or,* and *so* to connect ideas, as well as the subordinating conjunctions listed on page 34.

EXAMPLE 1 I have three reasons for not going to work on this dreadful winter day. I slipped on an icy sidewalk and injured my foot. I cannot wear my shoe. My son is not going to school. He has the flu. The heat is off at work. I would not be able to get much done there anyway.

EXAMPLE 2 I have three reasons for not going to work on this dreadful winter day. First, I slipped on an icy sidewalk. As a result, I hurt my foot and cannot wear my shoe. Also, my son is not going to school because he has the flu. Finally, the heat is off at work, so I wouldn't get much done there anyway.

What does the second example have that the first one does not? Notice the words *first, as a result, and, also, because, finally* and *so* that link ideas.

Write one connecting word or phrase from the box above to link each set of ideas. The first one is done for you.

1. I am not going out today with my bad cold. __Besides__, it is raining.

2. Mika made dinner. _____ he washed the dishes.

3. Frances studied hard for the GED. _____, she passed the exam.

4. Julio put an ad in the paper. _____, he put signs on the bulletin board at work.

5. The storm damaged the roof. _____, it could have been worse.

6. Hong's mother is ill. _____, he is flying to visit her.

7. Mei Lee worked hard. _____, she got a raise.

Check your answers on page 233.

Connecting Words for Style

There is no one "right" word or phrase to use when connecting ideas in your expository writing. Pick the one that best joins your ideas and makes your point. The words you choose help create your writing style—your own special way of putting your ideas on paper. Here is the same idea joined three ways.

EXAMPLES I like living in this building; as a result, I renewed my lease.

I like living in this building; thus, I renewed my lease.

I like living in this building, so I renewed my lease.

Punctuation also helps to show the connection between ideas.

- Use a comma to separate two complete thoughts that are joined by the coordinating conjunctions *and, but, or, nor, yet,* or *so.*
- Use a semicolon to connect two complete thoughts that are not joined by the connecting words *and, but, or, nor, yet,* or *so.*
- Use a comma after connecting words such as *however* and *for example.*

Rewrite this paragraph to make the ideas flow more smoothly. You can add, take away, or replace words and phrases.

People who win big prizes in the lottery often find that the money does not make them happy. They have to deal with lots of people trying to get a piece of the pie. Winners find that their friends expect them to hand over some of the winnings. They have to be on guard all the time. Lottery winners find that they often cannot trust anyone. All this pressure takes the fun out of winning. They can no longer relax and enjoy life. I am willing to give it a try!

_____

_____

_____

_____

_____

WRITE Someone once said, "There is only one success—to be able to spend your life in your own way."

On a separate piece of paper, write a paragraph explaining what success means to you.

Prewrite: List specific examples to explain the word *success.*

Write: Write your ideas so that your reader can follow your train of thought. Use connecting words and phrases to link your ideas.

Expository Writing

Expanding Your Vocabulary with Synonyms

The purpose of an expository essay is to explain something. When you speak, you have a chance to explain what you mean. But when you write, you do not have a second chance. Therefore, you want to choose words carefully so that your meaning is clear to your readers.

You can choose words more carefully when you know many words. One way to learn new words is to read a newspaper. Another way is to use a thesaurus.

The word *thesaurus* comes from a Latin word meaning "storehouse of knowledge." A thesaurus has lists of **synonyms,** or words that have the same or similar meaning. It also has **antonyms,** or words that have the opposite meaning. For example, look up the word *big* in a thesaurus. Here are just a few of the words you will find under *big*.

EXAMPLES

Synonyms for *big*			Antonyms for *big*		
large	huge	grown	little	small	tiny
immense	ample	adult	minute	modest	young
enormous	great	vast	minor	humble	little

A thesaurus entry can give you many synonyms to choose from. The thesaurus may remind you of words that you already know but might not think of on your own. As you read thesaurus entries, notice that different synonyms may express slightly different meanings. Using synonyms can help make your writing more vivid and more precise.

PRACTICE

Use a thesaurus. Write four synonyms for each word.

1. red _____ _____ _____ _____
2. win _____ _____ _____ _____
3. walk _____ _____ _____ _____
4. money _____ _____ _____ _____

WRITE On a separate piece of paper, write a paragraph explaining what *money* means to you.

Prewrite: List ideas that come to mind when you think of the word *money*. Write down as many ideas as you can. Then choose the three best.

Write: Use your ideas to explain what money means to you. In your paragraph, use at least two of the synonyms you found for *money* in the Practice above.

Choosing the Best Synonym

Words have varied shades of meaning. For instance, there are many words that mean "to hit." Although *bump* and *smash* both mean "to hit," *smash* suggests a harder action that may be more painful. When you write, use the word that says exactly what you want to say.

PRACTICE

A. Each line has four words. Three are synonyms; one word does not belong. Write the word that is <u>not</u> a synonym for the others.

_____	1. careless	hasty	rushed	neat
_____	2. still	racket	hushed	quiet
_____	3. mansion	cabin	hut	cottage
_____	4. decrease	explore	survey	probe
_____	5. stony	rigid	steely	gentle
_____	6. yearn	crave	scorn	wish

B. Select the best synonym for the underlined word or phrase in each sentence. Write the letter in the blank.

_____ 1. The <u>belligerent</u> dog bit the mail carrier again.

(A) hostile (B) unfriendly (C) warlike

_____ 2. That woman is a <u>brilliant</u> research scientist.

(A) glorious (B) colorful (C) distinguished

_____ 3. The group was <u>upset</u> when the power went out during the Super Bowl.

(A) overturned (B) distressed (C) sad

_____ 4. The ad states that the new cereal is <u>good</u> for you.

(A) nutritious (B) sufficient (C) benign

_____ 5. The redhead was made <u>the person in charge</u> of the bowling team.

(A) moderator (B) ruler (C) captain

WRITE On a separate piece of paper, write a paragraph explaining the different ways people laugh.

Prewrite: Use a thesaurus to list synonyms for *laugh*.

Write: For each synonym you write about, add details that help a reader picture and hear a person laugh in that way.

Expository Writing

Point of View

In expository writing, you can write from different **points of view.** This chart shows how to choose and use points of view.

Point of View	
If you are writing . . .	**Use . . .**
• as yourself or about yourself	• I (I am special.)
• to someone	• you (You are special.)
• about someone	• he, she, or they (He is special.)
• as a member of a group	• we (We are special.)

Be careful not to change your point of view in the middle of a sentence or passage. As you revise your writing, look for errors in point of view.

EXAMPLE **Change in point of view:** Many people say they like to work hard, but when a job is hard, you sometimes get upset.
Revised: Many people say they like to work hard, but when a job is hard, they sometimes get upset.

PRACTICE

Revise the sentences to correct changes in point of view. The sentences can be revised several different ways. If the sentence is correct, write *correct*.

1. I like to read forecasts of the future, but you have to wonder if any of them are true.

   _____

2. When people are treated with respect at work, you feel better about your work.

   _____

3. This morning I could not find my keys, so I left the back door unlocked when I left.

   _____

4. When one looks for a loan, you find who has the best rate.

   _____

WRITE On a separate piece of paper, write a paragraph to define the word *happiness.*

Prewrite: Jot down all the ideas that come to mind when you think of the word *happiness.* Decide how to organize them.

Write: Use your prewriting ideas to write a paragraph defining happiness and giving examples of it. Use the same point of view throughout the paragraph.

Expository Writing

Polishing Your Work

Your expository writing does not end with your first draft. If you want to make your writing shine, you must take time to polish your work. Check for correct spelling and punctuation. Be sure no letters or words have been left out. To polish your work, ask yourself these questions.

1. Does each sentence begin with a capital letter?

2. Does each proper noun begin with a capital letter?

3. Does each sentence end with a period, exclamation point, or question mark?

4. Is each word spelled correctly?

Read the paragraph. Then circle the best answer to each question.

(1) When I was in school, the teachers did not try to erase our backrounds. (2) they tried to say our real names, even though they did not speak our language. (3) We were never punished for speaking our native langauge in class.

1. Sentence 1: **When I was in school, the teachers did not try to erase our backrounds.** What correction should be made to this sentence?
   (1) Change *backrounds* to *backgrounds*.
   (2) Insert a comma after *teachers*.
   (3) Change *teachers* to *Teachers*.
   (4) Put a question mark at the end of the sentence.
   (5) No correction is necessary.

2. Sentence 2: **they tried to say our real names, even though they did not speak our language.** What correction should be made to this sentence?
   (1) Remove the comma after *names*.
   (2) Insert a comma after *tried*.
   (3) Change *they* to *They*.
   (4) Change *language* to *langauge*.
   (5) No correction is necessary.

3. Sentence 3: **We were never punished for speaking our native langauge in class.** What correction should be made to this sentence?
   (1) Change *were* to *are*.
   (2) Put a question mark at the end of the sentence.
   (3) Change *langauge* to *language*.
   (4) Add a comma after *langauge*.
   (5) No correction is necessary.

Language Link
Active and Passive Voice

In good expository writing, like Mae Jemison's piece on page 40, verbs like *explore* and *test* tell <u>what</u> actions happen. The **voice** of a verb helps show <u>how</u> an action happens. In the **active voice,** the subject of the sentence does the action. In the **passive voice,** someone or something else does the action to the subject.

EXAMPLES

Active Voice	Passive Voice
Sammy hit the ball.	The ball was hit by Sammy.
Crops need rain.	Rain is needed by crops.
Jen opened the book.	The book was opened by Jen.

Language Exercise A

Find the verb in each sentence. On the line, write *active* if the verb is in the active voice or *passive* if the verb is in the passive voice.

_____ 1. The pill was taken by my wife.

_____ 2. We bought a few extra hot dogs for later.

_____ 3. I read the newspaper every night after supper.

_____ 4. New York was reached by the Mexican tourists in a day.

In most cases, use the active voice in your writing. It helps you write crisp, clear sentences. It is strong and direct. It usually saves words. But there are three cases when the passive voice is good to use: (1) when you want to focus on the action, not the actor, (2) when you do not know the name of the actor, or (3) when the actor is not important.

EXAMPLES **Focus on action:** A mistake has been made.
(<u>not</u> You made a mistake.)
Name unknown: A woman has been charged with theft.
Actor not important: The check was mailed on Tuesday.

Language Exercise B

Choose the reason passive voice is used in each sentence. Write 1 (focus is on the action) or 2 (name is not known) or 3 (the actor is not important) on each line below.

_____ 1. My friend was struck by a car.

_____ 2. A bad check was written in the food store.

_____ 3. The phone call was made at 2:00 A.M.

_____ 4. At 10:00 A.M. the doors to the store were unlocked.

Changing Voice

To change a sentence from the active voice to the passive voice, switch the subject and the object. Change the form of the verb, too.

EXAMPLE

Active Voice	to	Passive Voice
The <u>players</u> wore new <u>hats</u>.		New <u>hats</u> were worn by the
subject ___ *object*		*subject*
		<u>players</u>.
		object

To change a sentence from the passive voice to the active voice, make the subject the object. Make the person or thing that acted the subject.

EXAMPLE

Passive Voice	to	Active Voice
The <u>soda</u> was sold by <u>them</u>.		<u>They</u> sold the <u>soda</u>.
subject ___ *object*		*subject* ___ *object*

Language Exercise A

Rewrite each passive sentence in the active voice.

1. passive voice: With great force, the lock was broken by the thief.

   active voice: _____

   _____

2. passive voice: The moon was landed on by the crew of *Apollo 11*.

   active voice: _____

3. passive voice: A plaque was left on the moon by them.

   active voice: _____

   _____

Language Exercise B

Choose the best way to write the underlined phrase or sentence. Write the letter in the blank.

_____ 1. <u>A creature has been seen in Loch Ness.</u>
   (A) Some people who have been to Loch Ness have seen a creature there.
   (B) No change is needed.

_____ 2. <u>These sightings have been doubted by many experts.</u>
   (A) Many experts have doubted these sightings.
   (B) No change is needed.

_____ 3. <u>Tests have been done by experts</u> to see if a monster is in the lake.
   (A) Experts have done tests.
   (B) No change is needed.

Sentence Revision

You can improve your writing by revising sentences to take out unnecessary words. Every word in every sentence should be there for a reason. If a word does not make your writing more vivid or precise, get rid of it. If too many words make it hard for a reader to get to the point, rewrite all or part of the sentence.

EXAMPLE 1 **Too Wordy:** The hikers saw the big, massive, dark, black cloud covering over the sun.

Revised: The hikers saw the massive, black cloud covering the sun.

EXAMPLE 2 **Too Wordy:** Mike is of the belief that the death penalty should be allowed.

Revised: Mike believes the death penalty should be allowed.

Language Exercise **Rewrite each sentence to get rid of extra words. Be sure not to lose any of the meaning.**

1. At the same time that he was driving a taxi, he was also working at a lawn-care type of business.

   _____

2. It goes without saying that in this day and age, many people do not vote.

   _____

3. The dog was very large in size and gave a nasty and fierce growling sound when anyone walked by the yard.

   _____

4. Because of the fact that it took a really very long time to get to his work, Sam quit his job.

   _____

5. Far away in the distance, we could see the little, small ships.

   _____

6. Modern cars of today can be driven faster than the old cars of the past.

   _____

7. I asked the speaker to repeat again what he had said.

   _____

For more practice on revising sentences, turn to pages 180–181.

Language Link
Style and Word Choice

Expository writing often has a formal style. When you write to explain, you may write for many readers or for readers you don't know personally. In these situations, your style needs to be especially clear and formal. To write in a clear, formal style, choose your words and phrases carefully. You should choose different words for formal writing than you choose for informal speaking or writing.

Informal or incorrect expression	Appropriate formal language
Being that you are the supervisor, you should decide.	Because you are the supervisor, you should decide.
We might could go to the concert.	We may be able to go to the concert.
You shouldn't ought to wear those jeans.	You shouldn't wear those jeans.
My friends, they said that I should apply for the job.	My friends said that I should apply for the job.
Try and arrive on time.	Try to arrive on time.
The reason is because the power was off.	The reason is that the power was off.
I am fixing to go to the store.	I am getting ready to go to the store.
I heard where you are coming with us.	I heard that you are coming with us.

Language Exercise — Rewrite each sentence by changing the informal or incorrect expressions to clear, formal, and appropriate language.

1. Being that the subway is more crowded, I prefer the bus.

   _____

2. You might could get a ticket if you are willing to wait in line.

   _____

3. The reason I am late is because my car broke down.

   _____

4. The minister, she says that new families are always welcome.

   _____

5. This boy's parents are fixing to take him to the doctor.

   _____

6. We shouldn't ought to lose these insurance papers.

   _____

Slang and Word Choice

Another way to write in a clear, formal style is to avoid using slang. A slang expression does not always mean the same thing to everyone who hears or reads it. Slang is fine in many situations—such as talking to friends or writing personal e-mail. However, you should not use slang in expository writing.

Slang: It's cool with me.
Formal: I approve.

Slang: His boss gave him grief for being late.
Formal: His boss reprimanded him for being late.

Slang: I'm bummed because I can't get the vacation time I requested.
Formal: I'm disappointed because I can't get the vacation time I requested.

Language Exercise A

Replace each of the underlined slang expressions with more formal words or phrases. Write the new word or phrase.

1. At the end of each week, I am flat broke. _____

2. The painters goofed off while we were out of town. _____

3. The president is really into this idea. _____

4. Leonard dissed his friend one too many times. _____

Language Exercise B

Revise the following paragraph. Rewrite the informal and slang expressions in a clear, more formal style.

You ticked me off when you accused me of taking the tools that got swiped. I'm not the one who ripped them off. Alvin, he says they disappeared right around the time Annette quit. You've been treating me lousy all week, and the reason is because you don't trust me. Try and believe what I tell you, or I'm out of here.

_____

_____

_____

_____

_____

_____

_____

GED Essay Link

Expository Writing

Using Examples

On the GED Writing Test, you will write an expository essay. In your essay, you can use examples to help explain the points you want to make. Read the sample topic below.

SAMPLE TOPIC

> **TOPIC B**
> What kind of work do you enjoy the most or get the most satisfaction from?
>
> In your essay, explain your choice. Use your personal observations, experience, and knowledge to support your essay

To write a strong GED essay on this topic, you might give examples of the types of work you enjoy most. Perhaps you like to work with your hands. Maybe you like to work with children. Or, you might like creative kinds of work. For all these types of work, there are many possible examples.

In the sample response below, a student writer has written about one kind of work he particularly likes. Notice how he uses examples to explain this type of work.

SAMPLE RESPONSE

> The kind of work I get the most satisfaction from is carpentry. I like to make complicated things, but I don't like to follow anyone else's directions. For example, last year I built a treehouse with my children. We made all the plans ourselves. So, nobody else in the world has a treehouse like ours. I also built a deck for my parents. It's shaped to the house just right, and I made the railings in a fancy way that my mom thinks is beautiful.

Planning a Response

You know that good expository writing offers a clear explanation with:

- examples of important ideas

- defined words and terms, as well as precise synonyms

When you plan a piece of expository writing, you will want to think of examples to help you explain your ideas and terms to define.

A. The writer of the paragraph on page 52 began by listing some ideas and examples of different types of work.

Carpentry

kids' treehouse

Mom and Dad's deck

deck chairs

Yardwork

mowing grass

raking leaves

planting new stuff

hate weeding!!

Driving

family driver

drive a cab

delivery truck

long haul trucking

Working with kids

camp counselor

kids' sports coach

church youth program

B. Read Topic B on page 52 again. What different types of paid or unpaid work do you do? Think about the types of work you enjoy, the ones that give you a feeling of satisfaction?

1. **Prewrite:** Use the planner below to list types of work and examples.

Type of work: _____

Examples:

_____

_____

Type of work: _____

Examples:

_____

Type of work: _____

Examples:

_____

_____

Type of work: _____

Examples:

_____

2. **Write:** On a separate piece of paper, write a paragraph response to Topic B. Write about one kind of work that you enjoy or get satisfaction from. Use examples from your list to help explain this kind of work.

Apply Your Writing Skills

Write an Expository Essay

Now you are ready to apply what you have learned by writing an expository essay.

An expository essay:
- explains an idea or point of view
- uses specific words and carefully chosen synonyms in clear examples
- uses the active voice and a formal style
- keeps the same point of view

As you write, follow the steps in the writing process outlined below.

ASSIGNMENT

Some people believe that "progress" always means new buildings and roads. Other people believe that "progress" also includes keeping older buildings, parks, and open spaces. Think about something old in your community that has been replaced by something new. Write a four-paragraph expository essay to explain how you feel about this change. Tell whether you think it was an example of progress.

Prewriting

1. List some changes in your community that you could write about. Circle any that seem particularly important to you personally.

   _____

   _____

2. Choose one change to write about. List any personal observations, experiences, or knowledge you have about this change.

   _____

   _____

   _____

   _____

3. Do you think this change was an example of progress? List your reasons why or why not.

   _____

   _____

   _____

Writing the First Draft

Write an opening sentence that states the main idea of your essay. What is the main point about this change that you want to get across? Try writing the opening sentence several different ways. Write your final version below.

_____

On a separate piece of paper, write your first draft.

Write an introductory paragraph. Use your opening sentence. Add any background information about the change that will help your reader understand the point you will make in the body of your essay.

Write <u>two</u> body paragraphs. Use your notes from page 54.

- The first body paragraph should explain your personal observations, experiences, or knowledge about this change.
- The second body paragraph should explain why you think this change is or is not an example of progress. (Hint: It may help to define what you think progress is.)

Write a concluding paragraph. Write a sentence to wrap up all the points you made. Add another sentence or two to leave the reader with a final viewpoint, a question, or an idea to think about.

Revising and Editing

Review, revise, and edit. Read your essay to see if you accomplished what you set out to do. Then use the checklist on page 216 to revise and edit it. Also, pay special attention to these points.

- ☐ Did you use good synonyms for overused words? _See pages 43–44._
- ☐ Did you use connecting words and phrases? _See pages 41–42._
- ☐ Did you replace the passive voice with the active voice? _See pages 47–48._
- ☐ Did you revise your work to cut extra words? _See page 49._
- ☐ Did you revise so there are no changes in point of view? _See page 45._
- ☐ Did you use two separate paragraphs to organize the body of your essay?

Writing the Final Draft

Write a final draft. Then read it one last time. If necessary, recopy or retype it.

Sharing the Final Draft

Publish. Let another person read your final draft. Ask if your message was clear and what else you could do to improve the essay. Make some notes and attach them to a copy of the essay. File the essay in your writing portfolio.

LESSON 4

Persuasive Writing

Elements of Persuasive Writing

Persuasive writing shows your readers your side of an issue, why they should agree with it, or why they should take a certain action. First, you state your position clearly. Then you give facts, opinions, or reasons that support it. You must back up your opinion with specific details so the reader knows <u>why</u> you feel the way you do.

Ads and sales messages, letters to the editor, and requests from charities are all forms of persuasive writing. A cover letter to an employer is also a form of persuasive writing that you may need to write.

Persuasive writing may appeal to readers' reason, emotions, or sense of right and wrong. A good piece of persuasive writing might appeal to all three.

EXAMPLE Below is part of a letter from the leader of a nonprofit group against family violence. She wants to persuade her readers to support the group's work with a donation.

Your support will help us continue sending our teaching materials, *Safe Homes/Safe Families,* free to teachers across the country. Last year we mailed information to over 350,000 teachers who requested it. The sample lessons, discussion topics, and classroom activities help teachers show their students how to recognize violence in the home, how to work toward solutions, and where to find help.

The problem of family violence is growing. It occurs in all parts of the country—in cities, suburbs, small towns, and rural areas. It occurs in families of all social, economic, and educational levels. Children who grow up in violent homes are often unaware that the behavior they experience is a problem. And, unfortunately, they may grow into violent adults. We believe that getting information into the hands of students and teachers can help break the cycle of family violence.

WRITE In the example, the writer believes in a cause. She wants to persuade you to believe in it, too, and to act by supporting her group.

On a separate piece of paper, write a paragraph about a cause you believe in. Persuade your reader to believe in it, too, or to take some specific action to help it. Choose an issue that you have a strong opinion about—crime, politics, rights. Give specific reasons and examples to support your opinion.

Using Connecting Words

Your opinion will make more sense to your reader if your ideas are connected. As you learned in the previous section on expository writing, connecting words join your ideas and help your writing flow smoothly.

EXAMPLE   **No connecting word:** People have the most energy at 10:00 A.M. You should read and do other memory tasks at that time.
Connecting word: People have the most energy at 10:00 A.M. Therefore, you should read and do other memory tasks at that time.

EXAMPLE   **No connecting word:** Your body goes into an energy slump at 2:00 P.M. You should do easier tasks in the afternoon.
Connecting word: Your body goes into an energy slump at 2:00 P.M., so you should do easier tasks in the afternoon.

Review the list of connecting words on page 41 and the rules for punctuation with connecting words on page 42.

PRACTICE

Fill in each blank with the connecting word that best joins the two thoughts.

1. Bran cereal is high in fiber. _____ , it is a good choice for breakfast.

   In summary   **Finally**   **Therefore**

2. People react to caffeine in many ways, _____ whether you drink coffee is up to you.

   in summary   **in brief**   **so**

3. Any exercise that speeds up your heart rate is good. _____, walking, running, and jogging are good exercise choices.

   Finally   **In brief**   **For example**

4. Eat plenty of vegetables and fruits. _____, limit foods high in fat, such as ice cream, peanuts, and cheese.

   In addition   **Finally**   **As a result**

5. I like to exercise every day, _____ I joined a health club.

   after   **so**   **whenever**

WRITE On a separate piece of paper, write a letter to ask a friend to give up smoking, drinking, overeating, or some other bad habit.

Prewrite: Choose your topic. List facts, examples, and reasons to give up the bad habit.

Write: Use connecting words to join your thoughts and to make your points easier to follow.

Writing Compare and Contrast Sentences

You can help persuade your readers to agree with your opinion by writing sentences that compare and contrast. To **compare** is to show how things are the same. To **contrast** is to show how things are <u>not</u> the same.

EXAMPLES

Compare
Both political parties have plans for the extra money.

Contrast
The Republicans want to cut taxes. The Democrats want to pay off part of the debt.

A. Write *compare* if the sentence shows how two things are the same. Write *contrast* if the sentence shows how two things are not the same.

_____ 1. People who walk to work are healthier than those who drive.

_____ 2. A half cup of ice cream has the same fat content as ten peanuts.

_____ 3. Japan exports more cars to the U.S. than France does.

_____ 4. Lake Superior is the largest of the five Great Lakes.

Compare and contrast sentences make your point clear when the ideas are smoothly joined. Here are some connecting words and phrases you can use to join ideas that compare and contrast.

Words that compare: *and, also, too, same as, as . . . as, like, similarly, in the same way, likewise*
Words that contrast: *but, yet, than, still, however, likewise, in contrast, on the other hand*

EXAMPLE I like to shop on weekends as much as I like to shop during the week.

Review the rules for punctuation with connecting words on page 42.

B. Complete each sentence to compare or contrast. The connecting words are in bold type. The first sentence has been done for you.

1. I liked the movie, **but** _it wasn't as interesting as the book._

2. The movie told the ending in the first scene, **in contrast to** _____.

3. I like his acting **as much as** _____.

Remember these three points when you compare and contrast.

1. **Avoid obvious statements.** If you want to compare and contrast two books, for example, it would be pointless to say that both have words.

2. **Stick to two subjects at a time.** You cannot compare and contrast more than two subjects in one sentence.

3. **Compare and contrast subjects that belong to the same category.** For example, you can easily compare two athletes. However, to compare an athlete with a politician, you must find a category they both belong to, such as *role models*.

One way to compare and contrast is first to write down your two subjects as headings. Then list points on which they are the same or different. For example, here are lists that a writer made to compare and contrast some abilities of males and females.

In general, males	In general, females
speak later than girls	speak earlier
stutter more	speak more clearly
catch up by age eight	speak better from age ten
solve mazes better as teenagers	do worse on mazes as teenagers
are better at mazes as adults	are better at language as adults

EXAMPLE Here is how the writer used the lists to write a paragraph.

People wonder why men and women seem to do better at different tasks. Experts have discovered some facts about male and female development. First, girls generally learn to speak earlier and better than boys, and boys have more speech problems. Far more boys than girls stutter, for example. Boys catch up by age eight, though. From age ten on, most girls again speak better than boys, and women generally do better than men on speech and language tasks. Meanwhile, teenage boys tend to do better than teenage girls on tests with mazes. The same is true for men and women. Even after much research, no one can tell why there are these differences in males and females.

WRITE Write one sentence that compares and one that contrasts.

1. Topic: two friends

   compare _____

   contrast _____

2. Topic: two homes that you have lived in or visited

   compare _____

   contrast _____

Persuasive Writing

Using Specific and Fresh Language

It is important in all your writing to choose your words with care. In Lesson 2, you learned that precise words create an interesting word picture. In persuasive writing, specific words help you persuade your reader that your belief or opinion has value. By using specific words, you help your reader understand your way of thinking.

EXAMPLES   **Vague:** Many people work too hard.
                    Specific: Tool-and-die machinists may work ten hours a day, six days a week.

The first sentence may seem to give you a fact, but look closely at the words. What does "many people" mean? What does "too hard" mean? The second sentence states an example of the idea with specific words.

PRACTICE

Rewrite each sentence. Replace each underlined part with a more specific word or phrase.

1. **Vague:** Sabrina's new <u>dog</u> is <u>great</u>.

   Specific: Sabrina's new fox terrier is good-natured.

2. **Vague:** My leg was <u>hurt</u> in the crash.

   Specific: _____

3. **Vague:** Mr. Mori drives a <u>truck</u> <u>part-time</u>.

   Specific: _____

4. **Vague:** The <u>man</u> <u>went</u> to the boss' office for an answer.

   Specific: _____

5. **Vague:** They were <u>eating</u> candy in the next row and <u>making</u> <u>noise</u>.

   Specific: _____

Words and phrases often become stale through overuse. Phrases such as "in the doghouse" and "cry wolf" have been used so often that readers are tired of them. The phrases no longer mean much. Replace stale phrases with fresh words that help your reader understand your meaning.

EXAMPLES
Stale	Fresh
eat humble pie	take back your words ten times over
hit the ceiling	holler until your throat hurts

A. Underline the stale phrase in each sentence.

1. We stayed friends through thick and thin.

2. Baseball is as American as Mom's apple pie.

3. The stamps are selling like hotcakes.

4. "This is a tried and true cure," the doctor said.

5. It's raining cats and dogs today.

6. "I am sick and tired of your lateness," the boss said.

7. The old gum was as hard as nails.

8. If you want to do well, you have to take the bull by the horns.

B. Rewrite each sentence. Replace the underlined stale phrase with fresh words.

1. **Stale:** I've had my ups and downs today.

   Fresh: _____

2. **Stale:** "Now it's time to face the music," the congressman said.

   Fresh: _____

3. **Stale:** If you eat well, get enough rest, and have a good outlook, you will live to a ripe old age.

   Fresh: _____

4. **Stale:** A summer cold is no tea party.

   Fresh: _____

WRITE On a separate piece of paper, write a persuasive paragraph on one of the topics below.

Cigarettes should (should not) be declared illegal.
The space program should (should not) be ended.
There should (should not) be speed limits on highways.

Prewrite: List the reasons you believe the way you do. Draw on your personal observations, experiences, and knowledge about this topic.

Write: State your position clearly. Support it with the reasons and examples you listed. Use specific and fresh language.

Persuasive Writing

Supporting the Main Idea

In a persuasive piece, you want the reader to agree with your main point. Therefore, you support it by giving facts, opinions, and reasons.

Facts

A **fact** is a statement that is true. The writer can prove the statement is true by giving examples. Writers often use facts to support the main idea of an essay. Here is how one writer used facts in a letter to the editor.

EXAMPLE Today, as I was walking to work, I saw a newspaper in the street. I lifted a corner of the paper and found a thin cat mewing with hunger. I could not leave the cat on the street, so I took it to an animal shelter for care. The man in charge told me that was the tenth animal that had been dropped off that day. In fact, more than 500 cats and 1,000 dogs are dropped off every year at animal shelters in our town alone. The shelter does not have the money to feed and treat all these animals, so more than half must be killed. I hope that the cat I left there today will live and that others like it will not suffer from lack of care. Please give what you can to the local animal shelter.

Opinions

An **opinion** is a point or belief that cannot always be proved. Writers use opinions as well as facts to support their main ideas. Good writers back up their opinions with reasons or logic. The next example offers the opinion that child-care workers should be licensed. Look for the logic the writer uses.

EXAMPLE Taking care of children is more difficult than many people realize. That is why all child-care workers should be licensed by the state. People who mind children in day care centers or in their homes must be trained to watch for possible dangers and know how to prevent accidents. They also need to know how to get help fast. Specific courses should be given in how to feed and handle infants and small children. Child-care workers must also know how to choose safe toys and games for children, and how to help children get along with others.

PRACTICE

Write *O* if the sentence is an opinion or *F* if the sentence is a fact.

_____ 1. Main Street is ten blocks long.

_____ 2. Main Street has the best shopping around.

_____ 3. Cigarette smoking is America's worst health problem.

_____ 4. Men should have shorter hair than women.

_____ 5. Juan's sister has three children.

_____ 6. The United States government consists of three branches.

Reasons

Your opinions should be supported with logical reasons. <u>Avoid</u> the following three kinds of false reasoning.

A. Jumping to Conclusions: Sometimes a writer reaches a decision without having enough facts. This is called jumping to a conclusion.

EXAMPLE Our union will not support the new overtime rules. I know because I spoke to Mike.

The writer draws the conclusion that Mike speaks for the entire union. An opinion from one union member is not enough to reach this conclusion.

B. Quoting False Experts: If you rely on experts who are not qualified to support your opinions, your proof will be false.

EXAMPLE Dr. O. Malhot, an eye doctor, says people should run five miles a day.

Dr. Malhot is an expert on eyes, not exercise. Quote a fitness expert to make your point.

C. Mistaking Cause and Effect: A **cause** is the reason things happen. The result of a cause is an **effect**. If you cannot prove that a reason (cause) results in a specific outcome (effect), your belief is not supported.

EXAMPLE When parents do not keep their teenagers at home at night, crime increases all over the city.

The writer has mistakenly seen a cause-and-effect relationship where none may exist. There is no reason to believe that allowing teenagers out at night affects crime. Other things may cause an increase in crime.

PRACTICE

Write the letter that names the kind of false reasoning: (A) jumping to conclusions, (B) quoting false experts, or (C) mistaking cause and effect.

_____ 1. The local radio station never plays good CDs. There is nothing good on the radio.

_____ 2. Shaun says that Flair makes the best slacks. He knows because he saw a hockey star wear this brand.

_____ 3. Since Marc started dating Lucy, his work has been poor. If he were to stop dating her, his work would improve.

_____ 4. I eat bran and fruit every day. That is why I never get colds.

Language Link
Subject-Verb Agreement

Your essay will be more persuasive if the subjects and verbs in your sentences are in the same form. Make a singular subject agree with a singular verb, and a plural subject agree with a plural verb. For subject-verb agreement, follow these steps.

1. Find the subject in the sentence. The subject tells <u>who</u> or <u>what</u>.

2. See if the subject is singular (one) or plural (more than one).

3. If the subject is singular, add *-s* or *-es* to most verbs.

4. If the subject is plural, use the base form of most verbs.

5. *I* and *you* use the base form of the verb: *I think* (not *thinks*), *I eat* (not *eats*), *you think* (not *thinks*), *you eat* (not *eats*).

6. Use the correct forms of the irregular verbs *be* and *have*.

   be: *I am; you are; he, she, or it is; we are; you are; they are*

   have: *I have; you have; he, she, or it has; we have; you have; they have*

EXAMPLES

Regular Verbs		Irregular Verbs *be* and *have*	
Singular subject	**Plural subject**	**Singular subject**	**Plural subject**
The cat <u>jumps</u>.	The cats <u>jump</u>.	The star <u>is</u> bright.	The stars <u>are</u> bright.
He <u>dances</u>.	They <u>dance</u>.	I <u>have</u> to dance.	He <u>has</u> to dance.

Language Exercise A

Circle the correct verb form for each sentence.

1. I (**hope, hopes**) the store will be open late.

2. We (**takes, take**) our daughter to that child-care center.

3. The egg (**has, have**) a strange taste.

4. She (**works, work**) hard at her new job.

EXAMPLE The box of gifts contains food, clothing, and books.

The subject in this sentence is *box*, not *gifts*. The verb is *contains*. The words *of gifts* that come between the subject and the verb do not affect agreement.

Language Exercise B

Underline the subject in each sentence. Cross out any words that come between the subject and the verb. Then circle the correct verb.

1. A salad with extra carrots (**is, are**) my usual lunch.

2. The people in the back of the crowd (**needs, need**) to be heard.

3. Ned, with his three dogs, (**run, runs**) around the block after work.

4. The leader of the union (**say, says**) dues will go up.

For more practice on subject-verb agreement, turn to pages 165–167.

Compound Subjects

A **compound subject** is two or more nouns or pronouns joined by *and, or,* or *nor.* A compound subject joined by *and* needs a plural verb. When a compound subject is joined by *or* or *nor,* the verb must agree with the subject that is closer to the verb.

EXAMPLES   Plural verb: The bus and subway stop here.
Singular verb: Neither the bus nor the subway stops here.

Language Exercise A

Write the correct form of the verb in each sentence.

1. The roof and the window _____ (**leak**) when it rains.

2. Marie or Juan _____ (**give**) me a ride to work on Thursdays.

3. My boss and I _____ (**bring**) our lunches to work every day.

Singular and Plural Words

A **collective noun** is one that refers to a group of people or things as a single unit. Examples of collective nouns are *class, team, staff, crew, troop, jury, public, group.* These nouns are often singular and use singular verbs.

When the subject is a pronoun, verb agreement may be more difficult. Some pronouns are always singular, some are always plural, and some can be either.

Singular	Plural	Singular or Plural	
words with *one:* someone, no one	several	all	any
words with *other:* another, other	few	some	part
words with *body:* somebody, nobody	both	none	half
words with *thing:* nothing, something	most		
other words: each, either, much, neither	many		

EXAMPLE Singular   Plural
No one gives a better haircut.   A few of the people drive to work.

Language Exercise B

For more practice on subject-verb agreement, turn to pages 165–167.

Decide if the verb used in each sentence is correct. If so, write *C.* If not, write the correct form of the verb.

_____ 1. Each of those restaurants serves fast food.

_____ 2. Some eat burgers and fries nearly every night.

_____ 3. Nobody love fast food more than I do.

_____ 4. My family take it home at least once a week, as a matter of fact.

Check your answers on page 236.   **65**

Persuasive Writing

Using Cause-and-Effect Relationships

On the GED Writing Test, you may be able to use cause-effect reasoning to support your essay. In fact, for many essay topics, you will be asked to discuss why something happens (cause) or state what happens as the result of a certain action (effect). Read the sample topic below.

SAMPLE TOPIC

> ### TOPIC C
>
> Why do Americans watch so much television?
>
> In your essay, explain why television is so popular. Use your personal observations, experience, and knowledge to support your essay.

To write a strong GED essay on this topic, you must discuss the cause of an effect. Americans watch a lot of TV—but why? What is the <u>cause</u> of, or reason for, TV's popularity?

In the sample response below, a student writer has written about one reason for TV's popularity.

SAMPLE RESPONSE

> I believe that TV is popular mostly because people are so tired. All we do is rush nowadays. We hurry through rush hour to get to work on time. We work hard all morning. We punch out for lunch, which is supposed to be a break, but we rush to do errands. Then we rush back to punch in on time. After work, we ride the rush hour back home. Even my kids have busy schedules. No one in my family wants to make any effort in the evenings. TV is easy—you just turn it on, lie back on the couch, and watch.

Planning a Response

You know that persuasive writing offers support for a viewpoint or opinion with:

- cause-effect reasoning
- supporting details presented in order of importance

Before you write about cause-and-effect relationships, you will want to think about the causes and/or effects to include in your writing as well as the order you will put them in.

A. The writer of the paragraph on page 66 made a cause-effect chart. Here is part of it. She listed different causes, or reasons, why people watch TV. She also listed supporting details under each cause. Then she numbered the causes in order of importance. The paragraph on page 66 is the third body paragraph of her essay.

Effect: People watch TV a lot.

Causes/Reasons

They enjoy the shows	It's easy	They like the news
• comedies • sports • reality TV	• people work hard all day • rush to work, rush home • even kids are busy	• get local news • get national news • news bulletins, like 9/11
second in importance—2	most important—3	least important—1

B. Read Topic C on page 66 again. Think of reasons for TV's popularity. Why do you watch TV? Why do other people that you know watch TV?

1. **Prewrite:** Use the planner below to list two reasons why you think people watch TV. Add details and examples to explain those reasons. Choose which reason is more important.

Effect: People watch TV a lot.

Causes/Reasons

2. **Write:** On a separate piece of paper, write a two-paragraph response to Topic C. Give two important reasons you believe TV is so popular. Save the more important reason for the second paragraph. Support your reasons with details and examples from your planner.

Apply Your Writing Skills

Write a Persuasive Essay

Now you are ready to apply what you have learned by writing a persuasive essay.

A persuasive essay:

- tells the reader why he or she should agree with your opinion
- uses facts, examples, and reasons to support your main point
- uses specific, fresh language

As you write, follow the steps in the writing process outlined below.

ASSIGNMENT

Write a five-paragraph persuasive essay about an issue you feel strongly about, such as prayer in schools, smoking, or healthcare.

Prewriting

1. List some issues that you feel strongly about.

   _____

   _____

2. Choose one issue to write about. Write your opinion or viewpoint. Then list facts, examples, and reasons from your personal experience related to the issue.

   _____

   _____

   _____

   _____

3. Look for three major supporting ideas on your list. On a separate piece of paper, draw an idea map like this one. Write your three supporting ideas in the boxes and, under each idea, add related details, examples, facts, or reasons.

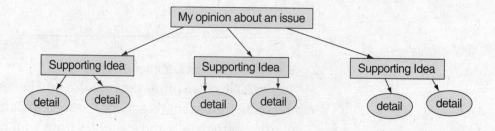

Writing the First Draft

Write an opening sentence that states the main idea of your essay. What is your opinion or viewpoint that you want to persuade your reader to agree with? Try writing the opening sentence several different ways. Write your final version below.

_____

On a separate piece of paper, write your first draft.

Write an introductory paragraph. Use your opening sentence. Then add any background information that will help introduce your opinion to your reader.

Write three body paragraphs. Use the three groups of supporting ideas and details on your idea map for <u>each</u> of your body paragraphs.

- Write a sentence about the major supporting idea. This is the topic sentence of the paragraph. Make sure each topic sentence supports your overall main idea.
- Add details to each topic sentence. Use examples, facts, and reasons.
- Make your writing fresh and vivid.

Write a concluding paragraph. Write a sentence to wrap up all the points you made. Add another sentence or two to leave the reader with a final question or an idea to think about.

Revising and Editing

Review, revise, and edit. Read your essay to see if you accomplished what you set out to do. Ask yourself, "If I were reading this essay, would it persuade me?" Then use the checklist on page 216 to revise and edit it. Also, pay special attention to these points.

- ☐ Did you write compare and contrast sentences? _See pages 58–59._
- ☐ Did you replace vague, stale words with specific, fresh language? _See pages 60–61._
- ☐ Do all your subjects and verbs agree? _See pages 64–65._
- ☐ Did you use connecting words to link your ideas? _See page 57._
- ☐ Did you support your ideas with facts, opinions, and reasons? _See page 62._
- ☐ Are your details in a logical order, and do they all support the main idea? _See page 62._

Writing the Final Draft

Write a final draft. Then read it one last time. If necessary, recopy or retype it.

Sharing the Final Draft

Publish. Let another person read your final draft. Ask if your message was clear and what else you could do to improve the essay. Make some notes and attach them to a copy of the essay. File the essay in your writing portfolio.

LESSON 5

The Writing Process

In Lessons 1 through 4, you have followed a process to write essays. The complete writing process consists of these steps.

Step 1:   Prewriting
Step 2:   Writing the First Draft
Step 3:   Revising and Editing
Step 4:   Writing the Final Draft
Step 5:   Publishing (Sharing the Final Draft)

Step 1: Prewriting

Prewriting means planning before you begin to write. This first step in the writing process involves defining your topic, generating ideas about it, and organizing those ideas.

Define Your Topic

To define your topic, first define your **purpose** for writing and the **audience** for whom you are writing.

- **Identify Your Purpose** Ask, *Why am I writing?* Possible answers are to tell a story, to describe, to explain, or to persuade.
- **Identify Your Audience** Ask, *Who will read what I am writing?* Possible answers are a friend, a coworker, a teacher, or a potential employer.

EXAMPLE Melissa Sanchez attends a preGED class at a community college. The first night, her instructor asked the students to write an essay. The essay topic was "How Can I Achieve Success in This Class?" Melissa thought about what she might write. First, she defined her purpose and her audience.

Purpose: To explain   **Audience:** My instructor and I

Then she made the following list of possible topics.

1. Everyday math practice
2. Good study habits
3. Improve my reading

Melissa selected "improve my reading" as her topic.

Essay Writing

Choose a topic that is neither too general nor too limited. For example, suppose you are asked to write a two-page essay on hobbies. This is a general subject that could fill a book. But some topics that you could cover in a brief essay are "refinishing old furniture" or "getting started in photography."

A topic that is too narrow or limited is also hard to write about because you may run out of things to say. For example, the topic of "wood-refinishing tools" is too limited for a two-page essay on hobbies.

Choose a topic that you already know something about or one that you find interesting. This will make your writing task easier.

PRACTICE

Below each general subject, list two topics that you could write about. The first one has been started for you.

1. Subject: Sports
   Purpose: To explain
   Audience: A group of children
   Topic 1: _How to Play Soccer_
   Topic 2: _____

2. Subject: Jobs
   Purpose: To describe
   Audience: Your friends
   Topic 1: _____
   Topic 2: _____

3. Subject: Movies
   Purpose: To describe
   Audience: Your friends
   Topic 1: _____
   Topic 2: _____

4. Subject: Animals
   Purpose: To persuade
   Audience: Fellow students
   Topic 1: _____
   Topic 2: _____

Generate Ideas

After your purpose, audience, and topic are clear in your mind, you are ready to generate ideas about your topic.

- **Explore your thoughts about the topic.** What interests you about the topic? What would interest your readers?
- **Brainstorm ideas.** To brainstorm, let your mind work freely as one thought leads to the next. Write down everything that comes to mind, without making any decisions about which ideas are good or bad. (That will come later).
- **Ask yourself questions.** Try applying the reporter's basic questions: Who? What? When? Where? Why? How? Write down everything that comes to mind, and keep writing anytime one idea leads to another.
- **Use what you know.** Your own personal observations, knowledge, and experiences are your best sources for ideas. You learn every day, just by living, observing people, reading the newspaper, and watching TV. What else can you say about this topic?

Organize Your Ideas

While you are generating ideas, write them down. You can refer to them when you begin to write. First, make a list of your ideas. Next, organize the ideas in the order that you want to write about them. Writing an **outline** and drawing an **idea map** are two ways to organize your ideas.

EXAMPLE Melissa thought about different ways she could improve her reading. She listed her ideas. Then she made this outline to organize them.

How I Can Improve My Reading Skills

I. **Read every day**

    A. set aside a time to read each day

    B. read 10 minutes before I get up

    C. read 10 minutes before I go to sleep at night

II. **Read with other people**

    A. join a book club

    B. read to my child

    C. volunteer to read to a blind person

III. **Read lots of different things**

    A. check out books from library

    B. subscribe to a magazine

    C. find interesting Internet sites

    D. read the newspaper

Instead of an outline, Melissa could have created an idea map like this one.

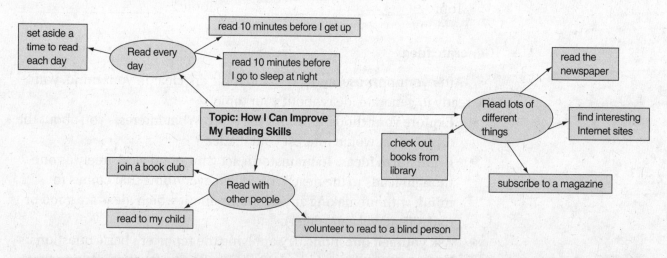

PRACTICE

Brainstorm and list your ideas for this topic: What are the advantages (or disadvantages) of a small (or large) family? Write an outline to organize your ideas. Then make an idea map. Which way of organizing ideas works best for you? Use a separate piece of paper.

Step 2: Writing the First Draft

In Step 1 of the writing process, you created a plan for what you are going to write. In Step 2 you will follow your plan and write the first draft. A **first draft** is the first version of your piece of writing. Sometimes you'll need to write two or three drafts before your piece is final. With each draft you will improve the piece.

When writing the first draft, the main goal is to get your ideas on paper in an organized way. Choose words and develop sentences that express your ideas. Don't worry about perfect word choice, spelling, and punctuation at this stage.

The first draft of the essay will have several paragraphs. Each paragraph will have a topic sentence and supporting details. The **topic sentence** states the main idea that you will develop in the paragraph. The **supporting details** are sentences that relate to the main idea.

Writing an Opening Sentence

An opening sentence tells the **main idea** of your essay. It tells the reader your purpose for writing the essay. If you write a good opening sentence, you can refer back to it as you continue writing to make sure you have not drifted away from your point.

A good opening sentence should be a clearly written summary of the main idea. It should be general enough to introduce the points you will cover in the rest of the piece. Avoid making opening statements that are vague (unclear) or statements that simply announce the topic.

EXAMPLE Melissa reviewed her outline. Then she wrote her main idea.

I can achieve success and improve my reading with just a few simple changes.

Melissa wrote three possible opening sentences.

1. This essay is about success in improving my reading.
2. Improving my reading successfully will not be that hard.
3. I can achieve success and improve my reading by making some changes in my daily life.

Sentence 1 just announces what the essay is about in general terms. Sentence 2 states the main idea, but it is vague. Since Melissa's goal was to show that she could make a difference in her reading skills fairly easily, she decided that the third sentence was the best opening statement.

Each topic below is followed by three opening statements. Put an X in front of the best statement to introduce each topic.

1. **Topic:** The Case Against Gun Control

    _____ A. Owning guns is a constitutional right of all Americans.

    _____ B. Some people want gun control, but many others don't.

    _____ C. I am going to write about gun control.

2. **Topic:** Every Citizen Should Vote

    _____ A. Voting is not a right; it is a duty of every citizen.

    _____ B. Voting has been expanded to include almost all adults.

    _____ C. Some people don't believe in voting.

3. **Topic:** Avoiding Sun Exposure

    _____ A. Many people like to spend hot summer days outside.

    _____ B. You don't have to stay inside to avoid getting too much sun.

    _____ C. There are all kinds of sunscreens on the market.

Developing Supporting Details

Your outline or idea map will guide you through the main points of the essay. As you get to each main point, begin a new paragraph. Each paragraph in an essay has a topic sentence and other sentences that support the topic sentence. You can write several types of detail sentences to support a topic sentence.

Details may:

- be **facts** or **reasons** that prove or disprove a point
- be **examples** that explain or prove a main idea
- be listed in **time order,** according to the order in which they occur
- be listed in **order of importance,** from the most important to the least important or from the least important to the most important
- show **cause and effect,** how one thing causes another thing to happen
- **compare or contrast** to show how things are alike or different

As you write paragraphs, use several types of details to support your topic sentences.

Here are the first two paragraphs of Melissa's essay. Compare these paragraphs to her outline and idea map. Notice that she wrote a topic sentence for each main point and then wrote supporting details to explain those statements.

Essay Writing

EXAMPLE Introductory paragraph I can acheive success and improve my reading by making some changes in my daily life. Reading is essential to success. At first, I thought it might be hard to get to be a better reader but after careful thought, I realized it doesn't have to be.

Body paragraph 1 My first goal is to make sure I read every day. I can read cereal boxes, junk mail, and coupons. I'll read for 10 minutes before I get up in the morning. I can put off having to work out that way. I can also read in bed—what could be nicer? I'll read for another 10 minutes before I go to sleep at night. I can learn a lot from reading with other people. I might join a book club at the community center. I can also read to my daughter. Children's books are fun! Finally, if I find the time, and as my skills improve, I might even read as a volunteer.

PRACTICE

Place a check mark next to each detail that could be used in a paragraph with this topic sentence: <u>New sports have been catching the interest of Americans everywhere.</u>

_____ 1. Cable sports networks have brought us sports we have never seen before.

_____ 2. Football still has its raving fans.

_____ 3. Americans are in love with soccer these days.

_____ 4. Snowboarding and skateboarding are becoming very popular.

_____ 5. We shouldn't leave out an old favorite like baseball.

_____ 6. Figure skating now gets the largest TV audiences during the Olympics.

WRITE Write a paragraph about a topic related to sports.

Prewrite:

A. Jot down a list of possible topics related to sports. Choose one.

B. Make a list of possible supporting details.

- Try to think of examples, facts, and reasons.
- Look for a logical way to include details to compare or contrast.
- See if you can show any cause-and-effect relationships.

Write: Write a topic sentence that states the main idea of your paragraph. Make it specific enough to tell the point you want to make. Then write at least three sentences using details from your list that support your topic sentence.

Review: How did you decide the order for your supporting details? Make sure they are in an order that helps readers understand the paragraph.

Check your answers on page 237.

Organizing Details

When you write supporting details, organize them in the clearest, most logical order. This way, the reader can easily follow your train of thought.

A. Each set of sentences below has a topic sentence and supporting details. Find the topic sentence and write 1 by it. Then number the details in the clearest, most logical order. The first paragraph is started for you.

Paragraph 1

_____ First, make sure you have all the ingredients you need.

___1___ Good cooking habits are worth developing.

_____ As you work, follow each step of the recipe carefully.

_____ Then read through all the directions in the recipe before you begin.

_____ Finally, keep your workspace clear by putting things away as you go.

Paragraph 2

_____ If you don't eat before an interview, you might feel weak and less talkative.

_____ Don't let nervousness spoil your appetite.

_____ Your physical condition can be important in a job interview.

_____ Otherwise, you might not be alert during the interview.

_____ Go to bed early the night before.

B. Circle the type(s) of supporting details used in Practice A.

Paragraph 1	examples	time order	cause/effect
Paragraph 2	facts/reasons	compare/contrast	cause/effect

WRITE On a separate piece of paper, write a paragraph about one of the topics below.

- Morning people and night people are very different.
- Learning to organize your time will change your life.
- Friendship is one of the most important things in life.

Prewrite: List supporting details. Decide how to organize them.

Write: Write the topic sentence and then supporting detail sentences.

Writing the Conclusion

The last paragraph of your essay is the **conclusion.** The topic sentence of the last paragraph should signal that the essay is drawing to a close. The other sentences should highlight what you want the reader to remember.

Certain words and phrases signal a conclusion. The most commonly used are *in conclusion, to conclude, finally, last, as a result, consequently,* and *therefore.* Here are four methods for writing conclusions.

End with a summary and a final thought.

EXAMPLE As I've shown, I don't think it will be very difficult to improve my reading skills. I can make improvements just by making small changes in my personal habits. I can't wait to get started!

End with a prediction for the future.

EXAMPLE If I can follow through with my plan, I know I will become a better reader. In fact, I predict that I'll begin to notice my skills improving very soon.

End with a recommendation.

EXAMPLE Finally, I recommend you consider improving your reading skills too. Think about which ways would work best for you—maybe some of mine, maybe some of your own. Then start building your skills right away.

End with a question.

EXAMPLE Now that I have figured out how easy it will be to improve my reading skills, which strategies should I try first? Perhaps I will talk with my preGED teacher. She should know.

PRACTICE

Review the concluding paragraphs you wrote for your essays in the "Apply Your Writing Skills" sections in Lessons 1 through 4. Choose one to rewrite. Use one of the four methods described above.

_____

_____

_____

_____

_____

_____

Step 3: Revising and Editing

The next step of the writing process is to review and evaluate your work. This is your chance to improve your first draft. When you **revise,** you review the **content** of your writing. Does it contain good supporting details? Are they well-organized? Can they be clearer? When you **edit,** you look carefully at the sentences and words. You review word choice, usage, sentence structure, and mechanics—that is, spelling, punctuation, and capitalization.

Revising

When you revise, you check the content, organization, and clarity of your writing. The Revising Checklist below tells you what to look for when you revise.

Revising Checklist	YES	NO
Does the content achieve your purpose?	☐	☐
Is the content right for your audience?	☐	☐
Is your main idea stated clearly?	☐	☐
Does each paragraph have a topic sentence?	☐	☐
Are topic sentences supported by details?	☐	☐
Are details written in a logical order?	☐	☐
Is the right amount of information included?	☐	☐
(Check for details that are missing or not needed.)		
Will the writing hold the reader's interest?	☐	☐
Are thoughts and ideas expressed clearly?	☐	☐

EXAMPLE Here is the first body paragraph from the first draft of Melissa's essay on page 75. You can see how Melissa used the Revising Checklist. She also used editing marks to indicate the revisions to make. Turn to page 81 and look over these marks.

My first goal is to make sure I read everyday. I can read ˄ *signs,* ← add new detail

cereal boxes, junk mail, and coupons. I'll read for 10 minutes

move this sentence for more logical order → before I get up in the morning. ~~I can put off having to workout~~ ← delete unnecessary detail

~~that way!~~ I can also read in bed—what could be nicer? I'll read

for another 10 minutes before I go to sleep at night. ¶I can learn ← begin new paragraph

add cause-effect detail → a lot from reading with other people. I might join a book club at *I understand better when I talk about what I've read with other people, and that will help my reading improve.* the commnity center. ˄I can also read to my daughter. Children's

books are fun! Finally, if I find the time, and as my skills

to a blind person ← add new detail improve, I might even read as a volunter˄

Essay Writing

EXAMPLE Here is the revised version of the paragraphs on page 78. Read the new version and compare it with the previous one.

My first goal is to make sure I read every day. I can read signs, cereal boxes, junk mail, and coupons. I can also read in bed—what could be nicer? I'll read for 10 minutes before I get up in the morning. I'll read for another 10 minutes before I go to sleep at night.

I can learn a lot from reading with other people. I might join a book club at the community center. I understand better when I talk about what I've read with other people, and that will help my reading improve. I can also read to my daughter. Children's books are fun! Finally, if I find the time, and as my skills improve, I might even read as a volunteer to a blind person.

PRACTICE

A. Read the following paragraph. Using the revising checklist, make at least three changes to improve the paragraph. Mark the paragraph using the editing marks on page 81.

Kingston Heritage Chorus is a great group. The spring retreat is one of the highlights of our year. We go away for a long weekend to a camp in the mountains. We learn a lot of music for our spring program. We always plan our concert outfits earlier in the fall. We also get to know each other better and have a lot of fun. Organizing the retreat is a big job. The committee members make all the arrangements. They arrange transportation, make room assignments, coordinate meals, and plan free-time activities. The Retreat Coordinator needs a committee of at least six people. They also set up our rehearsal room and bring all the supplies and snacks.

B. Now that you have marked the paragraph for revision, write the new version on a separate piece of paper.

WRITE Using the Revising Checklist on page 78, revise one of the paragraphs you wrote for the GED Essay Links in Lessons 1 through 4. Mark your changes using the editing marks on page 81. Then write your revised paragraph on a separate piece of paper.

Editing

When you edit, you smooth out and correct words, sentences, and mechanics. The Editing Checklist below tells you what to look for when you edit.

Editing Checklist	YES	NO
Are any ideas repeated?	☐	☐
Are some words used too many times?	☐	☐
Are precise words and fresh language used?	☐	☐
Are all sentences complete sentences?	☐	☐
Are any sentences too long and hard to understand?	☐	☐
Are any sentences too short and choppy?	☐	☐
Are nouns and pronouns used correctly?	☐	☐
Are verbs used correctly?	☐	☐
Are adjectives and adverbs used correctly?	☐	☐
Are all words spelled correctly?	☐	☐
Is punctuation used correctly?	☐	☐
Are words capitalized correctly?	☐	☐

EXAMPLE Melissa Sanchez is now editing the introductory paragraph of her essay (from page 75). Notice how she has used editing marks to show where she will make changes.

                    achieve   *easy*
I can (acheive) success and improve my reading by making some ∧

changes in my daily life. Reading is essential to success. At first, I

                                 become
thought it might be hard to ~~get to be~~ a better reader ∧but after careful

thought, I realized it doesn't have to be.

A.   Write the new version of Melissa's introduction on a separate piece of paper. Make the changes she has marked.

B.   Edit one of the paragraphs you wrote for the GED Essay Links in Lessons 1 through 4. Use the editing marks on page 81.

Step 4: Writing the Final Draft

Your **final draft** will incorporate all the changes you have marked while revising and editing. There are special symbols you can use to mark changes when you are revising and editing. These marks help you spot the changes you want to make when you rewrite or retype your final draft. Some basic marks are shown below.

Editing Marks

b̲	B	change to a capital letter
B̸	b	change to a lowercase letter
red, white‸and blue.		insert a comma or period
Will you go?		insert a question mark
Will you‸go? (and Sue)		insert word(s)
SP (there) car		check spelling
end. ¶We will		insert a paragraph indent
go ~~on~~ away		delete a word or punctuation mark
and‸a half (#)		add a space between words

After you have finished writing your final draft, it's time to read your essay one last time. When you read, make sure that you really have made all the changes and corrections you marked. Also make sure that you did not make any new errors. If your final version is typed, look for "typos"— reversed letters, missing words, missing spaces, and so on.

Step 5: Publishing (Sharing the Final Draft)

The final step in the writing process is **publishing** or **sharing the final draft.** Before sharing your final draft, read it aloud to yourself. As you read, think about what you enjoyed most about writing it and what you found to be the hardest part. Make notes.

Then read your essay to a partner or have your partner read it. Ask, *Is the writing clear? Is the piece interesting to read? Is the message clear? What parts need improvement?* Make notes. Use the notes to help you improve your writing.

Date your final draft and notes and keep them in a special folder or notebook. Keep an ongoing record of everything you write. Review your work weekly and add the best pieces to your **writing portfolio.**

  Check your answers on page 238.

Writing at Work

Office: Administrative Assistant

Office workers need to be able to write clearly. If their written work is unclear, problems or mistakes can occur. Office workers cannot follow their written work around and explain what it means to the reader. The writing must be able to stand on its own.

Administrative assistants are often called upon to use their writing skills. Administrative assistants may need to draft memos, letters, email, and other types of written correspondence. Their writing must include a clear introduction, supporting details, and an effective conclusion.

Look at the box showing some office careers.

- Do any of the careers interest you? If so, which ones?

- How could you find out more about those careers? On a separate piece of paper, write some questions that you would like to have answered. You can find out more information about those careers in the *Occupational Outlook Handbook* at your local library and online.

Some Office Careers

Administrative Assistant maintains files, writes correspondence, makes appointments, and runs office operations

Human Resources Clerk keeps important, private information about a company's employees

Receptionist represents company at entrance area; receives and routes phone calls

Typist or Word Processor uses computers to enter text or data, format the material, and print the final copy

An administrative assistant at a shelter for homeless mothers and children wrote the letter below.

Read the letter. Then answer the questions that follow.

Dear Neighbor:

Each year Judy's House gives hope to mothers and children in our town who are unable to make ends meet on their own. Our organization offers shelter, food, and clothing for our guests. Through your generous support, we are able to give services to over 400 women and children each year.

This year we hope to begin two new programs for our guests. One is a counseling program. The other is an educational program.

In the past your gifts have allowed us to buy toys and cribs, transportation services, and a washer and dryer for our residents. Won't you help us again by sending a donation to help those in the community less fortunate than yourself?

Thank you for your support.

Sincerely,

Tamara Jones

1. What is the purpose of Tamara Jones' letter?
   (1) to ask for transportation services
   (2) to thank past contributors
   (3) to persuade people to donate money
   (4) to show off her writing skills
   (5) to start counseling and education programs

2. Which paragraph or paragraphs could be made stronger by adding specific supporting details?
   (1) paragraph 1
   (2) paragraph 2
   (3) paragraph 3
   (4) none of the paragraphs
   (5) all of the paragraphs

3. On a separate piece of paper explain your answer to number 2 above. Then write two sentences for that paragraph to add specific supporting details.

Unit 1 Review
Creative and Essay Writing

Write pronouns to replace the underlined nouns. Choose from these pronouns: *he, she, they, her, him, them, his,* **and** *their*.

1. Gloria and Michael are planning a vacation. _____

2. Michael wants to go to Florida. _____

3. Gloria's brother Mario lives in Miami. _____

4. Gloria and Michael decide to stay with Mario. _____

For more practice with pronouns, turn to pages 152–156.

Write the correct pronoun to complete each sentence.

5. Lilly and _____ (**he, him**) drive to work together.

6. Oscar gave Otis and _____ (**she, her**) a ride.

7. Rick and _____ (**I, me**) want to buy a used car.

8. It's hard for _____ (**we, us**) to decide what kind of car to buy.

For more practice correcting sentence fragments, turn to pages 168–169.

Put an *S* next to each complete sentence. Put an *F* next to each fragment.

_____ 9. The groceries in the car.

_____ 10. Ms. Valdez wrote a check.

_____ 11. The clerk opened another checkout line.

_____ 12. Before the end of the day.

Complete each sentence by adding information. Use the connecting word shown. Add a comma if one is needed.

13. (**unless**) I can't give you a refund _____.

14. (**although**) _____,
Rudy and Ana went on a date.

15. (**when**) _____,
Carlos gave the file to Ms. Webb.

16. (**because**) You are ready for this test _____.

Unit 1 Review

For more practice with run-on sentences, turn to pages 170–171

Correct these sentences. Write each one with a comma and an appropriate coordinating conjunction—*and, or, but,* or *so*—or as two sentences.

17. She read his resume and liked it, it was neat and well organized.

   _____

18. Ms. Golov offered George a job, he would have to work Saturdays.

   _____

19. The job pays well the company also offers good benefits.

   _____

20. He likes the company he'll probably take the job.

   _____

For more practice with adjectives and adverbs, turn to pages 157–160.

Write the correct form of the adjective or adverb to complete each sentence.

21. Of all our employees, Anita is the _____ typist.

   fast   faster   fastest

22. Anita also writes _____.

   well   better   good

23. Of our two new employees, Jesse works _____ than Maurice.

   hard   harder   hardest

For more practice with subject-verb agreement, turn to pages 165–167

Write the correct form of the verb to complete each sentence.

24. My son and daughter _____ (**help**) me with housework every Saturday.

25. Darnell _____ (**be**) the man to see about your problem.

26. The shirts _____ (**cost**) $50; the tie _____ (**cost**) $10.

Write a five-paragraph expository essay on the following topic.

   An old saying is "A bird in the hand is worth two in the bush." It means that it is better to keep what you have than take a risk and try to get something else. Do you agree or disagree with that saying? Give facts, reasons, and examples to support your answer.

Writing Extension

   Use your writing skills to write a narrative. The narrative can be a true story about yourself that you want to tell. Or it can be a fictional story that you want to write. Follow the writing process when you write.

Mini-Test • Unit 1

This is a 15-minute practice test. After 15 minutes, mark the last number you finished. Then complete the test and check your answers. If most of your answers were correct but you did not finish, try to work faster next time.

Directions: Choose the one best answer to each question.

Questions 1 through 4 refer to the following letter.

Dear Neighbor:

(A)

(1) We is very excited to announce the opening of our new restaurant. (2) Hammonds' Place is a diner-style eatery with a friendly atmosphere. (3) Our menu appeals to all kinds of folks, we have many value options. (4) If you're looking for a delicious, inexpensive meal. (5) Hammonds' Place *is* the place.

(B)

(6) Because you're a neighbor of ours, we would like to offer you a special deal. (7) See the enclosed coupon for details. (8) They just can't wait to see you, so take advantage of this offer!

Sincerely yours,

Henry & Ella Hammond

1. Sentence 1: **We is very excited to announce the opening of our new restaurant.**

   Which is the best way to write the underlined portion of this sentence? If the original is the best way, choose option (1).

   (1) is
   (2) was
   (3) been
   (4) were
   (5) are

2. Sentence 3: **Our menu appeals to all kinds of folks, we have many value options.**

   Which correction should be made to sentence 3?

   (1) change appeals to appeal
   (2) remove the comma
   (3) insert and before we
   (4) change have to has
   (5) no correction is necessary

3. Sentences 4 and 5: **If you're looking for a delicious, inexpensive meal. Hammond's Place *is* the place.**

   Which is the best way to write the underlined portion of this sentence? If the original is the best way, choose option (1).

   (1) meal. Hammond's
   (2) meal, Hammond's
   (3) meal Hammond's
   (4) meal, but Hammond's
   (5) meal, and Hammond's

4. Sentence 8: **They just can't wait to see you, so take advantage of this offer!**

   Which correction should be made to sentence 8?

   (1) replace They with We
   (2) remove the comma after you
   (3) replace so with but
   (4) remove so
   (5) change take to took

Questions 5 through 8 refer to the following article.

A NEW USE FOR DUCT TAPE!

(A)

(1) Most people are familiar with that wide, silver, waterproof tape known as duct tape. (2) You can buy it at any hardware store you can use it for almost anything. (3) For example, are you feeling too lazy to do a proper window repair job? (4) If you use a piece of duct tape to seal your leaky window frame it will probably outlast your house anyway.

(B)

(5) It turns out that duct tape is good for warts. (6) In the study, people wore patches of duct tape over their warts for extended periods. (7) The study did not consider acne or other skin conditions. (8) The treatment also involved soaking and scraping the warts. (9) The duct tape treatment was found less painful and more effective than freezing.

5. Sentence 2: **You can buy it at any hardware store you can use it for almost anything.**

    Which is the best way to write the underlined portion of this sentence? If the original is the best way, choose option (1).

    (1) store you
    (2) store, so you
    (3) store, and you
    (4) store, you
    (5) store unless you

6. Sentence 4: **If you use a piece of duct tape to seal your leaky window frame it will probably outlast your house anyway.**

    Which correction should be made to sentence 4?

    (1) replace If with Unless
    (2) replace you with they
    (3) insert a comma after frame
    (4) insert and after frame
    (5) no correction is necessary

7. Which sentence would be most effective if inserted at the beginning of paragraph B?

    (1) Now a medical research study has found a surprising new use for duct tape.
    (2) Duct tape is not just for household repairs.
    (3) Duct tape is ideal for patching air leaks in air mattresses, children's pools, and water toys.
    (4) You can find duct tape in the hardware and adhesive section of any variety store.
    (5) no revision is necessary

8. Which revision would improve the effectiveness of the article?

    (1) remove sentence 3
    (2) remove sentence 6
    (3) remove sentence 7
    (4) remove sentence 8
    (5) remove sentence 9

  Check your answers on page 239.

Personal and Workplace Writing
Personal and Workplace Writing
Personal and Workplace Writing

UNIT 2

Personal and Workplace Writing

Personal and workplace writing is a way to communicate with others. Personal correspondence helps you keep in touch with family and friends. Everyone loves a letter! Written correspondence is essential in the workplace. It can both help you get a job and perform that job well.

What friend or family member would you like to write a letter to? What would you write about?

_____

What do you think you might need to write in order to get a job?

_____

Thinking About Personal and Workplace Writing

You may not realize how familiar you already are with personal and workplace writing. Think about what you have written recently.

Check the box for each activity you did.

☐ Did you write a letter to a friend or relative?

☐ Did you write a personal email message?

☐ Did you write a "to do" list?

☐ Did you write a memo at work?

☐ Did you fill out a form?

☐ Did you take down a message from a phone call?

☐ Did you write a letter to explain a problem or make a suggestion?

List some other kinds of writing you have done at home or on the job.

_____

_____

_____

_____

Previewing the Unit

In this unit, you will learn:

● how to write personal and business correspondence

● how to use your writing skills when you apply for a job

● how to complete common workplace writing tasks

● how to write a good explanation

Lesson 6	**Letter Writing**
Lesson 7	**Job Search Writing**
Lesson 8	**Workplace Writing**
Lesson 9	**Explanatory Writing**

LESSON 6

Letter Writing

You have many choices when you communicate with others. A phone call may be easy, but sometimes it is better, or even necessary, to write. You may write a letter on paper or send an email message. Either way, there are two main types of written correspondence: personal and business.

Personal Correspondence

A **personal letter** or email is usually written to someone you know well. The purpose may be to keep in touch with a friend or relative. It may be to say thank you for a gift or a favor, or to invite someone to visit you. Other reasons for writing personal correspondence are to ask someone to do something or to tell someone something that has happened.

EXAMPLE

> 140 W. 116 St., Apt. 10
> New York, NY 10026
> July 25, 2002
>
> Dear Toni,
>
> How are you? I hope you're enjoying the summer. The weather here has been miserable. I would love to leave the city for a few days to visit you and Vernon. I will be able to take some time off in a couple of weeks. Please write or call to let me know if that would be a good time for me to visit. I would have called you, but my phone bill last month was high. See you soon.
>
> Love,
> Yolanda

WRITE Notice the parts of Yolanda's letter to her friend Toni. Yolanda began by writing her own address and the date she was writing the letter. Use Yolanda's letter as a model.

On a separate piece of paper, write a short personal letter. Assume you are writing to a friend in another town to invite him or her to visit you.

Business Correspondence

A **business letter** or email is written to a company or an organization, or directly to a person who works for a company or an organization. You may be writing for yourself or as an employee. Business correspondence has two purposes: (1) to communicate a specific message and (2) to produce a record. Four common types of business correspondence are listed below.

- **Letter of request**—written to ask for something, to get information, to place an order, to issue an invitation
- **Letter of reply or confirmation**—written to respond to a message (written or oral) or a request, or to produce a written record of a spoken agreement
- **Follow-up letter**—written to remind someone of something, to thank someone, or to provide additional information
- **Letter to conduct business**—written to document a decision, process, complaint, or suggestion within a business

EXAMPLE Letter of Request

> **Overland Medical Center**
> **39000 South Oak Drive, Overland Park, MA 02115**
> **404-555-3200**
>
>   October 6, 2003
>
> Mr. Antonio Torres
> 201 Lowell Avenue
> Overland Park, MA 02110
>
> Dear Mr. Torres:
>
>   Thank you for your call inquiring about our medical technician training program at Overland Medical Center. Enclosed is a description of our program. Please send me your resume and a cover letter stating your reason for wanting to join the program. We will review your application and get back to you as soon as possible.
>
>   Sincerely,
>
>   *Joyce Hawkins*
>
>   Joyce Hawkins
>   Human Resources Dept.

WRITE On a separate piece of paper, write a letter of reply to Ms. Hawkins.

Say that your resume is enclosed, and give two reasons you would like to be admitted to the training program for medical technicians at Overland Medical Center.

Writing Style

Your **writing style** is the way you choose your words and sentences to express yourself. Personal letters and email are written in an **informal** style. Your written words and sentences are like those you use when talking to your friends. Your letter "sounds" like the way you talk.

Business letters and email are written in a **formal style.** You may be writing to someone you do not know. The letter should state its message in a direct yet polite way.

EXAMPLES

Informal Style: Dear John,
I've been calling you for two weeks, and you haven't called me back.

Formal Style: Dear Mr. Smith:
I have called your office several times, but I have not been able to reach you.

Informal Style: Mary,
I'm busy on Friday, so we'll have to change our lunch plans. Can you make it on Monday instead? Call me.

Formal Style: Dear Ms. Yazzie:
Thank you for your invitation to the Community Center luncheon on Friday. I am sorry that I will not be able to attend. Please keep me in mind for the next one.

PRACTICE

Practice informal and formal writing styles by writing a few sentences for each situation.

1. **Informal:** Write to your friend Kareem, asking him to help you move a piece of furniture this weekend.

   _____

   _____

   _____

2. **Formal:** Write to the president of the large company you work for. Ask her to speak at a meeting of a group you belong to on "Success in Your Career."

   _____

   _____

   _____

Personal Letter Format

Personal letters may be handwritten on plain paper, notepaper, or stationery, or they may be written on a computer and printed. Below are the parts of a personal letter.

- **Return address**—the writer's address
- **Date**—the date on which the letter is written
- **Salutation**—an opening greeting, such as *Dear Jake*, followed by a comma
- **Body**—the contents or message of the letter
- **Closing**—a parting phrase, such as *Sincerely*, followed by a comma
- **Signature**—the writer's signed name. In a letter written on a computer, the name is typed as well as written.

All personal letters should follow a specific format. The **format** is the way the parts of the letter are set up on the page.

EXAMPLE

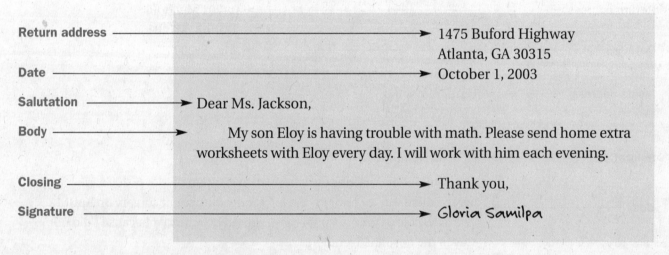

Return address	1475 Buford Highway Atlanta, GA 30315
Date	October 1, 2003
Salutation	Dear Ms. Jackson,
Body	My son Eloy is having trouble with math. Please send home extra worksheets with Eloy every day. I will work with him each evening.
Closing	Thank you,
Signature	Gloria Samilpa

A personal email message is similar to a personal letter. However, the format of an email is set up by the email program you use. It formats the date and the sender and receiver's email addresses for you.

PRACTICE

Below is a personal letter. Copy it onto a separate piece of paper, putting it in the proper format.

P.O. Box 32 Eden Prairie, MN 55344 October 20, 2003 Dear Aunt Frances, Thanks for the beautiful sweaters! It gets really cold up here this time of year, so your timing was perfect. After living in Florida for so long, I had forgotten what cold weather feels like. Give my love to Uncle Harold. Tell him I'll visit soon. Your nephew, Danny

Business Letter Format

Business letters from an individual can be handwritten on plain paper, typed, or written on a computer and printed. Business letters from an employee are written on a computer and printed out on letterhead paper. **Letterhead** is stationery that has a company name and address printed at the top.

The parts of a business letter are similar to the parts of a personal letter. However, there are a few differences.

- **Inside address**—The name and address of the company to which the letter is written is included. If the letter is written to a specific employee of the company, the employee's name goes on a line before the inside address.
- **Salutation**—The opening greeting is followed by a colon, not a comma.
- **Signature**—The signed name is always followed by the name typed.

EXAMPLE

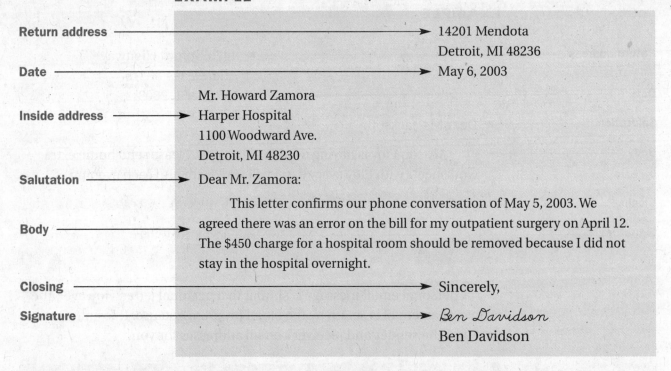

Return address →

14201 Mendota
Detroit, MI 48236

Date →

May 6, 2003

Inside address →

Mr. Howard Zamora
Harper Hospital
1100 Woodward Ave.
Detroit, MI 48230

Salutation →

Dear Mr. Zamora:

Body →

This letter confirms our phone conversation of May 5, 2003. We agreed there was an error on the bill for my outpatient surgery on April 12. The $450 charge for a hospital room should be removed because I did not stay in the hospital overnight.

Closing →

Sincerely,

Signature →

Ben Davidson
Ben Davidson

PRACTICE

Below is a business letter. Copy it on a separate piece of paper, putting it in the proper business letter format.

222 East 24th St. Philadelphia, PA 19135 June 14, 2003 Mr. Bernard Adams, Travelworld, 901 Harrison Avenue, Philadelphia, PA 19139 Dear Mr. Adams: Thank you for talking to me about the position in your word processing unit. I know my skills would fit your needs. Our meeting made me eager to work at Travelworld. I look forward to hearing from you about the job. Sincerely, Elaine Evans

Organizing Business Correspondence

A business letter should not be more than one page unless absolutely necessary. Two to four paragraphs are usually enough. Paragraphs should be short, usually just three or four sentences. A paragraph with only one sentence is acceptable. Business email should also be short, with short paragraphs.

EXAMPLE Here is a sample business letter with a few more tips to help you write business correspondence.

Universal Computer Company
509 Union Square
Lexington, KY 40527

January 3, 2003

Ms. Irma Salinas
Meeting Planner
Crown Plaza Hotel
1 City Plaza
Lexington, KY 40521

Dear Ms. Salinas:

Topic sentence comes first in paragraph and directly states a request. →

Universal Computers wishes to reserve a meeting room in your hotel for a computer-training program. We need the space from April 9–11 or April 20–22 from 9:00 a.m. to 4:00 p.m. Below is a list of our specific needs.

- Meeting room for twenty people

Details are listed in brief statements, not complete sentences. →

- Table space for ten computers
- Electrical wiring and outlets to accommodate the equipment
- Refreshments for a morning and an afternoon break

Conclusion states what will happen next and thanks the reader. →

Please let me know the cost of the items listed and the dates you can best serve our group. After I receive this information, I will call you to finalize the plans. Thank you for your help.

Sincerely,

Janice Adams

Janice Adams
Administrative Assistant

Check your answers on page 240.

WRITE Reply to the letter below. Use the tips on page 95. On the lines provided, write the body of the letter only. Do not copy the formatting.

Family Day Care Center
3300 North Beach Drive
Los Angeles, CA 90033
212-555-8899

September 23, 2003

Mr. Calvin Simpson
304 West End Blvd.
Los Angeles, CA 90011

Dear Mr. Simpson:

We are seriously considering your application for the position of administrative assistant at the Family Day Care Center.

It is our policy to screen all applicants by checking their references. Would you please send me the names of two people we can contact regarding your past work experience and personal background? I need the name, address, telephone number, and a brief description of your relationship with each person.

As soon as we have this information, we can complete the processing of your application.

Sincerely,

George Walker

George Walker
Director, Human Resources

_____

_____

_____

_____

_____

_____

_____

Language Link

Your business correspondence creates an impression of you in your reader's mind. If you are writing as an employee, it also creates an impression of your company. Even if you are writing a personal letter to a friend, you will want it to be correct. Therefore, capitalizing and punctuating correctly are important when you write correspondence.

Capitalization

1. Always capitalize the first word of a sentence.

EXAMPLE Please send me a copy of your latest catalog.

2. Capitalize each part of a person's name.

EXAMPLES Louise Guccione   Samuel C. Johnston

3. Capitalize titles and abbreviations that come before and after people's names. Do not capitalize when a title stands alone.

EXAMPLES Mr. Zell D. Moore, Jr.   Mrs. Barbara Westmass
Dr. Katherine Lord
No capital: The doctor has an office downtown.

4. Capitalize words showing family relationships when they are used as a title or in place of a name. Do not capitalize when the word stands alone.

EXAMPLE Aunt Jane will not be able to go, but Dad will.
No capital: My aunt will not be able to go.

5. Capitalize names of cities, states, and sections of the country.

EXAMPLES **City and state:** Chicago, Illinois   **Section:** Midwest

6. Capitalize names of countries, languages, nationalities, religions, and regions of the world.

EXAMPLES **Country:** Saudi Arabia   **Language:** Arabic
Nationality: Arabian   **Religion:** Islam
Region: Middle East

7. Capitalize names of streets, highways, bodies of water, buildings, monuments, and bridges.

EXAMPLES **Street:** Wall Street   **Highway:** New Jersey Turnpike
Water: Atlantic Ocean   **Monument:** Statue of Liberty
Building: Empire State Building

8. Capitalize months, days, and holidays.

EXAMPLES September   Wednesday   Thanksgiving

9. Capitalize names of companies and organizations.

EXAMPLES **Company:** Adams-Clarke Associates
Organization: Veterans Society

Check your answers on page 240.

Letter Writing

Language
Exercise A

Rewrite each sentence using correct capital letters.

1. last year I worked on senator smith's campaign.

   _____

2. the campaign office was on fifth avenue in the chrysler building.

   _____

3. a debate was sponsored by a group called independent voters of america at their building on the hudson river.

   _____

4. laura washington, vice president of the organization, made a speech.

   _____

Language
Exercise B

Use the editing mark to show where capital letters are needed. The mark to capitalize is three lines under the letter: a = A.

Bradley Advertising Agency
45 Capital Street
Columbus, OH 43225

may 20, 2003

supreme computer, inc.
958 alexander street
river tower
Columbus, oh 43221

dear mr. Potter:

   my supervisor, doris healy, director of sales here at bradley associates, asked me to send you the enclosed brochure detailing the services our company provides to computer stores like yours. If interested, you can take advantage of our free trial offer by calling before may 31. We are closed next Monday because of memorial day.

Sincerely,

James Hobson

james hobson
sales assistant

For more practice
on capitalization,
turn to pages
187–189.

Punctuation

1. End a sentence with a period, question mark, or exclamation point.

EXAMPLES   The party was over too soon.   How did you like the party?
The party was terrific!

2. Use a period after an abbreviation or an initial.

EXAMPLES   Sharon A. Kaufman   Co. (Company)
Inc. (Incorporated)

3. Use a comma after each item before *and* in a list of three or more items.

EXAMPLE   We need a new supply of red, green, and white labels.

4. Use a comma between the name of a city and state, and between the day and year in a date.

EXAMPLES   New Orleans, Louisiana   June 2, 2003

5. Use a comma after the salutation in a personal letter and after the closing of a personal or business letter. Use a colon after the salutation of a business letter.

EXAMPLES   Dear Toni,   Sincerely,   Dear Ms. Thomas:

Language Exercise C

Add correct punctuation marks where they are needed in the letter.

1670 Evergreen Road
Houston TX 77023
January 25 2003

Ms. Vanessa Lewis
Lewis and Evans Assoc
Houston TX 77025

Dear Ms Lewis

I attended your career planning workshop at the Valley College Library on December 15 2002. Your presentation was just what I needed to organize myself Would it be possible for you to send me copies of your resume-writing guidelines the worksheet and the sample Unfortunately, you ran out of these three handouts before you got to me

Sincerely

Joseph Wallach

Joseph Wallach

For more practice on punctuation, turn to pages 184–186.

Apply Your Writing Skills

Write a Complaint or Suggestion Letter

Now you are ready to apply what you have learned by writing a business letter.

A business letter:

- is written in a formal style
- follows a specific format
- is organized to request or give information directly and briefly

As you write, follow the steps in the writing process outlined below.

ASSIGNMENT

Many businesses are very eager to receive feedback from their customers. If you have a problem with a business, you might be able to get it solved by writing a letter. For example, you may have bought a product that doesn't work. If you write a letter of complaint, you might be able to get your money back or get a replacement for that product. Or maybe you had a problem with an employee or a service. By writing a letter of complaint, you might receive an apology—or at least a promise of better service for the future. You might also write a letter of suggestion if you have an idea about how a business could improve its merchandise, service, or facilities.

Prewriting

1. List some situations you could write a letter of complaint or suggestion about. Then choose one for your letter.

    _____

    _____

2. Use the questions below to think of strong details for your letter.

    What situation is your complaint or suggestion based on?

    _____

    Where and when did the situation take place?

    _____

    What are your feelings or attitude about this situation?

    _____

    What do you want your reader to do as a result of reading your letter?

    _____

Writing the First Draft

On a separate piece of paper, write your first draft.

Format the Letter. Write your return address, the date, and your inside address. Use "Dear Sir or Madam:" for the salutation.

Write the Message. In your introductory paragraph, briefly explain why you are writing. Use the details you listed on page 100 to write your body paragraphs. In your conclusion, state what you want your reader to do about the situation. Then write your closing, leaving space for your signature.

Revising and Editing

Review, revise, and edit. Read your letter to see if you accomplished what you set out to do. Then use the checklist on page 216 to revise and edit it. Also, pay special attention to these points.

Check the organization of your letter. *See page 95.*

- ☐ Is the letter brief, with short paragraphs?
- ☐ Does the topic sentence come first and directly state your request?
- ☐ Does the conclusion state what you expect to happen next and thank the reader?

Check the mechanics of your letter.

- ☐ Did you use correct capitalization? *See pages 97–98.*
- ☐ Did you use correct punctuation? *See page 99.*

Writing the Final Draft

Write a final draft. Then read it one last time. If necessary, recopy or retype it.

Sharing the Final Draft

Publish. Let another person read your letter. Ask if you explained the situation clearly. Make some notes and attach them to a copy of the letter. File the letter in your writing portfolio.

Write a Letter in Response to an Ad

Now you are ready to apply what you have learned by writing a job application letter.

As you write, follow the steps in the writing process outlined below.

On a separate piece of paper, write a letter to apply for one of the jobs in the want ads below. Or, if you wish, find a real ad for a job you want.

Want Ad 1	Want Ad 2
Security Guards for Warehouse	**Retail Sales Clothing Store**
Day or night positions available. No experience required. Will train. Send letter of application to Mike Anderson, XYZ Packing Company, 655 Landers Avenue, Chicago, IL 60612.	Some experience preferred, but will train. Must be willing to work evenings & weekends. Send letter of application to Antonia Lucci, Rave Wear, 243 W. Madison, Suite 2200, Chicago, IL 60620.

Prewriting

1. Select the ad you want to answer. Think about the working hours, the experience required, and why you might be good at this job.

2. List any information you might need or questions you might have.

   _____

   _____

   _____

3. List the main ideas you want to put in your letter. Why are you interested in applying for the job? What qualifications do you have for the job? What do you want the person reading the letter to do after he or she receives it?

   _____

   _____

   _____

4. On a separate piece of paper, organize your ideas in an outline or on an idea map.

Writing the First Draft

On a separate piece of paper, write your first draft.

Format the Letter. Write your return address, the date, the inside address, and the salutation.

Write the Message. In your introductory paragraph, briefly explain why you are writing. Use your prewriting ideas to write your body paragraphs. In your conclusion, state what you would like your reader to do. Then write your closing, leaving room for your signature.

Revising and Editing

Review, revise, and edit. Read your letter to see if you accomplished what you set out to do. Then use the checklist on page 216 to revise and edit it. Also, pay special attention to these points.

Check the organization of your letter. *See page 95.*

☐   Is the letter brief, with short paragraphs?

☐   Does the topic sentence come first and directly state your request?

☐   Does the conclusion state what you expect to happen next and thank the reader?

Check the mechanics of your letter.

☐   Did you use correct capitalization? *See pages 97–98.*

☐   Did you use correct punctuation? *See page 99.*

Writing the Final Draft

Write a final draft. Then read it one last time. If necessary, recopy or retype it.

Sharing the Final Draft

Publish. Let another person read your letter. Ask if your message was clear. Show the person the ad you are responding to so that he or she can judge whether you asked appropriate questions and discussed appropriate skills you have. Make some notes and attach them to a copy of the letter. File the letter in your writing portfolio.

LESSON 7

Job Search Writing

When you are looking for a job, you will have many chances to use your writing skills. For some jobs, you may need to prepare a resume. For almost all jobs, you will be asked to fill out a job application form.

Resumes

A **resume** is a written summary of your qualifications for a job. Your resume should have one goal: to get you interviews. It should make employers want to meet you. Employers will often spend only a few minutes looking at your resume. So, it should be carefully written to *sell* you and your skills to employers.

There are many things about you that will help you sell yourself to an employer. Write your resume to present the best possible picture of yourself. Always be honest about your background, but include only information that makes you look good. A resume usually includes the following parts.

1. **Personal data:** Your name, address, and telephone number
2. **Objective:** The position you are seeking or goal you want to achieve
3. **Work experience:** Your employment record or employment skills
4. **Education:** The schools you attended and courses you took
5. **Other experience, skills, activities, or interests:** Any items an employer might find useful or interesting, such as your knowledge of a second language and volunteer or community work you have done

Do not include this personal information on a resume.

- Your age
- Your race or ethnic origin
- Your marital status
- Your height or weight
- Your health status

An employer's request for information in some of these personal areas is not legal. However, some jobs, such as police officer or firefighter, may have special physical requirements. Find out what is required before you apply for the job, and be prepared to provide the necessary information.

Do not list personal references on your resume. Employers may request references on job application forms. If so, list them there.

PRACTICE

Look over the resumes on pages 105 and 106. What are the common categories on both resumes?

EXAMPLE 1 The resume below shows how someone with a few years of work experience highlights her skills and experiences.

Juanita Diaz
1225 Pharr Road South
Los Angeles, CA 90011
213-555-3509

OBJECTIVE

To use customer service and people skills in a sales position with potential for career growth

WORK EXPERIENCE

Sales Associate, Baldwin's Department Store, Los Angeles, CA, January 2002–present. Member of a five-person sales team in the children's department for a large department store chain in Los Angeles. Responsibilities include:

- Training new sales clerks to use computer system
- Handling return of damaged merchandise to manufacturers
- Assisting in inventory records maintenance
- Stocking shelves and keeping merchandise in order

Sales Clerk, Power Video, Los Angeles, CA, June 1999 to December 2001. Responsibilities included:

- Processing sales and rentals of videotapes
- Assisting customers in finding merchandise
- Recording inventory of incoming stock

EDUCATION

- Southview Learning Center, Los Angeles, CA
  Basic Computer Skills Certificate, September 2002
  GED Certificate, June 2002
- Dover High School, Los Angeles, CA

SKILLS

Computer skills
Fluent in Spanish and English

REFERENCES

Available upon request

Comment: Juanita Diaz is looking for a sales position with potential for growth. Although she has only a few years of work experience, she details her job responsibilities very specifically. She also highlights her computer and language skills, which are very important in many workplaces.

EXAMPLE 2 The resume below shows how a person with limited work experience presents his skills and background.

Jonathan Sowell
26047 Birch Road
Detroit, MI 48234
313-555-2310

OBJECTIVE

Entry-level position in data entry or computer operations

WORK EXPERIENCE

Messenger, Reed Printing Company, 19000 Jefferson Ave., Detroit, MI 48232. July 2002 to present.

EDUCATION

Attended Northern High School 1997–2000
Attended night school at J. P. Alexander Adult Learning Center; received GED Certificate June 2002
Completed courses in record keeping and accounting

SKILLS

- Keyboarding and computer literacy
- Ability to listen, follow instructions, and learn quickly
- Dependability and ability to work with little supervision
- Experience operating photocopy and fax machines

OTHER EXPERIENCE

Worked as group leader in summer day camp program

REFERENCES

Available upon request

Comment: Jonathan Sowell does not have all of the work experience he needs, but his resume emphasizes that he is hardworking, mature, and willing to learn. The resume also lists courses he has taken to gain the computer and math-related skills that a data-entry operator needs. It also mentions a leadership role in a day camp program, which illustrates a sense of maturity and responsibility.

Personal Data Sheet

Before you write your resume, you need to gather and organize the information, or data, for it. One way to do this is to complete a **personal data sheet.** Even if you do not use all the information on the data sheet, completing it will help you make sure you don't leave anything out. It may also help you discover things about yourself that you would not have thought of putting on your resume. Finally, it will help you think about questions that you may be asked when you have a job interview.

WRITE Complete the personal data sheet on this and the next two pages.

Personal Data Sheet

Personal Data

Name _____

Address _____

City, State, Zip Code _____

Telephone _____

Objective

An *objective* is a goal or something you want. Right now your objective may be to get a job. Or perhaps you already have a job, but you would like a better one. The type of work you choose should interest you. It should make good use of your skills and talents. It should also give you a chance to learn and grow. What type of work do you want to do? Write a statement that summarizes your objective.

_____

_____

_____

_____

Education

High School _____ Years Attended _____

Address _____

Other Courses or Educational Achievement _____

_____

Work Experience

Complete a copy of this page for each job you have held.

Company _____ Telephone _____

Address _____

Dates of Employment _____

Type of Business _____

Name and Title of Supervisor _____

_____

Your Title _____

Your Job Duties _____

_____

_____

Did you receive any special training on the job, such
as training in using equipment, handling customer
problems, or anything not described in your job duties?

_____

_____

_____

_____

What did you like best about this job? _____

_____

_____

What did you like least? _____

_____

_____

Why did you leave? _____

_____

_____

What was your salary when you started the job? _____

What was your salary when you left? _____

Other Experiences, Skills, Activities, Interests

What personal strengths will help you achieve your objective? For instance, if you want to be a salesperson, you should enjoy working with people. Are you good at solving problems, making decisions, or organizing things? Can you draw? Can you fix things? Ask someone who knows you well to help you identify your strengths.

_____

_____

_____

What are your interests, hobbies, or accomplishments? Are you an athlete? A singer? A dancer? An artist? Have you done volunteer work?

_____

_____

_____

Do you have training in any technical skills? Do you know how to operate any kind of equipment used in the job you want?

_____

_____

_____

References

Ask three people if they would recommend you for a job. If they agree, fill in the information for each of them.

1. Name _____ Title _____

   Company _____

   Address _____ Telephone _____

2. Name _____ Title _____

   Company _____

   Address _____ Telephone _____

3. Name _____ Title _____

   Company _____

   Address _____ Telephone _____

Job Application Forms

The information you put on a job application form is similar to the data on your resume. A job application usually asks for the following categories of information:

1. **Name, address, telephone number.**

2. **Position desired.** List the specific job opening or a general job category such as secretary, trainee, or supervisor. You can also write *entry-level position*.

3. **Salary required.** State the salary you are currently making or hoping to make, given your qualifications. If you do not know the salary range for a certain type of job, learn this before you apply. Check the want ads, talk with people who do similar kinds of work, or ask the interviewing company's personnel office.

4. **Social Security number.** If you don't have a Social Security number, you can apply for one at a local Social Security office. You must have a Social Security number in order to be employed.

5. **U.S. citizenship.** If you are not a U.S. citizen, the company will inform you of their requirements for hiring noncitizens. Also, U.S. citizens are required to prove citizenship after they are hired by showing a passport, birth certificate, driver's license, or other proof of identity.

6. **Educational data.** Include formal schooling and any additional courses.

7. **Skills.** Although you may be applying for a particular position, there may be other jobs in the company for which you are also qualified. List all your skills here so the employer can see that.

8. **Employment history.**
   - Names and addresses of companies you worked for in the past.
   - Names and titles of supervisors. If the person you worked for is no longer with the company, you should still give his or her name.
   - If asked, include the reason you left a job. Some common reasons for leaving are returning to school, seeking a better position, or staff reduction or layoffs. Do not state personal reasons for leaving a job, such as not having anyone to care for your children or not getting along with the boss. The phrase "to seek a better position" covers these kinds of reasons.
   - Your starting and ending salary for each job. Most employers consider this routine and expect an answer.

9. **References.** Most job application forms will ask whether the company can contact your present employer. If you do not want your present employer to know you are looking for a new job, ask the company not to call at this time.

Language Link
Action Verbs and Phrases

Business people look for short resumes. They are busy, and long resumes take time to read. You can limit your resume and hold the attention of an employer by using phrases rather than sentences. When you state your objective, use a phrase.

Sentence: I would like a position as a sales clerk and eventually hope to become a supervisor.

Phrase: Sales position with potential for promotion

When you describe your experience and skills, use phrases with **action verbs.** Action verbs tell your employer what you have done or can do. They are commonly used to describe work experience and skills.

Sentence: My neighborhood had a fund-raising drive for victims of last summer's flood, and I helped plan the bake sale.

Phrase with action verb: Planned fund-raising activity

When you use the action verbs listed below, you help create an image of yourself as a capable person. In fact, some companies use computers to scan for keywords in resumes. These keywords are qualities that companies are looking for in the people they want to hire. Keywords are often action verbs.

Action Verbs			
accomplished	developed	performed	taught
achieved	directed	planned	trained
answered	handled	processed	typed
approved	input	repaired	used
assisted	led	scheduled	won
completed	managed	sold	
created	operated	solved	
designed	organized	supervised	

Language Exercise A

Write the best action verb to complete each phrase.

1. _____ letters and memos for department staff

   Typed   Solved   Supervised

2. _____ telephone calls for two executives

   Completed   Trained   Handled

3. _____ weekly reports on service calls

   Taught   Accomplished   Completed

4. _____ computer equipment and a fax machine

   Operated   Developed   Processed

**Language
Exercise B**

Rewrite the sentences to change them into phrases with action verbs. The first one has been done for you.

1. When the copier broke down, I was able to repair it.

   Repaired equipment, such as a photocopier
   _____

2. I drew all the signs we used in the window of the hardware store.

   _____

3. I made up schedules for covering the reception desk.

   _____

4. When the newsstand owner was out or on vacation, I took over.

   _____

5. I got awards for running track when I was in high school.

   _____

**Language
Exercise C**

Write phrases with action verbs to explain your work experience and skills.

Use the information on your personal data sheet. If the verbs listed on page 111 do not fit, think of other action verbs to use.

Job Duties	Skills
_____	_____
_____	_____
_____	_____
_____	_____

Other Experience	Skills
_____	_____
_____	_____
_____	_____

Special Training/Equipment	Skills
_____	_____
_____	_____
_____	_____

Apply Your Writing Skills

Write Your Resume

Now you are ready to apply what you have learned by writing a resume.

A resume:

- is an outline of a person's work experience, education, and training
- is intended to get a person an interview for a job
- describes skills in a way that presents the best possible picture of the person

As you write, follow the steps in the writing process outlined below.

ASSIGNMENT

Write a resume that presents your education and skills in the best way. Include information that will "sell" you to an employer.

Prewriting

1. Review the personal data sheet you completed on pages 107–109. It is actually the prewriting for your resume.

2. List some questions an employer might want answered about your skills or education. Think of ways you might answer those questions. Your answers may provide you with more "selling points" to put on your resume.

   _____

   _____

   _____

   _____

Writing the First Draft

On a separate piece of paper, write your first draft.

Format the Resume. Follow the format used in Example 1 on page 105 or Example 2 on page 106. Use these headings.

Personal Data

Objective

Work Experience

Education

Other Experience, Skills, Activities, or Interests

   Check your answers on page 241.   113

Write the Information. Include information from your personal data sheet under the appropriate headings of the resume. Use action verbs and phrases to describe your skills and experience.

Revising and Editing

Review, revise, and edit. Read your resume to see if you accomplished what you set out to do. Then use the checklist on page 216 to revise and edit it. Also, pay special attention to these points.

☐ Did you use action verbs to tell what you did in each job? *See pages 111–112.*

☐ Did you use phrases instead of complete sentences? *See pages 111–112.*

Check the formatting of your resume. Did you include the following information?

☐ Personal data

☐ Objective

☐ Work experience

☐ Education

☐ Other experience, skills, activities, or interests

Writing the Final Draft

Write a final draft. Then read it one last time. If necessary, recopy or retype it.

Sharing the Final Draft

Publish. Let another person read your resume. Ask if the resume presents your skills clearly. Ask what else you might include to make an employer want to interview you for a job. Make some notes and attach them to a copy of the resume. File the resume in your writing portfolio.

Complete a Job Application Form

Now you are ready to apply what you have learned by completing a job application form. Use the information from your personal data sheet and resume to fill in the following job application from Belvedere Hospital. Apply for a job as an orderly, nurse's aide, or receptionist at the hospital.

BELVEDERE HOSPITAL

Employment Application

An Equal Opportunity Employer

Belvedere policy and federal law forbid discrimination because of race, religion, age, sex, marital status, disability, or national origin.

Date _____

Personal Data

Applying for position as _____ Salary required _____

Name _____
        (Last)   (First)   (Middle)

Address _____
       (Street)   (City)   (State)   (Zip)

Telephone _____ Social Security Number _____

Are you a U.S. citizen? _____ Yes _____ No

If noncitizen, give Alien Registration Number _____

Person to notify in case of emergency:

Name _____ Telephone _____

Address _____

Have you ever been employed by Belvedere? _____ Yes _____ No

If yes, list department _____ Dates _____

Have you previously applied for employment with Belvedere?

_____ Yes _____ No

If yes, give date _____

How were you referred to Belvedere? _____ Agency _____ School

_____ Advertisement _____ Belvedere Employee _____ Other

Name of referral source above _____

(continue on the next page)

Military Data

Have you served in the military service of the United States?

_____ Yes _____ No

If yes, branch of service _____ From _____ To _____

Rank _____ Service duties that apply to civilian jobs _____

_____

Educational Data

List school name/address; dates attended; type course/major; degree received.

High School _____

_____

College _____

_____

Trade, Business _____

_____

Other _____

_____

Grade Point Average: High School _____ College _____

Skills

List any special skills _____

_____

_____

Business machines you can operate _____

_____

Computer skills _____

_____

(continue on the next page)

Employment Data

List all full-time, part-time, temporary, or self-employment. Begin with current or most recent employer.

Company Name _____

Address

_____
(Street)　　　　　　(City)　　　　(State)　　　(Zip)

Employed From/To　　　Salary or Earnings　　Name/Title of Supervisor

_____

Your Title and Duties

_____

_____

Reason for Leaving _____

_____

Company Name _____

Address

_____
(Street)　　　　　　(City)　　　　(State)　　　(Zip)

Employed From/To　　　Salary or Earnings　　Name/Title of Supervisor

_____

Your Title and Duties

_____

_____

Reason for Leaving _____

_____

I confirm that all information in this employment application is accurate and complete. I understand that employment is contingent upon the accuracy, completeness, and acceptability of the information furnished. Permission is granted to verify all statements in this employment application.

_____　　_____
Date　　　　　　　Signature of Applicant

Workplace writing is any kind of writing you do on the job. In the workplace, you may use your writing skills in a number of different ways.

The format you use depends on the kind of information you are writing. To take telephone messages, you may use special printed forms. To write and send messages to another company, you may write a business letter. To send information to a coworker, you may write a memo. You might also fax or email your messages.

Your workplace writing begins as soon as you start a new job. For example, new employees must fill out certain employment forms.

EXAMPLE This W-4 form gives your employer information needed to take federal income tax from your paycheck.

Form **W-4**
Department of the Treasury
Internal Revenue Service

Employee's Withholding Allowance Certificate

For Privacy Act and Paperwork Reduction Act Notice, see page 2

DMB No. 1525INC10

2002

1. Type or print your first name and middle initial	Last Name	2. Your social security number
Frank M.	Nava	555 00 1212

Home address (number and street or rural route)
4243 Meems Avenue

3. [X] Single [ ] Married [ ] Married, but withhold at higher single rate
Note: If married, but legally separated, or spouse is a nonresident alien, check the single box.

City or town, state, and zip code
Chicago, IL 60601

4. If your last name differs from that on your social security card, check here and call 1-800-772-1213 for a new card . . . . ▶ [ ]

5. Total number of allowances you are claiming (from line H above or from the worksheets on page 2 if they apply) .   **5.** 1
6. Additional amount, if any, you want withheld from each paycheck.   **6.** $ — O —
7. I claim exemption from withholding for 2002, and I certify that I meet **BOTH** of the following conditions for exemption:
 • Last year I had a right to a refund of **ALL** Federal Income Tax withheld because I had **NO** tax liability **AND**
 • This year I expect a refund of **ALL** Federal Income Tax withheld because I expect to have **NO** tax liability.
 If you meet both conditions, enter "**EXEMPT**" here . . . . ▶ **7.** —

Under penalty of perjury, I certify that I am entitled to the number of withholding allowances claimed on this certificate or entitled to claim exempt status

Employee's signature ▶ *Frank M. Nava*   Date ▶ August 15   20 02

8. Employee's name and address   (Complete 9 and 10 only if sending to the IRS) | 9. Office code (optional) | 10. Employer identification number |

WRITE Explain why complete and accurate information is necessary when you fill out a workplace form like the W-4 form above.

_____

_____

_____

Forms

A **form** is a printed document or a computer entry screen with spaces for filling in information. Forms help workers give and receive complete, accurate information.

To fill out a form, look at it carefully to see what kinds of information it asks for and where you write or type each piece of information. If you are handwriting the form, print neatly so that others can read the information.

Some common business forms are order forms, invoices, and shipping forms.

Order Forms

An **order form** is a written statement of what a customer ordered from a company. It also records who ordered the item, who sold it, and how payment will be made.

EXAMPLE Here is part of an order form used by an office supply store.

CUSTOMER ORDER			DATE 10-01-03	
NAME Marlin Fisher				
ADDRESS 111 E. Main St.			ORDER NO. 23201	
CITY, STATE, ZIP Jonesville, IL 60623				
SOLD BY SM	CASH	CHECK	CHARGE	ACCT. NO. 4909

	QUAN.	DESCRIPTION	PRICE	AMOUNT
1	12	binders, imprinted	3 00	36 00
2				
3				

RECEIVED BY M. Fisher	TAX	2 00
	TOTAL	38 00

Answer these questions about the order form above.

1. Who placed the order? _____ Marlin Fisher _____

2. Where does he live? _____

3. What did he order? _____

4. When did he order it? _____

5. Did the customer pay in cash? _____

6. What is the total amount to be paid? _____

Invoices

An **invoice** is a form used to bill customers for what they owe. It shows what they have bought, just as an order form does. It also shows the price of each item and the number of items bought. Because order forms and invoices contain much of the same information, some companies use the same form for both.

EXAMPLE Here is a partly completed invoice used in a hardware store.

INVOICE	TAYLOR HARDWARE		INVOICE NO. 7602

SOLD TO Anne Johnson	SHIP TO same
ADDRESS	ADDRESS
CITY, STATE, ZIP	CITY, STATE, ZIP

ORDER NO. 6626	SOLD BY M. Jones	TERMS 30 days	DATE 10-3-03

ORDERED	SHIPPED	DESCRIPTION	PRICE	UNITS	AMOUNT
10-3		wood paneling, pine	30.00	8	240:00
				TAX	
				TOTAL	

WRITE Complete the invoice above. Use the following information.

In addition to 8 sheets of wood paneling at $30.00 a sheet, Anne Johnson, of 21 Ford Avenue in Detroit, MI 48011, also ordered these items on October 3: 1 package of 3'' wood nails at $5 a package and 1 decorative mirror at $75.00. The tax is $16.00, for a total of $336.00. On October 8, all the items were shipped.

Shipping Forms

A **shipping form** is used to send a letter or package through a delivery service. A shipping form contains information about who is sending the package and who is receiving it. The form also shows facts about the kind of item being sent and who is paying for the shipment. Information on the form must be accurate and easy to read. Otherwise, the package may not get to the right place.

EXAMPLE Below is an example of a completed shipping form.

FedEx® USA Airbill   FedEx Tracking Number 8109 0674 3968   Form I.D. No. 0200   Sender's Copy

1 From Please print and press hard.

Date 11-15-03   Sender's FedEx Account Number N/A

Sender's Name Ben Martinez   Phone (312) 228-1128

Company Martinez, Inc.

Address 1800 W. Chicago Avenue

City Chicago   State IL   ZIP 60601

2 Your Internal Billing Reference
First 24 characters will appear on invoice.

3 To

Recipient's Name Glenn Bono   Phone (512) 555-6111

Company Bono Construction

Address 21 N. Main St.
We cannot deliver to P.O. boxes or P.O. ZIP codes.

To "HOLD" at FedEx location, print FedEx address here.

City Austin   State TX   ZIP 78755

Questions? Call 1·800·Go·FedEx® (800-463-3339)
Visit our Web site at www.fedex.com

By using this Airbill you agree to the service conditions on the back of this Airbill and in our current Service Guide, including terms that limit our liability.

4a Express Package Service   Packages up to 150 lbs.
[X] FedEx Priority Overnight   [ ] FedEx Standard Overnight   [ ] FedEx First Overnight
[ ] FedEx 2Day*   [ ] FedEx Express Saver*

4b Express Freight Service   Packages over 150 lbs.
[ ] FedEx 1Day Freight*   [ ] FedEx 2Day Freight   [ ] FedEx 3Day Freight

5 Packaging
[X] FedEx Letter*   [ ] FedEx Pak*   [ ] Other Pkg.

6 Special Handling
[ ] Saturday Delivery   [ ] Sunday Delivery   [ ] HOLD Weekday   [ ] HOLD Saturday

Does this shipment contain dangerous goods?
One box must be checked.
[X] No   [ ] Yes As per attached Shipper's Declaration   [ ] Yes Shipper's Declaration not required   [ ] Dry Ice   [ ] Cargo Aircraft Only

7 Payment Bill to:
[X] Sender   [ ] Recipient   [ ] Third Party   [ ] Credit Card   [X] Cash/Check

FedEx Acct. No.
Credit Card No.

Total Packages 1   Total Weight 2 (oz)   Total Declared Value $ 12 .00

8 Release Signature Sign to authorize delivery without obtaining signature.

360

Study the form above to see where each piece of information is written. Then answer the following questions.

1. What is being sent, a letter or a package? _____

2. Who is sending the item? _____

3. To whom and where is the item being sent? _____

4. Who is paying to send this item? _____

Messages

Workers need to give and receive information all the time. Therefore, being able to write clear and accurate messages is a valuable work skill. A good message gives all the facts a reader needs. It also presents the information in a way the reader can easily understand.

EXAMPLE Here is a phone message a worker took for his boss.

While You Were Out

Mr. Rice,

Barbara Slade called at 9:00 to say she will not be able

to come to work today. Her daughter is ill. Please call her

when you have time. Her number is 555-4391.

Raoul

The information is complete and clear. The message explained who called, when she called, why she called, and what Mr. Rice should do.

Read the message. Compare it with the example message above. Then answer the questions.

Ms. Luther,

Call Jim Cowens because he won't be in.

Terry

1. What three important facts are missing from this message?

2. What information seems out of order in this message?

Fax Messages

One way to send messages quickly is by using a fax machine. *Fax* is the shortened form of the word *facsimile*. A fax machine sends pages of written material to another fax machine over telephone lines. A fax message usually includes a cover sheet with important information.

EXAMPLE Below is a sample fax cover sheet. It is partly filled in.

FAX TRANSMITTAL SHEET		
TO: Abdel Tahiri	FROM: John Mandel	
COMPANY: Tahiri Retail	DATE: 12-5-03	
FAX NUMBER: 847-555-1212	PHONE NUMBER:	
CONTENTS: Parts information	TOTAL NUMBER OF PAGES INCLUDING COVER:	
NOTE:		

WRITE A Complete the fax cover sheet above. Use this information.

1. Mr. Mandel's phone number is 847-555-3311.

2. He is faxing four pages of catalog information about parts, along with the cover sheet.

3. On a separate piece of paper, write a note to Mr. Tahiri saying that the items he ordered last week are now in stock. Mr. Tahiri should call to say when he would like them delivered.

Email Messages

Another way to send messages quickly is by using email. With email, you write a message on your computer and send it electronically to another computer. Different email systems use different formats. You always need to insert the receiver's email address after the word *To*. The date and your email address are included automatically on a message.

WRITE B Write the email message with this information.

1. You are writing to your coworker, Marty Cox. His email address is Mcox.

2. Your boss, Alicia Stoppen, would like Marty and his team to attend a meeting from 9 to 10 a.m. on Monday, Oct. 1, in the conference room.

3. Anyone with questions should contact you at extension 7224.

TO:	SUBJECT:

Workplace Writing

Memos

A **memo** (short for *memorandum*) is a written workplace message. Memos are written between coworkers to explain, to announce, or to inform, as well as to produce a written record. Like all workplace writing, a memo should include all the facts a reader will need to understand the message.

Memos are prepared in a standard format. A memo includes the date, the sender's name, and the receiver's name. Memos also usually have a subject line to tell the topic of the message.

Workplace memos are often sent by email. Most mail programs create a memo format automatically.

EXAMPLE Below is an example of a memo written about a company policy.

> Date: January 2, 2003
> To: All Employees
> From: Beverly Smith, Human Resources
> Subject: Vacation Requests
>
> We want to be sure that everyone enjoys a two-week vacation this year. If you have not requested a specific time for your vacation, please do so before January 15. If we receive your request by that date, you will have a better chance of receiving the vacation dates you prefer.

PRACTICE

Answer these questions about the memo above.

1. What is the memo about? _____

2. Who wrote the memo? _____

3. Who is the memo to? _____

4. Do you think the message is clear? Is all of the important information included? Explain your answer.

_____

WRITE On a separate piece of paper, write a short memo.

Ask your supervisor, Art Balsam, for permission to leave work an hour early one day next week. You have an appointment with the doctor. You can work an extra hour this week to make up the time.

Prewrite: List the important information you need to include in your memo.

Write: Write your memo, making sure you include all necessary information.

Language Link

Your messages and other pieces of workplace writing should be free of errors. Spelling or punctuation errors can confuse your reader and make you look like a careless worker. Always edit your messages to be sure you are using plurals, possessives, and contractions correctly.

Plurals

Plural means "more than one."

1. To form the plural of most nouns, add *s* or *es*. Add *es* to nouns that end in *s*, *ch*, *sh*, *x*, or *z*.

   EXAMPLES form–forms   tax–taxes   match–matches

2. Many nouns ending in *f* or *fe* form the plural by changing the *f* to *v* and adding *es*.

   EXAMPLES half–halves   wife–wives   knife–knives

3. Nouns that end in a consonant followed by *y* form the plural by changing the *y* to *i* and adding *es*. If there is a vowel before the *y*, just add *s*.

   EXAMPLES company–companies   baby–babies
                      boy–boys   key–keys

4. Some nouns form the plural irregularly. Many dictionaries list irregular plurals.

   EXAMPLES child–children   man–men
                      woman–women   tooth–teeth

Language Exercise

Complete each sentence with the correct plural form of the noun in parentheses.

1. (business) We own both painting and carpeting ____businesses____.

2. (wharf) Oil tankers dock at the _____ in the harbor.

3. (man) The other four _____ in our store are clerks.

4. (attorney) Three _____ wrote the employee manual.

5. (secretary) All the _____ went to lunch together.

6. (woman) Several _____ applied for the welding job.

7. (tooth) Kari brushes her _____ after she eats lunch in the cafeteria.

For more practice with plurals, turn to page 190.

Possessives

The **possessive** form of a noun shows that something is owned and to whom it belongs. Possessive nouns can be singular or plural.

1. Form the possessive of singular nouns and plural nouns that don't end with an *s* by adding an apostrophe (') and *s*. If a singular noun ends in *s*, just add an apostrophe (').

EXAMPLES

Singular: The father's workday began early in the morning.
Bernard's computer was very expensive.
The business' hours are from 10 to 8.

Plural: Women's pay is sometimes less than men's.

2. To form the possessive of plural nouns ending in *s*, add only an apostrophe (').

EXAMPLES

Plural: Both of my sisters' husbands are carpenters.
The Greens' store has been family-owned for years.

Language Exercise

Circle the correct possessive form of the word in each sentence.

1. A (**secretary's**, secretaries') job duties usually include typing letters and memos.

2. A day care center in our office building provides the (**childrens'**, **children's**) breakfast and lunch.

3. My (**friend's, friends'**) spouses take turns driving to work.

4. He is going to work in his (**company's, companies'**) headquarters.

5. My (**boss', bosses'**) name is Hector Ramirez.

6. All of (**Amos', Amos's**) equipment was damaged.

7. After (**everyones', everyone's**) work is done, we can leave for the day.

8. The (**worker's, workers'**) old desks were replaced with work stations.

9. The softball (**player's, players'**) uniforms have the company logo on them.

10. (**Women's, Womens'**) roles in the workplace have changed greatly.

11. The (**Jackson's, Jacksons'**) house was not damaged in the storm last week.

12. The (**machine's, machines'**) warranties all expired last year.

For more practice with possessives turn to page 191.

Contractions

A **contraction** is a word formed by joining two other words. An apostrophe (') shows where a letter or letters have been left out. Most people use contractions when they speak or when they write informal letters. Do not use contractions, however, in formal business writing.

Common Contractions

Contraction	Words It Replaces
I'm	I am
he's, she's, it's	he is, she is, it is
you're, we're, they're	you are, we are, they are
isn't, aren't, wasn't, weren't	is not, are not, was not, were not
he'll, she'll, you'll	he will, she will, you will
won't	will not
didn't	did not
I'd	I would
I've, we've	I have, we have
who's	who is, who has
let's	let us
can't	cannot
there's	there is

Language Exercise   Write the contraction for the underlined words.

_____ 1. I have recently learned to use a personal computer.

_____ 2. I did not know a computer could make my job easier.

_____ 3. There is a way to make many copies of the same letter.

_____ 4. There was not enough time to type every letter.

_____ 5. My co-workers were not happy about using computers.

_____ 6. You will not be surprised to hear that most people use computers.

_____ 7. Let us agree that computers changed the way business works.

_____ 8. We did not want to admit computers would be useful.

For more practice with contractions turn to page 192.

Apply Your Writing Skills

Complete a Form

Now you are ready to apply your writing skills by completing a form. A business form:

- has spaces in which information is entered
- must be accurate and complete
- must be neat so that someone else can read it

As you write, follow the steps in the writing process outlined below.

ASSIGNMENT

Complete the shipping form on page 129.

Prewriting

Assume the following information.

- You are sending an 8-oz. letter from your company, ABC Supplies, 100 Hudson Street, Detroit, MI 48255.
- The phone number is 313-555-0795.
- The letter is going to Mary Money at Adams Company, 1421 Wilson, Cleveland, OH 44101.
- Her phone number is 216-555-4875.
- The letter needs to arrive the next business morning but does not require special handling.
- Your company will pay the bill. Its account number is 584-906-792. The internal billing reference number is AC-34.
- Because the shipment is being charged to an account, you do not need to enter total charges.
- You do not need to enter a declared value.
- You do not want the letter left without someone at the Adams Company signing for it.

Writing

Write the information above in the appropriate spaces on the form on page 129. Be sure to read the form carefully so that you put the information in the correct spaces.

FedEx® *USA Airbill* FedEx Tracking Number **81090674396 8** Form I.D. No. **0200** Sender's Copy

1 From Please print and press hard.

Date _____ Sender's FedEx Account Number _____

Sender's Name _____ Phone ( )

Company _____

Address _____ Dept./Floor/Suite/Room

City _____ State _____ ZIP _____

2 Your Internal Billing Reference
First 24 characters will appear on invoice.

3 To

Recipient's Name _____ Phone ( )

Company _____

Address _____ Dept./Floor/Suite/Room
We cannot deliver to P.O. boxes or P.O. ZIP codes.

To "HOLD" at FedEx location, print FedEx address here.

City _____ State _____ ZIP _____

Questions? Call 1·800·Go·FedEx® (800-463-3339)
Visit our Web site at www.fedex.com

By using this Airbill you agree to the service conditions on the back of this Airbill and in our current Service Guide, including terms that limit our liability.

4a Express Package Service *Packages up to 150 lbs.*
Delivery commitment may be later in some areas.

☐ FedEx Priority Overnight
Next business morning

☐ FedEx Standard Overnight
Next business afternoon

☐ FedEx First Overnight
Earliest next business morning delivery to select locations

☐ FedEx 2Day*
Second business day

☐ FedEx Express Saver*
Third business day

* FedEx Letter Rate not available Minimum charge: One-pound rate

4b Express Freight Service *Packages over 150 lbs.*
Delivery commitment may be later in some areas.

☐ FedEx 1Day Freight*
Next business day

☐ FedEx 2Day Freight
Second business day

☐ FedEx 3Day Freight
Third business day

* Call for Confirmation: _____

5 Packaging * Declared value limit $500

☐ FedEx Letter* ☐ FedEx Pak* ☐ Other Pkg.
Includes FedEx Box, FedEx Tube, and customer pkg.

6 Special Handling

☐ Saturday Delivery
Available for FedEx Priority Overnight and FedEx 2Day to select ZIP codes.

☐ Sunday Delivery
Available for FedEx Priority Overnight to select ZIP codes

☐ HOLD Weekday
at FedEx Location
Not available with FedEx First Overnight

☐ HOLD Saturday
at FedEx Location
Available for FedEx Priority Overnight and FedEx 2Day to select locations

Does this shipment contain dangerous goods?
One box must be checked.

☐ No
☐ Yes
As per attached Shipper's Declaration
☐ Yes
Shipper's Declaration not required
☐ Dry Ice
Dry Ice, 9, UN 1845 _____ x _____ kg
☐ Cargo Aircraft Only

Dangerous Goods cannot be shipped in FedEx packaging.

7 Payment *Bill to:*
Enter FedEx Acct. No. or Credit Card No. below.

☐ Sender
Acct. No. in Section 1 will be billed.
☐ Recipient ☐ Third Party ☐ Credit Card ☐ Cash/Check

FedEx Acct. No.
Credit Card No. _____ Exp. Date _____

Total Packages _____ Total Weight _____ Total Declared Value†
$ _____ .00

†Our liability is limited to $100 unless you declare a higher value. See back for details. FedEx Use Only

8 Release Signature Sign to authorize delivery without obtaining signature.

By signing you authorize us to deliver this shipment without obtaining a signature and agree to indemnify and hold us harmless from any resulting claims.

360

Rev. Date 11/98•Part #154614•©1994-98 FedEx•PRINTED IN U.S.A. GBFE 1/99

Double-checking

After you have completed the form, check it to make sure you have filled it out accurately and completely.

☐ Are all the spaces that need to be completed filled in?

☐ Is all the information accurate?

☐ Did you spell names correctly?

☐ Did you capitalize correctly? *See pages 97–98.*

☐ Is your writing neat enough so that someone else can read it?

Write a Memo

Now you are ready to apply what you have learned by writing a memo to your coworkers.

A memo:

- is a written workplace message
- must include all important information
- uses a standard format

As you write, follow the steps in the writing process outlined below.

ASSIGNMENT

Assume you are an assistant manager in a grocery store. You have noticed that some of the checkout cashiers seem to have forgotten basic store policies about how to act with customers. Some don't smile and greet the customer. Others don't count back change. You think a refresher workshop in customer service for all checkout cashiers would be a good idea. Write a memo announcing the workshop and the reasons for it. Include a date, time, and place for the workshop.

Prewriting

1. List the details you will need to cover in your memo. (You may make up more details if you like.)

_____

_____

_____

_____

_____

_____

_____

2. Organize your ideas in an outline or idea map like the one below.

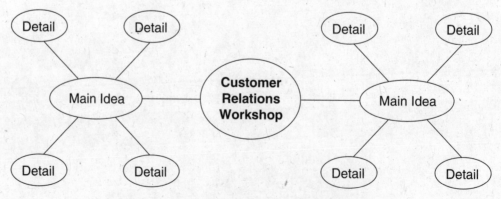

Writing the First Draft

On a separate piece of paper, write your first draft.

Write the Introduction. Briefly state the subject of your memo. Write a strong topic sentence that directly and clearly states the problem.

Develop Supporting Details. As you write your memo, remember to include all important information.

Write the Conclusion. Give the reader a person to contact and, if appropriate, a telephone number. Do not bring up any new points here.

Revising and Editing

Review, revise, and edit. Read your memo to see if you accomplished what you set out to do. Then use the checklist on page 216 to revise and edit it. Also, pay special attention to these points.

- ☐ Did you use the proper memo format? *See page 124.*
- ☐ Did you give readers all the details they need? *See page 124.*
- ☐ If you used plurals, possessives, or contractions, did you spell them correctly? *See pages 125–127.*

Writing the Final Draft

Write a final draft. Then read it one last time. If necessary, recopy or retype it.

Sharing the Final Draft

Publish. Let another person read your memo. Ask if your memo was clear. Ask what you might do to improve your writing. Make some notes and attach them to a copy of the memo. File the memo in your writing portfolio.

LESSON 9

Explanatory Writing

Explanatory writing explains, informs, or instructs. You can read explanatory writing in books, newspapers, and magazines. The writing in this textbook is explanatory.

Much of the writing that you do every day is also explanatory writing. You might write travel directions for someone or leave a note about where you are going. You might have to write down what you do to complete a certain job.

Explanatory writing contains clear and complete facts. The facts are arranged to help readers follow the point. Good explanatory writing also uses precise words so that the reader understands exactly what is being explained.

EXAMPLE Read the following paragraph. It explains how a camera works.

A camera works a little like your eye does. When you point a camera at something—say, your five-year-old daughter or the New York City skyline—light reflects from that subject and strikes the lens of your camera. The light passes through the lens and forms an image on the film. You sharpen that image by focusing. To form a sharp image of a subject close to your camera, such as your daughter, focus so that the lens is relatively far from the film. If the subject is far from your camera, such as a skyline, focus so that the lens is closer to the film. If you have an automatic camera, the camera focuses for you.

The explanation in the example uses a spatial explanation, light moving from outside a camera to within. From that explanation, you get a basic understanding of how a camera works.

WRITE Think of something you know about and can explain.

On a separate piece of paper, write a paragraph that explains how something works to a person who knows very little about your subject.

Think of something you use. Your topic could be as simple as the table of contents in a book or as complicated as a car engine. List specific details you could include. Decide the order in which to present them. Then follow the writing process you learned in Lesson 5 to write an explanation.

Explanatory Writing

Time-order Transition Words

One way to explain your ideas clearly is to include transition words in your paragraphs. **Transition words** link ideas in specific ways. For example, **time-order transition words** show the order of ideas through time. Common time-order transition words are listed below.

first	next	before	meanwhile
second	then	soon	when
third	last	later	while
fourth	after	during	earlier

EXAMPLE **No transition words:** Go north on Main Street for two miles. Turn left onto King Street. Take a left by the park.

Transition words: First, go north on Main Street for two miles. Next, turn left onto King Street. Finally, take a left by the park.

PRACTICE

Write time-order transition words to complete the paragraph. Use each word once.

when   second   last   then   first

_____, go north to the corner. _____ , turn right at the food store. Look for the sign for Smith Street. _____ you see the sign, walk a block more. _____ turn left. _____, stop at the dress shop. Our apartment is on the second floor.

WRITE On a separate piece of paper, write directions that a friend could use to go from your house or apartment to the nearest grocery store.

Prewrite: List the steps to get to the grocery store from your house.

Write: Put the steps into sentences. Then add time-order transition words to make the directions clearer. Begin your directions with the word *first*.

Explanatory Writing

Transition Words in "How-to" Writing

Time-order transition words are also used in "how-to" writing. "How-to" writing explains how things are made or done.

EXAMPLE Read the paragraph below about how to follow the writing process. Notice that the writer uses time-order transition words to join the steps.

Writing is a step-by-step process. **First,** decide what you want to write. **Second,** plan your message. Jot down ideas about what you want to cover in your writing and organize your ideas in an outline or idea map. **Next,** write a first draft. **Then** review, revise, and edit your draft to make it clear and correct. Write a final draft and read it again. **Finally,** share your writing with another person.

PRACTICE

Write time-order transition words to complete the paragraph. Use each word once.

next   during   after   second   last   then   first

Did you ever wonder how peanut butter is made?

_____ , the peanuts are shelled. _____ , they are sorted for size and value. _____ , they are roasted.

_____ they are cooked, the red outer skin is removed.

_____ , the nut is split, and the small piece called the "heart" is taken off. The heart makes the peanut butter sour.

_____ , the nuts are mashed. _____ the last step of mashing, workers add honey, sugar, and salt.

WRITE On a separate piece of paper, write a paragraph explaining something simple you know how to do.

Prewrite: Think of something you can explain. It could be diapering a baby, starting a car, going grocery shopping, or shooting a basketball. List all the steps. Then number the steps in order.

Write: Use your prewriting plan to write your paragraph. Use time-order transition words to connect the steps.

Explanatory Writing

Precise Words and Specific Details

Precise words and specific details help the reader understand an explanation. As you learned in Unit 1, Lesson 2, being precise and specific helps you create word pictures so the reader can "see" what you mean.

EXAMPLE Read the two explanations for grilling fish. The second one has precise words and specific details; the first one does not.

1.   Here's a way to cook fish on a grill. First, buy a plank of wood at the store. Clean the plank. Then soak it to prevent it from burning. Next, preheat the coals in your grill. Put the fish on the plank and some herbs on the fish. When the coals are hot, place the plank on the grill with the coals around the edges. Cook for 15 to 20 minutes.

2.   Here's a healthy, fat-free way of cooking fish that you can use on your barbecue—grilling fish on a wood plank. First, buy a cedar or fir plank at a lumberyard or home supply store. The plank should be cut to 1" by 8" by 18". Second, rinse the plank with water to clean it. Then soak the plank in water for one hour to prevent it from burning on the grill. Next, preheat the coals in your grill. Place the fish on the plank and sprinkle the top of it with fresh herbs. When the coals are hot, place the plank on the grill so that the fish is in the center with the coals around the edges. Cook over a medium fire for 15 to 20 minutes or until the fish is cooked throughout. Then enjoy!

Notice how the precise words (*cedar or fir, lumberyard or home supply store, sprinkle*) and specific details (*1" by 8" by 18", for one hour, medium fire*) in the second explanation help you understand much better what to do.

PRACTICE

Rewrite each sentence using precise words and specific details.

1. You can relax at night by listening to music and by taking a bath.

_____

2. You can protect yourself from crime by being careful and getting in shape.

_____

3. I can make my lifestyle healthier by watching what I eat and exercising.

_____

Completeness

If an explanation is missing important details or steps, the reader might do something wrong. Look again at the two explanations on page 135. The first explanation is missing the detail "Cook over a medium fire." If you read that explanation and cooked over a hot fire, you'd have burnt fish for dinner.

Write an answer for each question.

1. In the first explanation, what is missing in the step about soaking the plank?

   _____

2. What might happen as a result of this missing information?

   _____

Clear Presentation

Sometimes explanations are written in one or more paragraphs. Often, however, it is clearer to list the steps in an explanation. The clearest presentation depends on the topic and the number of steps involved.

EXAMPLE Here is the explanation for grilling fish written as a list of numbered steps.

1. Buy a cedar or fir plank at a lumberyard or home supply store. The plank should be cut to 1" by 8" by 18".
2. Rinse the plank with water to clean it. Then soak the plank in water for one hour to prevent it from burning.
3. Preheat the coals in your grill.
4. Place the fish on the plank and sprinkle the top of it with fresh herbs.
5. When the coals are hot, place the plank on the grill so that the fish is in the center with the coals around the edges.
6. Cook over a medium fire for 15 to 20 minutes, or until the fish is cooked throughout.

WRITE On a separate piece of paper, write an explanation about one of these topics or a topic of your own.

| how to relax at night | how to be safe from crime | how to cook a dish |
| how to quit smoking | how to do an exercise | how to tell a joke |

Prewrite: Picture in your mind what to do. List all the steps involved. Think of the clearest way to present the ideas: paragraph or list.

Write: Write your explanation in paragraph form or list form. Use precise words and specific details.

Language Link
Verb Tenses

Explanatory writing often deals with actions: "First, do this" or "Then, this happens." **Verbs** are words that show action. Verbs also show time, or **tense.** English has six verb tenses. There are three simple tenses and three perfect tenses. The **simple tenses** show present, past, and future time.

EXAMPLES   **Present tense:** I call my friend daily.
                                       She is my friend.

                Past tense: You smiled at me yesterday.
                                     They gave a party.

                Future tense: He will work late tonight.
                                        We shall call home.

The three **perfect tenses** show actions that have ended or that will end soon. They also can show the effect of actions.

For more practice on verb tenses, turn to pages 161–164.

EXAMPLES   **Present perfect:** My friend has offered to help me.

                Past perfect: The storm had ended when the power went off.

                Future perfect: By Tuesday, I will have been here three days.

Language Exercise A

Identify the tense of each underlined verb. Write *past, present,* or *future.*

1. We will give a party after work today. _____

2. Marge likes chips and dip. _____

3. I called all our friends last night. _____

4. He spent most of his money. _____

Language Exercise B

Circle the number of the best way to correct each underlined verb.

1. Your children grow so tall since last year!
    (1) have grown
    (2) will grow
    (3) had grown
    (4) grows

2. By the time you came home, I have cleaned up.
    (1) had cleaned
    (2) will clean
    (3) cleaning
    (4) cleans

3. Charles did visited his aunt every summer.
    (1) visiting
    (2) visits
    (3) have visited
    (4) visit

4. Steve has swum ten laps in the pool yesterday.
    (1) swimming
    (2) swims
    (3) will be swimming
    (4) swam

Misplaced and Dangling Modifiers

Using the wrong verb tense can make explanatory writing unclear. Placing **modifiers**—descriptive words and phrases—in the wrong place or leaving out the words they describe can also make explanations confusing.

Misplaced Modifiers

Place modifiers as close as possible to the part of the sentence they describe. Sentences are unclear when the modifiers are in the wrong place.

EXAMPLE

Wrong Place: John saw the train passing through the open window.

A train did not pass through the open window. The phrase "through the open window" should be closer to the word it describes, *saw.* Move the phrase.

Correct Place: Through the open window, John saw the train passing.

Dangling Modifiers

Don't forget to include the word that is being described in a sentence. A sentence with a dangling modifier has something missing.

EXAMPLE **Dangling Modifier:** Coming up the stairs, the clock struck one.

A clock cannot come up the stairs. The sentence does not say <u>who</u> did the action. *Coming up the stairs* is left dangling with nothing to modify. There are two ways to correct the sentence.

Correct: Coming up the stairs, he heard the clock strike one.
Correct: As he was coming up the stairs, the clock struck one.

Language Exercise A

Circle the number of each sentence that has a modifier in the wrong place.

1. Save a room for the couple with a bath.
2. I found a letter in the mailbox that is not mine.
3. To get to the plant, we went nearly ten miles.
4. We bought a cat for my son we call Fluff.

Language Exercise B

Circle the number of the best way to correct each sentence.

1. When driving, a fatal crash was seen.
   (1) When driving a fatal crash, we saw it.
   (2) A fatal crash, when driving, was seen.
   (3) When driving, we saw a fatal crash.
   (4) A fatal crash was seen when driving.

2. While passing a large rock, a noise made me jump.
   (1) While I was passing a large rock, a noise made me jump.
   (2) While a large rock passed a noise made me jump.
   (3) A noise made me pass a large rock.
   (4) While a large rock was passed, a noise made me jump.

For more practice on placing modifiers correctly, turn to pages 178–179.

Parallel Structure

Explanatory writing is clearer if all the ideas in a sentence are in the same form. When you list words or phrases in the same form, you are using **parallel structure.** The words or phrases may be used as nouns, verbs, adjectives, or adverbs.

EXAMPLES   **Not parallel:** TV is good for <u>news</u>, <u>movies</u>, and <u>to watch sports</u>.
Parallel: TV is good for <u>news</u>, <u>movies</u>, and <u>sports</u>. (nouns)

Not parallel: The cat likes <u>to sleep</u>, <u>scratch</u>, and <u>eating</u>.
Parallel: The cat likes to <u>sleep</u>, <u>scratch</u>, and <u>eat</u>. (verbs)

Not parallel: The room was <u>large</u>, <u>clean</u>, and <u>did not cost a lot</u>.
Parallel: The room was <u>large</u>, <u>clean</u>, and <u>inexpensive</u>. (adjectives)

Not parallel: For an interview, dress <u>neatly</u>, <u>appropriately</u>, and <u>comfortable</u>.
Parallel: For an interview, dress <u>neatly</u>, <u>appropriately</u>, and <u>comfortably</u>. (adverbs)

Language Exercise A

Circle the number of each sentence that is written in parallel structure.

1. Mr. Paul promised me a good job and a fair wage.

2. Hard workers are intense, motivated, and take care.

3. My friend is kind, generous, and interesting.

4. They like watching football, playing baseball, and to bowl.

Language Exercise B

Rewrite each sentence using parallel structure.

1. It is good for people to run, swim, and go jogging.

_____

2. Running, for example, helps you stay fit and to be in good health.

_____

3. Swimming can help in toning your muscles and to lower your blood pressure.

_____

4. You can start by walking a block a day and to eat good food.

_____

5. Exercise can help you look better, be stronger, and to have mental alertness.

_____

For more practice on parallel structure, turn to pages 174–175.

Apply Your Writing Skills

Write an Explanation

Now you are ready to apply what you have learned by writing an explanation.

Explanatory writing:

- explains, informs, or instructs
- includes transition words to link ideas or to show the order of ideas
- uses precise words and specific details, includes all important information, and is presented clearly

As you write, follow the steps in the writing process outlined below.

ASSIGNMENT

Suppose you must explain to a friend or family member how to perform some skill or explain to a co-worker how to do a job at work. Write an explanation that this person could use to learn the skill or complete the job.

Prewriting

1. List several skills that you have or jobs that you perform well.

   _____

   _____

   _____

2. Use the space below to organize your ideas in an outline or idea map. Arrange your ideas in a way that will help you best explain one skill or job you listed above. If you are writing step-by-step instructions, you may want to list and number them. If you are explaining or giving information, you may want to write about related ideas in paragraph form.

Writing the First Draft

On a separate piece of paper, write your first draft.

Write the Introduction. Briefly state the subject of your "how-to" explanation. Write a strong topic sentence that states your topic best.

Develop Supporting Details. As you develop your explanation, remember to include precise words and specific details. Follow your prewriting plan.

Write the Conclusion. Write a strong ending that ties together all the points you have made. Do not bring up any new points here.

Revising and Editing

Review, revise, and edit. Read your explanation to see if you accomplished what you set out to do. Could someone follow your explanation to complete this job? Then use the checklist on page 216 to revise and edit it. Also, pay special attention to these points.

- ☐ Did you use time-order transition words? *See pages 133–134.*
- ☐ Did you use precise words and specific details? *See page 135.*
- ☐ Did you include all necessary information? *See page 136.*
- ☐ Is your presentation clear? *See page 136.*
- ☐ Did you use correct verb tenses? *See page 137.*
- ☐ Did you place modifiers correctly? *See page 138.*
- ☐ Did you use parallel structure? *See page 139.*

Writing the Final Draft

Write a final draft. Then read it one last time. If necessary, recopy or retype it.

Sharing the Final Draft

Publish. Let another person read your explanation. Ask if your explanation was clear. Ask what you might do to improve it. Make some notes and attach them to a copy of the explanation. File the explanation in your writing portfolio.

Writing at Work

Office and Administrative Support: Customer Service Representative

Do you enjoy helping people solve problems? Do you pay attention to details? Do you like to follow tasks through from beginning to end? If so, you may be interested in becoming a customer service representative.

Customer service representatives are often the first contact that customers have with a company. Customer service representatives receive and process customers' orders. They answer customers' questions and help them solve any problems they may have.

In order to perform their job effectively, customer service representatives should have excellent listening and speaking skills. They should also have strong writing and grammar skills. Representatives must be able to write clearly and logically and include relevant details in their writing.

Look at the box showing some careers in office and administrative support.

- Do any of the careers interest you? If so, which ones?

- How could you find out more about those careers? On a separate piece of paper, write some questions that you would like to have answered. You can find out more information about those careers in the *Occupational Outlook Handbook* at your local library and online.

Admitting Interviewer records information from incoming patients in healthcare and nursing facilities

File Clerk classifies, stores, and retrieves information; performs data entry and word processing tasks

New Accounts Clerk records information from new customers to help them open financial accounts

Library Assistant issues library cards; checks materials in and out; updates records in computer databases

Use the material below to answer the questions that follow.

Creature Comforts
1900 Sleepy Hollow Drive ◆ Wake Forest, NC 27587

Dear Ms. Chambers:

Thank you for ordering our Fit for a King bedroom furniture. I was sorry to receive your phone call telling me that some pieces of your furniture arrived damaged and others did not arrive at all. Please be assured that Creature Comforts stands behind every piece of furniture we sell. We want our customers to be totally satisfied with their purchases.

I will send a truck to pick up your damaged dresser. Creature Comforts will cover the cost of this truck. I have also put out a tracer to find the night table you never received. If the table is not found within the next 72 hours, I will order a replacement for you.

If you have any questions or need any further assistance, please contact me at 555-7645.

Sincerely,

Lacey Curtin

Customer Service Representative

1. What is the purpose of the customer service letter?
    (1) to tell Ms. Chambers that her furniture was damaged
    (2) to let Ms. Chambers know that her night table did not arrive
    (3) to deny that there were problems with Ms. Chambers' order
    (4) to let Ms. Chambers know that the problems will be fixed
    (5) to tell Ms. Chambers to call and give more details about her order

2. Which of the following is a true statement about Ms. Chambers' order?
    (1) Nothing that she ordered arrived undamaged.
    (2) She ordered the Fit for a King bedroom set.
    (3) The delivery person damaged her front door.
    (4) Her night table was damaged.
    (5) It was her first time ordering from Creature Comforts.

3. In her letter, what does customer service representative Curtin tell Ms. Chambers?
    (1) She will receive all pieces of furniture within 72 hours.
    (2) She will need to pay for any damages to the furniture.
    (3) Creature Comforts will find the missing table within 72 hours.
    (4) All the Fit for a King bedroom furniture did not arrive.
    (5) Creature Comforts believes in keeping their customers happy.

Unit 2 Review: Personal and Workplace Writing

Write the best action verb to complete each phrase.

1. _____ telephone calls for two attorneys

   Completed   **Trained**   **Handled**

2. _____ computer and word processing equipment

   Operated   **Developed**   **Handled**

> For more practice with plurals, turn to page 190.

Write the plural form of each noun.

3. community _____

4. knife _____

5. tax _____

> For more practice with possessives, turn to page 191.

Write the possessive form of each word in parentheses.

6. The ten (**workers**) _____ paychecks were in the mail.

7. The (**people**) _____ rights are protected by law.

8. (**Charles**) _____ car is red.

> For more practice with contractions, turn to page 192.

Write the contraction to replace the underlined words in each sentence.

9. <u>I have</u> read everything I could find about cars. _____

10. <u>I would not</u> mind buying an electric car. _____

Identify the tense of each underlined verb. Write *past*, *present*, or *future*.

11. Gina <u>started</u> her own business last year. _____

12. Her business <u>will earn</u> a large profit this year. _____

13. She <u>makes</u> custom picture frames. _____

> For more practice with verb tenses, turn to pages 161–163.

Write the correct verb to complete each sentence.

14. I _____ before you called.

    will cook   **cook**   **had been cooking**

15. Doug _____ a mechanic for the last two years.

    will be   **has been**   **is being**

For more practice with irregular verbs, turn to page 164.

Write the correct verb form to complete each sentence.

16. Mei Lei had _____ before she left.

    wrote   written

17. Mr. Lucas _____ learning Spanish last year.

    began   begun

18. The TV had _____ $239 before the sale.

    cost   costed

For more practice with capitalization, turn to pages 187–189.

Use the editing mark to show where capital letters are needed (a = A).

19. Her uncle was a well-known mexican doctor.

20. He went to work for a texas company called lonestar.

For more practice with punctuation, turn to pages 184–186.

Add the correct punctuation to complete each sentence.

21. Is Mrs May serving hot dogs potato salad and baked beans

22. Sheila B Cohn was born on May 25 1965

For more practice with placing modifiers correctly, turn to pages 178–179.

Rewrite each sentence to correct the dangling or misplaced modifiers.

23. Broken beyond repair, Juan saw his motorcycle in the front yard.

    _____

24. When watching my son, he ran into the street.

    _____

For more practice with parallel structure, turn to pages 174–175.

Rewrite each sentence to give it parallel structure.

25. The meal was cheap, tasty, and the food was good for us.

    _____

26. I should walk, jog, or go swimming to stay in shape.

    _____

For a review of writing a business letter, turn to pages 91–92 and pages 94–96.

Write a business letter.

You ordered a set of three CDs, *Marco's Best Songs*. Two of the CDs were exactly what you wanted. The third CD was blank. Write a letter to Music-Pro, Inc. Return the blank CD and request a new one. The company's address is Music-Pro, Inc., 222 Mission Street, San Antonio, TX 78212.

Writing Extension

Use your writing skills to write a business letter to a company that makes a product you use. Explain why you like the product or why you don't like it. Follow the Writing Process when you write your letter. Share your final draft with your instructor or another student.

Mini-Test • Unit 2

This is a 15-minute practice test. After 15 minutes, mark the last number you finished. Then complete the test and check your answers. If most of your answers were correct but you did not finish, try to work faster next time.

Directions: Choose the <u>one best answer</u> to each question.

<u>Questions 1 through 4</u> refer to the following information.

HOLIDAY COOKING

(A)

(1) Once Halloween is over, the next round of holidays may be on your mind. (2) Special meals for thanksgiving and winter feasting are often fancy, with roast turkey, homemade mashed potatoes, and pie. (3) Keeping cost in mind, these two tips may help.

(B)

(4) Your Grandmother probably saved stale bread for turkey stuffing, and you can too. (5) Just stash any kind of old bread in your freezer, including those heels at the bottom of the bag. (6) Also, don't buy store-baked desserts because you were worried about having too much to do. (7) A pie or cookies made a day in advance will taste better anyway.

1. Sentence 2: **Special meals for thanksgiving and winter feasting are often fancy, with roast turkey, homemade mashed potatoes, and pie.**

   Which correction should be made to sentence 2?

   (1) change thanksgiving to <u>Thanksgiving</u>
   (2) change <u>winter</u> to <u>Winter</u>
   (3) remove the comma after <u>turkey</u>
   (4) remove the comma after <u>potatoes</u>
   (5) no correction is necessary

2. Sentence 3: **Keeping cost in mind, these two tips may help.**

   Which is the best way to write the underlined portion of this sentence? If the original is the best way, choose option (1).

   (1) Keeping cost in mind
   (2) If cost is on your mind
   (3) Keep cost in mind
   (4) Giving cost some thought
   (5) Having kept cost in mind

3. Sentence 4: **Your Grandmother probably saved stale bread for turkey stuffing, and you can too.**

   Which correction should be made to sentence 4?

   (1) change <u>Grandmother</u> to <u>grandmother</u>
   (2) insert <u>had</u> before <u>saved</u>
   (3) change <u>saved</u> to <u>saving</u>
   (4) change <u>can</u> to <u>could have</u>
   (5) no correction is necessary

4. Sentence 6: **Also, don't buy store-baked desserts because you were worried about having too much to do.**

   Which correction should be made to sentence 6?

   (1) change <u>don't</u> to <u>you didn't</u>
   (2) change <u>don't</u> to <u>do'nt</u>
   (3) change <u>were</u> to <u>are</u>
   (4) change <u>were</u> to <u>was</u>
   (5) no correction is necessary

Questions 5 through 8 refer to the following business advertisement.

HOW TO PLAN YOUR DRIVING VACATION WITH CAR MASTER MOTOR CLUB

(A)

(1) Take advantage of Car Master Motor Club's vacation travel planning service. (2) We'll get you from the West Coast to Maine or any state in between. (3) First, call our operator at the toll-free number on your membership card. (4) Be ready to give us your home address your destination address, and any attractions you want to visit along the way.

(B)

(5) Next, we will help you reserve your accommodations and with tickets to attractions. (6) Along your route, tell us where you want a campground or motel room. (7) Finally, order your discount passes to the places you want to visit, such as amusement parks and museums. (8) For ideas about where to stay and what to do purchase our Roadside Reference Book for $25.00. (9) It has over 500 recommendations for hotels, restaurants, and attractions. (10) It also has more than $200 worth of coupons. (11) Buy one today and have a great vacation tomorrow!

5. Sentence 4: **Be ready to give us your home address your destination address, and any attractions you want to visit along the way.**

   Which correction should be made to sentence 4?

   (1) insert a comma after home address
   (2) remove the comma after destination address
   (3) insert a comma after and
   (4) change attractions to Attractions
   (5) no correction is necessary

6. Sentence 5: **Next, we will help you reserve your accommodations and with tickets to attractions.**

   Which is the best way to write the underlined portion of this sentence? If the original is the best way, choose option (1).

   (1) with tickets to attractions
   (2) buying tickets to attractions
   (3) attract tickets
   (4) ticketing for attractions
   (5) purchase tickets to attractions

7. Sentence 6: **Along your route, tell us where you want a campground or motel room.**

   Which correction should be made to sentence 6?

   (1) move Along your route to the end of the sentence
   (2) remove the comma after route
   (3) insert a comma after campground
   (4) change motel to Motel
   (5) no correction is necessary

8. Which revision would improve the effectiveness of this advertisement?

   Begin a new paragraph with

   (1) sentence 6
   (2) sentence 7
   (3) sentence 8
   (4) sentence 9
   (5) sentence 11

Language Skills

nguage Skil

Good **language skills** are essential to your success in writing on the job, in school, or in your personal life. Writing good sentences, spelling correctly, using correct punctuation, and organizing paragraphs effectively are all language skills that help you communicate your ideas. From job applications, to accident reports, to the GED Test, not only what you write, but also how well you write will give an impression of you.

What language skills do you feel confident about when you write?

_____

What language skills do you feel you need help with when you write?

_____

Thinking About Language Skills

You use language skills every day—in some ways you may not even be aware of. Think about your day-to-day activities.

Check each activity you did.

☐ Did you notice a misspelled word on a piece of mail or a sign?

☐ Did you correct something you wrote because it had errors in it?

☐ Did you look up a word in a dictionary to see how it was spelled?

☐ Did you "look over" a piece of writing for a friend or coworker to find any mistakes?

☐ Did you stop in the middle of writing something and think, *Do I need a comma here?*

Write some other activities where you have used language skills.

_____

_____

_____

Previewing the Unit

In this unit, you will learn:

● how to use the basic parts of speech—nouns, pronouns, verbs, adjectives, and adverbs—to express yourself clearly and correctly

● how to create varied, interesting, and correct sentences

● what the basic rules for punctuation, spelling, and capitalization are

● how to write well-organized paragraphs

Lesson 10	**Usage**
Lesson 11	**Sentence Structure**
Lesson 12	**Mechanics**
Lesson 13	**Paragraph Organization**

Nouns

A **noun** is the name of a person, place, or thing. All nouns belong to one of two groups: common nouns or proper nouns.

Common Nouns

A **common noun** names a person, place, or thing.

Person		Place		Thing	
writer	athlete	street	country	movie	marriage
woman	actor	city	sea	car	year

Proper Nouns

A **proper noun** names a <u>specific</u> person, place, or thing. A proper noun always begins with a capital letter.

	Person	Place	Thing
Common noun:	writer	street	beverage
Proper noun:	Stephen King	Front Street	Zippy Cola

PRACTICE

Draw <u>one</u> line under each common noun and <u>two</u> lines under each proper noun.

1. The meeting between the lawyers of Martello Company and our client will take place on Tuesday, November 1.

2. The client has asked Ms. Robinson to be present at the meeting as well.

3. The first item on the agenda will be to discuss the accusations against Martello Company.

4. *Business Times* magazine has been reporting on the situation for several months now.

5. Our client plans to be at the Hartford Street office by nine o'clock.

6. Many businesses in the United States are interested in this investigation.

Collective Nouns and Mass Nouns

Collective Nouns

Collective nouns are nouns that name groups of people, places, or things.

family	team	jury
company	committee	group

A collective noun usually takes the singular form of the verb.

The <u>team</u> <u>begins</u> the tournament on Tuesday.

Mass Nouns

Mass nouns are nouns that name qualities and things that cannot be counted.

water	chaos	strength	anger
time	courage	hair	gold

Mass nouns do not have plural forms because the things they name cannot be counted. Use the singular form of the verb with a mass noun.

There <u>isn't</u> much <u>time</u> left.

<u>Water</u> <u>flows</u> downhill.

PRACTICE

Underline the collective or mass noun in each sentence. Then circle the correct verb.

1. Our company (**is, are**) sponsoring a race today.

2. The race begins, and the crowd (**cheer, cheers**) loudly.

3. Water (**is, are**) available on the sidelines.

4. A family (**wait, waits**) eagerly to root for one of the runners.

5. The athletes' speed (**seem, seems**) incredible.

6. A group (**has, have**) gathered at the finish line.

7. The winner's time (**is, are**) going to be a new record.

Complete each sentence.

Sample: After I go swimming, my hair _____ is dry and frizzy. _____

8. My favorite team _____.

9. During a game, the crowd _____.

Check your answers on page 246.

Pronouns

A **pronoun** is a word that takes the place of a noun.

When the Johnsons moved, <u>they</u> hired a moving company to help <u>them</u>.

(The pronouns *they* and *them* take the place of the noun *Johnsons*.)

Just like nouns, pronouns can be singular or plural. **First-person pronouns** refer to the speaker or speakers; **second-person pronouns** refer to the person or people being spoken to; **third-person pronouns** refer to the person, people, or things being spoken about.

	Singular	Plural
First-Person:	I, me, my, mine	we, us, our, ours
Second-Person:	you, your, yours	you, your, yours
Third-Person:	he, him, his/she, her, hers/it, its	they, them, their, theirs

These personal pronouns may be divided into three basic types: subject, object, and possessive.

Subject Pronouns

A **subject pronoun** can act as the subject of a sentence. A subject tells <u>who</u> or <u>what</u> the sentence is about. The subject pronouns are *I, you, he, she, it, we,* and *they.*

<u>We</u> are going to get married. (*We* is the subject.)

<u>I</u> need to rent a truck. (*I* is the subject.)

PRACTICE

Write a subject pronoun to replace the underlined word or words.

_____ 1. <u>My fiancé and I</u> also have to find a band.

_____ 2. <u>Mike</u> wants a band to play the hits.

_____ 3. <u>He and I</u> can't agree on a band at all.

_____ 4. <u>My mother</u> does not know much about music.

_____ 5. <u>My parents</u> will pay for part of the wedding.

Write a sentence to go with the one that is given. Use a subject pronoun.

Sample: <u>My neighborhood</u> is very friendly. _It is a good place to live._

6. <u>My neighbors</u> sometimes help me out.

_____

7. <u>My neighbors and I</u> usually get along.

_____

Object Pronouns

Object pronouns are pronouns that are used as the object of a verb or preposition. The object pronouns are *me, you, him, her, it, us,* and *them.*

1.　An object pronoun can be a **direct object.** A direct object receives the action of the verb in the sentence.

I met my new boss today, and I like her. (Whom do you like? *Her.*)

Take the glass, and put it in the sink. (What should you put in the sink? *It.*)

2.　An object pronoun can be an **indirect object.** An indirect object tells *to whom* or *for whom* the action of a verb is done.

My sister sent me a gift for my birthday. (To whom did she send a gift? *Me.*)

3.　An object pronoun can be the **object of a preposition.** The object of a preposition is simply the noun or pronoun that follows a preposition. Some common prepositions are *about, above, in, by, to, at, in front of, inside, into,* and *with.*

I have not spoken to him yet.

Remember to use an object pronoun correctly even when it is part of a compound object.

Correct: The award for excellent attendance was given to Ricardo and me.

PRACTICE

Write the correct object pronoun to complete each sentence.

1.　My aunt told my cousin and _____ (**I, me**) that she once heard Martin Luther King, Jr., speak.

2.　She heard _____ (**he, him**) speak when she was a little girl.

3.　My brother and I were excited when she told _____ (**we, us**) about how he sounded.

4.　At one point, she thought he looked directly at _____ (**she, her**).

5.　He was such a good speaker that all the people in the crowd thought he was speaking directly to _____ (**they, them**).

Write a sentence using each object pronoun.

Sample: (him) _____ I gave the tickets to him. _____

6.　(me) _____

7.　(them) _____

8.　(us) _____

Possessive Pronouns

Possessive pronouns show ownership.

1.   Use the **possessive pronouns** *my, your, his, her, its, our,* and *their* before nouns to show ownership. (These words are sometimes called **possessive adjectives.**)

> Nick left <u>his</u> glove in <u>our</u> car.   <u>Their</u> dog buried <u>its</u> bone.

2.   Use the **possessive pronouns** *my, your, his, her, its, our,* and *their* before a gerund. A **gerund,** such as the word *driving,* looks like the *-ing* form of a verb, but it acts as a noun.

> <u>Their</u> driving to Nashville was my idea.
>
> He did not agree with <u>my</u> changing jobs.

3.   Use the **possessive pronouns** *mine, yours, his, hers, its, ours,* and *theirs* alone to show ownership.

> Is this coat <u>his</u>?   <u>Mine</u> is in the closet.
>
> Are those papers <u>ours</u>?   No, they are <u>theirs</u>.

4.   A possessive pronoun is <u>never</u> written with an apostrophe. Spellings such as *their's, your's,* and *our's* are incorrect.

PRACTICE

Circle the correct word to complete each sentence.

1.   Antonio seemed to have a problem with (**he's, his**) eyes.

2.   (**His, Him**) squinting was obvious to everyone.

3.   "We are worried about (**you're, your**) vision," I told him.

4.   "My eyes are (**my, mine**), not (**yours, your's**)," he growled.

5.   He finally listened to (**our, ours**) concerns and went to an eye doctor.

Read each sentence about a man named Kim. Write two sentences comparing yourself with Kim. Use *mine* in one sentence and *my* in the other.

Sample: Kim's children are young. _____ Mine are grown up. _____

_____ My children are grown up. _____

6.   Kim's home is very messy. _____

_____

7.   Kim's hometown is a big city. _____

_____

Pronoun Antecedents

A pronoun gets its meaning from the noun to which it refers. This noun is called the **antecedent.** Pronouns usually have specific antecedents.

1. An **antecedent** is the word to which a pronoun refers. The antecedent usually comes before the pronoun.

   Louisa forgot to buy her weekly bus pass. She had to pay cash every day.

   (*Louisa* is the antecedent for *her* and *She.*)

   Every cat in the shelter received its shots.

   (*Cat* is the antecedent for *its.*)

   Carolyn and I left our keys on the desk. We didn't realize that until much later.

   (*Carolyn and I* is the antecedent for *our* and *We.*)

2. Sometimes the antecedent comes after the pronoun.

   Since they moved, Donna and Jim have not called us.

   (*Donna and Jim* is the antecedent for *they.*)

   Because of its climate, San Diego is my favorite city.

   (*San Diego* is the antecedent for *its.*)

PRACTICE

Circle the antecedent for the underlined pronoun in each sentence.

1. Cities that get a lot of snow must keep their snow plows in good condition.

2. When two snowstorms hit town last January, they nearly shut down the city.

3. On its front page, the newspaper had a photo of a snowplow stuck in the snow.

4. The mayor knew she had to act fast to clear the snow.

5. Even though it was his day off, the police chief met with the mayor to make a plan.

6. My brother worked overtime. He was one of fifty city snowplowers.

Write a sentence using each pronoun. Circle its antecedent.

Sample: (it) _____ When the (phone) rang at 7:00 a.m., it surprised me. _____

7. (it) _____

8. (he) _____

Pronoun Agreement

Pronouns and antecedents must match, or agree with one another.

1. A pronoun must **agree** with its antecedent in number, person, and gender. *Number* means that the words are either singular or plural. *Person* refers to first-person, second-person, or third-person. *Gender* refers to whether the words stand for males, females, or things.

> Lucy gave her bill to the clerk.
>
> (Both the antecedent *Lucy* and the pronoun *her* are singular, in the third-person, and used for females.)

2. Use a **plural pronoun** with two or more antecedents joined by *and*.

> My roommate and I disagree about our responsibilities.

3. Use a **singular pronoun** with two or more singular antecedents joined by *or* or *nor*.

> Either Steve or Ricardo should give up his seat for the elderly woman.

4. Be sure that the pronoun agrees with the antecedent in **person**.
   Correct: When students want to get a GED, they must work hard.
   (*Students* and *they* are both third-person pronouns.)
   Incorrect: When students want to get a GED, you must work hard.
   (*Students* is a third-person pronoun, but *you* is second-person.)

PRACTICE

Circle the correct pronoun to complete each sentence.

1. Most of us have (**our, their**) own views on women in sports.

2. In my opinion, female athletes don't get the recognition (**you, they**) deserve.

3. If a female athlete is very talented, (**she, they**) can become famous.

4. However, male athletes are more likely to be known for (**his, their**) skills.

5. My uncle or my brother will be happy to give (**his, their**) opinion.

Write a sentence with a pronoun that agrees with each antecedent. Underline the pronoun and its antecedent.

Sample: (man) _____ The man brought his date to the movie. _____

6. (actress) _____

7. (beef or chicken) _____

Adjectives

An **adjective** is a word that modifies, or helps describe, a person, place, or thing. Adjectives describe by answering one of these questions.

What kind?	<u>red</u> light	<u>good</u> dog	<u>hot</u> shower
How many?	<u>few</u> fish	<u>many</u> bills	<u>ten</u> cards
Which one?	<u>first</u> hit	<u>this</u> box	<u>any</u> choice
How much?	<u>more</u> tea	<u>little</u> time	<u>some</u> luck

1. An adjective can come before or after the noun or pronoun it describes.

The <u>sick</u> dog lay by the door.

He is <u>sick</u>.

I saw a movie about a <u>far-off</u> land.

Many of the workers say they are <u>underpaid</u>.

2. **Proper adjectives** are formed from proper nouns. Like proper nouns, they are capitalized.

We like <u>Mexican</u> food.

PRACTICE

Underline all the adjectives in these sentences.

1. In long-ago times, dogs served people as skilled hunters.

2. Irish setters and Russian wolfhounds are some examples of early dogs that hunted.

3. Dogs that were strong and intelligent often worked on farms.

4. German shepherds and English collies are part of this group.

5. Dogs make good hunters because they have sharp senses.

Write a sentence about each animal. Use at least one adjective in each sentence.

Sample: (dogs) _Dogs are friendly and loyal animals._

6. (cats) _____

7. (birds) _____

8. (horses) _____

9. (rats) _____

10. (elephants) _____

Adverbs

An **adverb** is a word that describes a verb, an adjective, or another adverb. Adverbs describe by answering one of these four questions.

How?	walked slowly	ate well	worked carefully
When?	left today	start now	arrived early
Where?	flew above	moves aside	climbs up
To what extent?	almost done	fully healed	barely open

1. When adverbs describe verbs, they can come before or after the verbs.

   We often eat chicken.   We eat chicken often.

   Chicken must be cooked well.   You need to check it frequently.

2. When adverbs describe adjectives, they often come right before the adjectives.

   I was very happy to hear about your success.

   Helene is never ready on time.

3. When adverbs describe other adverbs, they often come right before the adverbs they describe.

   Helene moves very slowly in the morning.

   She just barely catches her bus on time.

PRACTICE

Underline all the adverbs in this paragraph.

Are people ever really happy with their appearance? They must not be, judging by how warmly they greet each new diet. They must want to lose weight very badly. Some people hardly finish one diet before they begin another. My friend had just finished his powdered-drink diet when he quickly started a new diet.

Answer each question with a complete sentence.

Sample: What do you do well? _____ I play tennis well. _____

1. What do you do well? _____

2. What do you do badly? _____

3. What do you do carefully? _____

Comparing with Adjectives and Adverbs

When you compare people, places, things, or actions, use either the comparative or superlative form of the adjective or adverb.

	Adjectives		Adverbs	
	big	short	highly	slowly
Comparative:	bigger	shorter	more highly	more slowly
Superlative:	biggest	shortest	most highly	most slowly

1. Use the **comparative form** of the adjective or adverb to compare two people, places, or things. Add -er to one-syllable adjectives and adverbs to form the comparative. Use *more* or *less* before most adjectives and adverbs with two or more syllables to compare them.

This box is smaller than that one.

The turtle moves more slowly than the rabbit.

But: This box is heavier than the other one.

2. Use the **superlative form** of the adjective or adverb to compare three or more people, places, or things. Add -est to one-syllable adjectives and adverbs to form the superlative. Use *most* or *least* before most adjectives and adverbs with two or more syllables to compare them.

Of the three brothers, Jason drives fastest.

He is the most careless dresser, too.

But: He is also the funniest brother.

3. Never add both -er and *more* (or *less*), or both -est and *most* (or *least*), to an adjective or adverb.

Not correct: This is the most hardest thing I've ever done.

Correct: This is the hardest thing I've ever done.

PRACTICE

Circle the correct word or words to complete each sentence.

1. Shopping on Saturdays is (**more hard, harder**) than shopping during the week.

2. Of all the days, Saturday is when the stores are (**most crowded, more crowded**).

3. Traffic moves (**more slowly, more slowlier**) on Saturday than it does on other days.

4. Even so, I think Saturday is the (**most best, best**) day for shopping.

Check your answers on page 247. 159

Common Problems with Adjectives and Adverbs

1. Adjectives and adverbs usually have different forms. Many adverbs are formed by adding -ly to the end of an adjective.

    bright light (adjective)   brightly lit (adverb)

    To be certain whether to use an adjective or an adverb, see what kind of word it is describing. Use an adjective to describe a noun or a pronoun. Use an adverb to describe a verb, an adjective, or another adverb.

    Incorrect: They took their job serious.

    Correct: They took their job seriously.
                   (*Seriously* is an adverb describing the verb *took*.)

2. Not all adjectives and adverbs have regular comparative and superlative forms. Here are some common irregular adjectives and adverbs.

Adjective/Adverb	Comparative	Superlative
good	better	best
well	better	best
bad	worse	worst
badly	worse	worst
little	less	least
many/a lot of	more	most
much/a lot of	more	most
far	farther	farthest

Tuna is good, shrimp is even better, but lobster is the best seafood of all.

I get very little time off, my brother gets less, and my sister gets the least.

PRACTICE

Circle the correct word to complete each sentence.

1. Eric is not a good map reader, but Larry is even (**worst, worse**).

2. However, Chris reads maps very (**careful, carefully**).

3. Li is the (**best, better**) driver in the group.

4. Ellen has had (**more, most**) accidents than anyone else.

Write a sentence using each word correctly.

Sample: (worst) _____ Of everyone in my family, I am the worst dancer. _____

5. (farther) _____

6. (real) _____

Verbs

Verb Tense

Verbs are words that show action or a state of being. Every verb has four different forms. The forms of a verb are used to make the different verb tenses. **Tense** is the form of a verb that shows when the action takes place.

Verb Forms

Present	Present Participle	Past	Past Participle
talk/talks	talking	talked	talked
eat/eats	eating	ate	eaten

Simple Tenses

There are three simple tenses: present, past, and future. Form the present tense by using the present form of the verb. Form the past tense by using the past form of the verb. Form the future tense by using the helping verb *will* and the present form of the verb.

Tense	Form	Use
Present	talk/talks	repeated action or habit; general truth
Past	talked	action completed in the past
Future	will talk	action not yet completed

Present: I talk to my children on the phone every week.

Past: I talked to my daughter yesterday.

Future: I will talk to my son next week.

PRACTICE

In each sentence write *collect, collected,* or *will collect.*

1. I _____ coins when I was a child.

2. I still _____ coins.

3. Next year, I _____ stamps for a change.

Complete each sentence. Use the correct form of the verb *like.*

Sample: When she gets older, I think my daughter will like basketball.

4. As a child, I _____.

5. Now I _____.

6. Next year I _____.

Perfect Tenses

There are three perfect tenses: present perfect, past perfect, and future perfect. Use the correct form of the helping verb *to have* and the past participle to form all of the perfect tenses.

Tense	Form	Use
Present perfect	have/has worked have/has taken	A completed action or an action that continues into the present
Past perfect	had worked had taken	An action completed before another past action or event
Future perfect	will have worked will have taken	An action completed before another future action or event

Present perfect: Vernon has worked here for a long time.

Past perfect: He had worked at another job before he came here.

Future perfect: By May 1, he will have worked here for ten years.

PRACTICE

Circle the correct form of the verb to complete each sentence.

1. Shawn has asthma. He (**has suffered**, **had suffered**) from it since he was a child.

2. By the time he was ten years old, he (**had been**, **will have been**) to the emergency room several times.

3. Now that he is an adult, he (**had gotten**, **has gotten**) his asthma under control.

4. By this time next month, it (**had been**, **will have been**) exactly one year since his last asthma attack.

5. Shawn is glad his baby (**had not shown**, **has not shown**) any signs of asthma so far.

Write a sentence using each verb phrase.

Sample: (have lived) _____ I have lived here for two months. _____

6. (will have lived) _____

7. (has been) _____

8. (had wanted) _____

9. (have seen) _____

10. (will have written) _____

Clues to Verb Tense in Sentences

Often there are clue words in a sentence that tell you which tense to use.

Our group <u>will go</u> on an all-day retreat <u>tomorrow</u>.

The clue word *tomorrow* in the sentence tells you the action will be in the future. Therefore, the future tense *will go* is correct.

Clue words can often help you decide which verb tense is correct. Many words and phrases can be clues to a verb tense in a sentence. The chart below includes some common examples.

Past	Present	Future
yesterday	now	next week
last week	today	tomorrow
last year	currently	in the year 2010
in 1990	in the present	soon

Examples

Past: <u>Yesterday</u> Dan and his friends <u>went</u> to the stock car races.

Present: <u>Currently</u>, stock car racing <u>is</u> a very popular sport.

Future: The Daytona 500 <u>will be held</u> in Florida <u>next week</u>.

Note: Use the present simple tense with words like *always, usually, sometimes,* and *never.*

PRACTICE

Underline the tense clue in each sentence. Then circle the correct verb.

1. Your application (**was being reviewed, is being reviewed**) currently.

2. The documents (**are mailed, were mailed, will be mailed**) at the end of last month.

3. Most people (**mailed, mail, will mail**) their requests last week.

4. Next Monday, the committee (**made, will make**) its final decisions.

5. Your task right now (**is, was**) to wait patiently for the information.

Write a sentence using each tense clue. Be sure to use the correct verb tense.

6. (in 2008) _____

7. (in 1990) _____

8. (now) _____

Irregular Verbs

Most verbs in English are regular, but some verbs have irregular past and past participle forms. Here are some common irregular verbs.

Present	Past	Past Participle
am, is, are	was, were	been
begin	began	begun
break	broke	broken
bring	brought	brought
buy	bought	bought
choose	chose	chosen
do	did	done
drink	drank	drunk
eat	ate	eaten
get	got	gotten
give	gave	given
go	went	gone
has, have	had	had
know	knew	known
leave	left	left
lose	lost	lost
see	saw	seen
send	sent	sent
show	showed	showed/shown
speak	spoke	spoken
take	took	taken

PRACTICE

Circle the correct form of the verb to complete each sentence.

1. I (**leave, leaved, left**) high school when I was 16.

2. I (**lose, lost, losed**) years of education when I was a teenager.

3. I (**am, been, was**) unhappy during that time and wanted to go back to school.

4. Now that I have (**gone, went, go**) back, I have (**begin, began, begun**) to feel better.

Write a sentence using each irregular verb form.

Sample: (took) _____ When I was younger, I took too many risks. _____

5. (known) _____

6. (done) _____

7. (ate) _____

Subject-Verb Agreement

In some tenses, subjects and verbs must agree in number. A singular subject must have a singular verb. A plural subject must have a plural verb.

Singular subject and verb: A big ship sails into the harbor.

Plural subject and verb: We are waiting for the ship to arrive.

1. Words between the subject and verb do not affect the agreement.

   The insects on the oak tree are harmful.

   (The subject is *insects,* not *tree.* The verb is *are.* The phrase *on the oak tree* between the subject and verb does not affect the agreement.)

2. Use a plural verb for subjects joined by *and.*

   The door and window are both stuck.

3. Use a singular verb for singular subjects joined by *or* or *nor.*

   Each morning Julia or Lucy buys fresh rolls.

4. If a singular subject and a plural subject are joined by *or* or *nor,* the verb must agree with the subject that is closer to it.

   Neither the loaf of bread nor the eggs were fresh.

   Neither the eggs nor the loaf of bread was fresh.

PRACTICE

Circle the correct verb to complete each sentence.

1. The sky (**appears, appear**) blue as we look up from Earth.

2. In space, both the sun and moon (**is, are**) easy to see during the day.

3. The moon and the planet Venus (**glow, glows**) at night.

4. The Big Dipper, along with many other stars, (**shines, shine**) as well.

5. Neither Pluto nor Saturn (**is, are**) easy to find, though.

6. Meteors that shoot across the sky (**is, are**) a special treat.

Write a sentence using each word or phrase as the subject of the sentence.

Sample: (Tony or Leo) _____Either Tony or Leo is going to help us paint._____

7. (cars) _____

8. (buses or the train) _____

   _____

9. (the locks on the door) _____

   _____

More on Subject-Verb Agreement

1.   Sometimes the subject of a sentence follows the verb. Changing the order of the words in the sentence can help you decide the correct subject-verb agreement.

On the wall (<u>hangs</u> or <u>hang</u>?) Ray's GED certificate.

Ray's GED certificate <u>hangs</u> on the wall.

2.   In many sentences that begin with *here*, *there*, or *where*, the subject follows the verb. Be careful not to start a sentence with *here's (here is)*, *there's (there is)*, or *where's (where is)* when the subject is plural.

Incorrect:	Here's the paper rolls for the cash register.
Correct:	Here are the paper rolls for the cash register.
Correct:	The paper rolls for the cash register are here.
Incorrect:	There's several items of interest on the agenda for the meeting.
Correct:	There are several items of interest on the agenda for the meeting.
Correct:	Several items of interest are on the agenda for the meeting.
Incorrect:	Where's the screwdriver and the wrench?
Correct:	Where are the screwdriver and the wrench?
Correct:	The screwdriver and the wrench are where?

3.   Remember that a collective noun names a group of people, places, or things and is often singular. When the members of the group act as one, use a singular verb.

The <u>team</u> <u>is running</u> onto the field.

PRACTICE

Circle the correct verb to complete each sentence.

1.   Our family (**is, are**) giving a large party.

2.   The whole group (**wants, want**) to honor our grandfather, who's 75.

3.   Here (**is, are**) the decorations to hang.

4.   On top of that shelf (**is, are**) the cups I need.

5.   There (**seem, seems**) to be some crumbs on the table.

Complete each sentence. Use correct subject-verb agreement.

6.   Here _____

_____.

7.   The jury _____

_____.

Pronoun and Verb Agreement

A pronoun used as a subject must agree with the verb in number.

1. These pronouns always use singular verbs: *much, neither, no one, nothing, one, other, somebody, someone, something, another, anybody, anyone, anything, each, either, everybody, everyone, everything.*

> <u>Someone</u> <u>has been</u> in the house.
>
> <u>Everything</u> <u>is</u> fine, thanks.

2. These pronouns always use plural verbs: *both, few, many, others, several.*

> <u>Both</u> of the glasses <u>have been used</u>.
>
> <u>Several</u> of the glasses <u>are</u> broken.

3. These pronouns use singular or plural verbs, depending on what they refer to: *all, some, any, part, none, half.*

> <u>All</u> of the books <u>have been checked</u> out. *(All refers to books.)*
>
> <u>All</u> of the milk <u>was spilled</u> on the floor. *(All refers to milk.)*

PRACTICE

Circle the correct verb to complete each sentence.

1. Both of my children (**are, is**) planning to look for famous people in New York.

2. Everyone (**has, have**) told them not to be disappointed if they don't see any.

3. At 11:00 P.M. all of the actors (**take, takes**) their last bow and leave the theater.

4. Each of the actors (**gives, give**) my children a smile and an autograph.

5. Few (**is, are**) this nice.

6. Several (**has, have**) since answered letters from my children.

Complete each sentence. Use *is/are* or *has/have*.

Sample: Several of my friends _____have twins._____

7. Everyone in my family _____.

8. No one in my family _____.

9. All of my friends _____.

10. Several of my coworkers _____.

LESSON 11

Sentence Structure

Sentence Fragments

A **sentence fragment** is a group of words that does not express a complete thought. Even if a fragment begins with a capital letter and ends with a period, it is not a sentence. Some information is missing from it.

Fragment: Ran away with the bone. (missing a subject)
Correct: A dog ran away with the bone.

Fragment: Helped her get a job as a cashier. (missing a subject)
Correct: Her friend in the diner helped her get a job as a cashier.

Fragment: The rags under the sink. (missing a verb)
Correct: The rags under the sink are dirty.

PRACTICE

Write *C* if the group of words is a complete sentence. Write *F* if it is a fragment.

_____ 1. "Road rage" is an act of aggression similar to an assault.

_____ 2. Taking place after two drivers have a disagreement.

_____ 3. Tailgating, yelling curses, and flashing the headlights.

_____ 4. Also fall into this category.

_____ 5. Because driving can be very stressful.

_____ 6. Some drivers are unable to control themselves.

_____ 7. Often these drivers are already angry about a problem at home or work.

Change each fragment into a complete sentence.

Sample: One safety rule. _One safety rule is to use your seat belt._

8. The minimum driving age.

_____

9. Drive too fast.

_____

Sentence Structure

There are three ways to test whether a group of words is a fragment. If you answer *no* to one of the following questions, you have a fragment.

1. **Is there a verb?** If there is no verb, the group of words is a fragment. All parts of the verb must be present for a sentence to be complete. To correct this type of fragment, add or complete the verb.

   Fragment: Mark taking a GED class.
   Correct: Mark is taking a GED class.

2. **Is there a subject?** To find out if a sentence has a subject, ask <u>who</u> or <u>what</u> is doing the action. If there is no subject, the group of words is a fragment. To correct this type of fragment, add a subject.

   Fragment: Studied hard for the test. (Who studied?)
   Correct: Mark studied hard for the test.

3. **Does the group of words express a complete thought?** Even if the group of words has a subject and a verb, it is not a complete sentence if it does not express a complete thought. To correct this type of fragment, complete the thought.

   Fragment: After we studied a lot. (What is the complete thought?)
   Correct: After we studied a lot, we did well on the test.

PRACTICE

Explain why each of the following groups of words is a fragment.

1. In the last twenty years, the number of families with adult children living at home.

   This is a fragment because _____.

2. Increased by four percent.

   This is a fragment because _____.

3. Compared to a generation ago, fewer young adults.

   This is a fragment because _____.

4. Can afford to set up their own households.

   This is a fragment because _____.

Change each fragment into a complete sentence.

5. My older sister still living with our parents.

   _____

6. Enjoys spending time with them in the evenings.

   _____

Run-on Sentences

A **run-on** sentence is two or more complete thoughts that are not correctly separated. There are two kinds of run-on sentences.

1. One type is made up of two sentences that are not separated by punctuation.

Run-on: The storm got worse it turned toward the land.
Correct: The storm got worse. It turned toward the land.

Run-on: The Japanese subway is the fastest train it travels over 100 miles an hour.
Correct: The Japanese subway is the fastest train. It travels over 100 miles an hour.

2. The other type is made up of two sentences joined with a comma when they should be joined with a semicolon or a comma and a coordinating conjunction. This type of run-on is sometimes called a comma splice.

Run-on: We were not hungry, we had already had lunch.
Correct: We were not hungry; we had already had lunch.

Run-on: You can visit the White House, you can tour many rooms.
Correct: You can visit the White House, and you can tour many rooms.

PRACTICE

Write *RO* if the sentence is a run-on. Write *C* if the sentence is correct.

_____ 1. Bacteria in food can cause illness you should take care to store food properly.

_____ 2. Don't keep cooked food that's been standing out for two or more hours, don't even taste it.

_____ 3. Hamburgers should be eaten well-done, cooking kills bacteria.

_____ 4. Raw eggs are not safe to eat they may contain salmonella.

_____ 5. It's a good practice to date your leftovers and throw them out after three to five days.

_____ 6. Dishes should be washed right away it's better to air-dry them than to use a towel.

_____ 7. You can use soap to clean the kitchen counter, but bleach is better.

_____ 8. It's important to store food properly and to keep food preparation areas clean.

How to Correct Run-on Sentences

1. Use an end punctuation mark to separate the two complete thoughts.

    Run-on: Do most people like crowds I don't think so.
    Correct: Do most people like crowds? I don't think so.

2. Use a semicolon to connect two complete thoughts.

    Run-on: I couldn't wait to jump in the water looked so cool.
    Correct: I couldn't wait to jump in; the water looked so cool.

3. Use a comma and a coordinating conjunction—*and, but, or, so, for, nor, or yet*—to connect the two complete thoughts.

    Run-on: The sky got dark it started to rain.
    Correct: The sky got dark, and it started to rain.

PRACTICE

Correct each run-on sentence by using one of the three methods described above.

1. The Special Olympics was started more than 30 years ago it is a sports competition for people with disabilities.

    _____

2. More than 7,000 athletes attend they come from 150 nations.

    _____

3. Each nation competes in nineteen sporting events athletes do not have to enter every event.

    _____

4. Everyone is a winner each athlete gets a ribbon or medal.

    _____

5. Many people come to watch they are impressed by the athletes.

    _____

Add another complete thought to each complete thought below. Separate the thoughts with correct punctuation and/or a connecting word.

6. I enjoy watching the Olympic Games _____

    _____

7. Winning a gold medal must be a thrill _____

    _____

Compound Sentences

A **compound sentence** is made up of two or more complete thoughts. Each of these thoughts could stand alone as a sentence. There are two ways to create a compound sentence.

1.   Join the complete sentences with a comma and a **coordinating conjunction** such as *and, but, or, so, for, nor,* or *yet.*

> Jill wanted the job, and she knew she had the skills for it.
> She could accept the job, or she could reject it.
> The job had many good points, so she decided to accept it.

2.   Join the complete sentences with a semicolon. Use this method when you do not need a connecting word to show how the thoughts are related.

> Martin read the book in two hours; he wrote his essay in three.
> Jess liked the movie; she saw it last Friday.

Write *CS* if the sentence is a compound sentence. Write *S* if it is not.

_____   1.   Soap operas have earned a bad name, but they don't always deserve it.

_____   2.   Some people watch too many TV programs; other people take the plots too seriously.

_____   3.   This does not make the programs themselves bad.

_____   4.   Some people think soap opera viewers are not smart, but people from all walks of life watch soaps.

_____   5.   Even doctors, lawyers, and other highly educated people watch soap operas.

_____   6.   Some hospitals tell patients to watch the soaps, and some doctors tell depressed people to tune in as well.

Add another complete thought to each complete thought below to create a compound sentence. Use a coordinating conjunction and a comma.

7.   James watches soap operas every day _____

_____

8.   Some soap stars have been on the air for many years _____

_____

_____

3. Use a compound sentence to join related ideas. The sentence will not make sense unless the two ideas are related.

> **Not related:** Computers became popular in the 1970s, for they were very expensive. (The high prices did not make computers popular.)

> **Related:** Computers became popular in the 1970s, for they had many different uses.

4. Use a coordinating conjunction that helps show the relationship between the parts of a compound sentence. Each of these connecting words has a certain meaning. Use the word that shows a logical relationship.

Connecting Word	Meaning	Function
and	also	joins ideas
but	on the other hand	contrasts
or	a choice	shows a choice
so	thus	shows a result
for	because	shows a reason
nor	not	joins negative ideas
yet	but	contrasts

PRACTICE

Combine the two sentences to create a logical compound sentence.

1. My first week on the job was a disaster. My boss told me so.

   _____

   _____

2. I was really upset. I knew things had to get better.

   _____

   _____

3. I tried as hard as I could. I really wanted to keep the job.

   _____

   _____

4. My coworker gave me good advice. I felt more confident.

   _____

   _____

5. Next week has to be better. I'll think about quitting!

   _____

   _____

Parallel Structure

Your writing will be clearer if the ideas within each sentence are written in a similar way. Put them all in **parallel,** or similar, form. For example, all verbs should be in the same tense and form. To have **parallel structure,** use matching nouns, verbs, adjectives, and adverbs when you write a list.

Not parallel:	The store is good for fruit, meat, and to buy cheese.
Parallel:	The store is good for fruit, meat, and cheese. (nouns)
Not parallel:	Doctors say I should run, swim, and go walking.
Parallel:	Doctors say I should run, swim, and walk. (verbs)
Not parallel:	The meal was tasty, quick, and the food was good for you.
Parallel:	The meal was tasty, quick, and healthful. (adjectives)
Not parallel:	In the rain I drive slowly, carefully, and watch out for other drivers.
Parallel:	In the rain I drive slowly, carefully, and defensively. (adverbs)

PRACTICE

Write *P* if the sentence has parallel structure. Write *NP* if the sentence does not have parallel structure.

_____ 1. Eating the right foods will help you feel healthier, more attractive, and strongly.

_____ 2. Fruits, vegetables, and grains are important in a balanced diet.

_____ 3. They provide vitamins, minerals, and are low in fat.

_____ 4. Meat, fish, and poultry provide zinc, iron, and B vitamins.

_____ 5. Fiber, which is good for digestion, is found in plant foods like beans, peas, and whole grain cereals.

_____ 6. To lose weight, eat smaller portions and limiting second helpings.

_____ 7. Eat slowly and be careful; be sure to chew your food well.

Complete each sentence. Use parallel structure.

Sample: Three important paths to good health are diet, sleep, and exercise.

8. Three places you can buy food are a grocery store, a snack shop, and

   _____ .

9. When you are sick, you should stay home, drink fluids, and

   _____ .

In addition to using parallel words in lists, use parallel phrases in your writing. Write each parallel idea in the same grammatical structure.

Not parallel: The members of the council read the letter, discussed its points, and the decision was to ignore it.

Parallel: The members of the council <u>read</u> the letter, <u>discussed</u> its points, and <u>decided</u> to ignore it.

Not parallel: The members of the council, the person who wrote the letter, and people at the meeting then got into a shouting match.

Parallel: The <u>council members</u>, the <u>letter writer</u>, and the <u>audience</u> then got into a shouting match.

PRACTICE

Rewrite each sentence so that it has parallel structure.

1. Writing helps people think, speak, and be learning.

   _____

   _____

2. Those who can write well will be leaders in the community, state, and nationally in years to come.

   _____

   _____

3. By writing frequently, reading often, and to seek feedback, writers can improve.

   _____

   _____

4. Learning to write clearly, correctly, and be effective is a goal.

   _____

   _____

Answer each question with a complete sentence. Use parallel structure.

5. What different things can you write?

   _____

   _____

6. What are three qualities of good writing?

   _____

   _____

Complex Sentences

1. A **clause** is a group of words with its own subject and verb. A clause that can stand alone as a sentence is called an **independent clause.**

   He woke up at seven o'clock so that he could go fishing.

2. A clause that cannot stand alone as a complete sentence is a **dependent clause.**

   He woke up at seven o'clock so that he could go fishing.

3. Many dependent clauses begin with a connecting word called a **subordinating conjunction.** Here are some of the most common subordinating conjunctions:

after	although	as	as if	because
before	even though	if	since	so that
though	unless	until	when	while

4. A sentence with both an independent clause and a dependent clause is a **complex sentence.** The dependent clause can come at the beginning or the end of the sentence. Put it where it helps you state your point most clearly. If the dependent clause is at the beginning of the sentence, put a comma after it.

   Even though his alarm didn't go off, he woke up at seven o'clock.
   He woke up at seven o'clock even though his alarm didn't go off.

PRACTICE

Draw a line under the dependent clause in each complex sentence. This is the clause that cannot stand alone. Then add a comma if needed.

1. Although I have a car I usually take the bus.
2. I prefer the bus because I care about the environment.
3. If we don't help to reduce pollution the problem will only get worse.
4. Let's act before it's too late.

Write directions for walking from one place to another in your neighborhood. Include your favorite shortcuts. Use at least two dependent clauses.

Sample: Walk down Elm Road until you see a recreation center on the right. If the building is open, you can walk straight through it. After you come out on the other side, you'll see a dirt path.

_____

_____

_____

5. Use complex sentences to link related ideas. Make sure the ideas you link make sense together.

Ideas that are not related: Because Helen Keller was unable to speak and hear, her books have been in print for many years.

Ideas that are related: Because of a serious illness in childhood, Helen Keller was later unable to speak and hear.

6. Use a subordinating conjunction to show the relationship between the ideas in a complex sentence. Since each subordinating conjunction has a certain meaning, choose the conjunction that best links your ideas.

Time	Reason	Contrast
after	since, as	although
before, until	because	even though
once	so that	though

No dependent clause: You are late. You will not get a break.

Complex sentence: Because you are late, you will not get a break.

PRACTICE

Combine each pair of sentences by changing one sentence to a subordinate clause. Use an appropriate subordinating conjunction to link the ideas and use a comma if necessary.

Sample: I got tired. It was so late. ___I got tired because it was so late.___

1. I went to bed. I heard a loud crash in the kitchen.

    _____

2. I pulled the blankets over my head. I was afraid.

    _____

3. I finally got up. I heard the cat's meow.

    _____

4. I knew what had happened. I saw the cat sitting by the broken plate.

    _____

Continue the story by completing the sentences.

5. I went to get a broom so that _____

    _____.

6. I didn't get very much sleep that night because _____

    _____.

Misplaced and Dangling Modifiers

1.   Place a **modifier** (a descriptive word or phrase) as close as possible to the word or phrase it describes.

The woman who delivered the package spoke to the man at the desk.

The batter with the red shirt hit a home run.

2.   If the modifier is far from the word it describes, the sentence might not make sense. A **misplaced modifier** is a modifier in the wrong place in a sentence.

Misplaced modifier: The woman spoke to the man at the desk who delivered the package. (The sentence now means that the man, not the woman, delivered the package.)

Misplaced modifier: The batter hit a home run with the red shirt. (The sentence now means that the batter used the red shirt to hit the ball.)

PRACTICE

Write C if the underlined modifier is in the correct place in the sentence. Write M if the modifier is misplaced.

_____ 1. We saw many smashed houses driving through the storm.

_____ 2. The storm even wrecked the sidewalks.

_____ 3. Scarcely people could believe the damage.

_____ 4. The storm was barely over when people came to help.

_____ 5. Nearly everyone pitched in.

_____ 6. First, a list was given to each owner with many items.

_____ 7. Then Marta picked up the clothes for the children that had been left in the box.

_____ 8. A neighbor bought a pie with a crumb crust from the store.

_____ 9. The house was rebuilt by the owners destroyed by the storm.

Describe a bad storm that you experienced. You can make up details if you need to. Use at least three sentences that have correctly placed modifiers.

_____

_____

_____

_____

3. Every modifier must describe a specific word in a sentence.

<u>Coming up the stairs</u>, he heard the clock strike six.
(*Coming up the stairs* describes *he*.)

4. A sentence cannot make sense if the modified word is missing. A **dangling modifier** is a modifier that does not describe anything in the sentence. Watch for dangling modifiers and rewrite them.

Dangling modifier:	Driving down the road, a bad accident happened. (Who was driving down the road?)
Correct:	Driving down the road, they saw a bad accident happen.
Correct:	While they were driving down the road, a bad accident happened.

PRACTICE

Rewrite each sentence to correct the dangling modifier.

1. While passing a large rock, a clap of thunder made me scream.

   _____

2. Sailing up the harbor, the boat was seen.

   _____

3. Flying over the town, the cars and houses looked like toys.

   _____

4. While putting the chair together, the screw was lost.

   _____

5. Opening the jar, the sauce spilled all over the floor.

   _____

6. Walking up the steps, the packages fell.

   _____

Complete each sentence. Include a word that can be modified by the phrase that is already written.

Sample: Eagerly waiting for news, <u>I jumped at the ring of the phone</u>.

7. Going to my class, _____.

8. Angry at her husband, _____.

9. Already hungry, _____.

10. Without thinking, _____.

Revising Sentences

Eliminate Wordiness

After you write, revise your sentences to make your meaning as clear as possible. Remove any extra words that make it harder for your reader to grasp your point. If you are saying the same thing twice, you need to cut some words.

Too wordy: Please repeat your comment again.
Revised: Please repeat your comment.

Too wordy: Is that the real truth?
Revised: Is that the truth?

PRACTICE

Revise each sentence to get rid of the extra words.

1. The baseball game took place at 3 P.M. in the afternoon on Saturday.

   _____

2. When the game started to begin, the players relaxed, and the tension was over with.

   _____

3. The pitcher he did not know to whom to throw the ball to.

   _____

4. After each inning, they repeated their signals again.

   _____

5. In the last inning, the game ended with a home run with the bases loaded.

   _____

6. Up to this point, no one knows where the next game will be held at.

   _____

Describe a sport or game that you know very well. Include details. When you are finished, check your writing for extra words.

   _____
   _____
   _____
   _____
   _____

Sentence Structure

Correct Informal Speech

Another reason to revise your sentences is to get rid of expressions that are not correct to use in writing or in formal situations, even though they may be used in informal speech. Here is a list of some words and expressions to avoid in writing.

Avoid: What kind of a movie are you going to see?
Use: What kind of movie are you going to see?

Avoid: Being that I have been here longer, I can help you.
Use: Because I have been here longer, I can help you.

Avoid: We had ought to leave now.
Use: We ought to leave now.

Avoid: My boss, she says I am a good worker.
Use: My boss says I am a good worker.

Avoid: Try and work more.
Use: Try to work more.

Avoid: This here book will help you.
Use: This book will help you.

Avoid: The reason is because the bus was late.
Use: The reason is that the bus was late.

Avoid: Like I told you, he moved to the city.
Use: As I told you, he moved to the city.

Avoid: I saw on TV where a man was hurt.
Use: I saw on TV that a man was hurt.

PRACTICE

Write *C* if the sentence is correct. Write *W* if the sentence is wrong because of informal expressions.

_____ 1. Being that the food is good, the place is always crowded.

_____ 2. The critics say it is the best restaurant in town.

_____ 3. You had ought to get there early to get a seat.

_____ 4. The reason is that all the food is fresh.

_____ 5. Like I told you, the fish is excellent.

_____ 6. All the take-out food is listed on this here menu.

_____ 7. I heard on the radio that they are opening a new place.

_____ 8. We have to try and get there soon.

Construction Shift

You have learned about some common problems with sentence structure—sentence fragments, run-on sentences, and dangling or misplaced modifiers. On the multiple-choice part of the test, you will need to recognize the best way to rewrite sentences that contain these problems. One type of question is called a **construction shift** question. It presents a sentence that must be rewritten by revising the sentence structure. To answer these questions, think through the process of changing a sentence.

1. Identify the main person or thing the sentence is about. Make this the subject of the sentence. Put it first.

2. Identify the main action. Make this the verb. Put it next.

3. Place modifying words and phrases close to the words they modify.

4. Combine related ideas in parallel form.

5. Eliminate unnecessary words.

Unclear sentence: A garage sale can be held by you in order to get rid of things you don't want, and you can also make some money from things you don't want.

Revised sentence: · You can hold a garage sale to get rid of things you don't want and to make some money.

The revised sentence has a clear subject: *you.* The verb is in the active voice: *can hold.* Parallel form is used: *to get* and *to make.* The repeated words *things you don't want* are eliminated.

Circle the letter of the best revision of each sentence.

1. Garage sales have inexpensive things, and some people need to buy these things.
   a. Garage sales have inexpensive things needed by some people, so they buy them.
   b. Some people rely on garage sales to buy the things they need inexpensively.

2. Browsing and haggling are enjoyed by people who go to garage sales.
   a. People enjoy going to garage sales to browse and haggle.
   b. People who enjoy browsing and haggling are others who go to garage sales.

Revise this sentence to make it clear and direct. Keep the same meaning.

3. Things not needed or some things you just don't want anymore can probably be found in your own home.

Combining Sentences

Sometimes closely related sentences repeat words. The repetition does not help make the meaning clear. Instead, it just makes the writing sound wordy. These sentences can be combined by eliminating the repeated words.

Repetition: The newscaster gave her report on the 10 o'clock news. Her report gave unemployment figures for the past year.

Improved: On the 10 o'clock news, the newscaster reported unemployment figures for the past year.

When you combine sentences to eliminate repetition and wordiness, make sure you keep all the important information from the original sentences.

Repetition: Our manager created a plan, and she discussed it with the team. The team is the group that is responsible for writing company policies.

Incomplete: Our manager discussed a plan with the team that is responsible for writing company policies.

Complete: Our manager created a plan and discussed it with the team that is responsible for writing company policies.

PRACTICE

Circle the letter of the best reconstruction of each pair of sentences.

1. I make an award-winning bread using a special recipe. It is a recipe for bread that was handed down by my great-grandmother.
   a. I make an award-winning bread using a special recipe handed down by my great-grandmother.
   b. I make an award-winning bread using a special recipe, and it was handed down by my great-grandmother.

2. This request is made by me. I'd like this request to be considered with care, and I'd like what I request to be respected.
   a. This request is made by me and it should be considered carefully with respect.
   b. I'd like my request to be considered with care and respect.

Combine the sentences to eliminate repetition.

3. The witness said the accident took place last week, and it was on a Sunday. The witness stated that the accident involved a red sports car. It also involved a bike.

_____

_____

Mechanics

LESSON 12

End Punctuation

Punctuation is the set of symbols used in writing to guide the reader. A sentence always ends with a period, a question mark, or an exclamation point. Each type of punctuation signals something different to the reader.

1.   Use a **period** to end a statement—a sentence that gives information or states facts. Also use a period to show the end of a command.

I am studying right now**.**   Open your books to page 156**.**

2.   Use a **question mark** to end a question.

When are you planning to move**?**   Is heat included in the rent**?**

3.   Use an **exclamation point** to end a sentence that shows strong emotion.

That's great**!**   Watch out for that truck**!**

PRACTICE

Add the correct end punctuation to complete each sentence.

1.   When do you think the first soap opera was broadcast on TV

2.   The first TV soap opera was aired on October 2, 1946

3.   Called *Faraway Hill,* it was the only network show on Wednesday nights

4.   Amazingly, the show was done live—on a budget of less than $300 a week

5.   Soap operas were originally broadcast on the radio

6.   Do you know anyone who likes soap operas

7.   Some people say that soap operas help them relax

8.   What a ridiculous waste of time they are

Write three sentences about TV shows. Use correct end punctuation.

9.   (statement)

_____

10.   (question)

_____

11.   (strong emotion)

_____

Commas

Commas help to break up sentences to make them easier to read.

1. Use commas to separate three or more items in a list.

   Joe, Paul, Hector, and Luis are going camping.
   They plan to go fishing, take walks, and sleep late.

2. Use a comma between the two independent clauses of a compound sentence. Join the clauses with a coordinating conjunction: *and, but, or, so, yet, for,* and *nor.* Put the comma before the conjunction.

   They saw a lot of rabbits, but they didn't see any deer.
   The weather was bad the first day, so everyone stayed inside.

Do <u>not</u> use a comma between the two subjects in a compound subject or the two verbs in a compound predicate.

   Compound subject: <u>Joe and Paul</u> played cards that day.

   Compound predicate: Hector <u>read magazines and sorted his gear.</u>

3. Use commas with dates and place names. Place a comma between the day and the month and between the number of the day and the year. Also use a comma between the city and state or city and country.

Monday, May 8	January 1, 2000	Sunday, July 4, 1999
Chicago, Illinois	Paris, France	San Juan, Puerto Rico

PRACTICE

Add commas where they are needed in each sentence.

1. My aunt was born on January 13 1960.

2. She grew up in Toledo but she and her family moved to Los Angeles in 1975.

3. She is a store manager a swimmer and a mother of two.

Answer each question with a complete sentence. Use commas correctly.

4. Think of a relative. When was this person born? (Include month, day, and year.)

   _____

5. Tell something about the person. Use a compound sentence.

   _____

   _____

   Check your answers on page 251.

4. Use a comma after a dependent clause that comes at the beginning of a complex sentence. Do <u>not</u> use a comma before a dependent clause that comes at the end of a complex sentence.

> **Correct:** After Fred retired, I joined the company.
>
> **Correct:** I joined the company after Fred retired.
>
> **Incorrect:** I joined the company, after Fred retired.

5. An **appositive** is a noun or noun phrase that defines or explains another noun. Use commas to set off an appositive that is <u>not</u> essential to a sentence's meaning.

> **Not Essential:** Mrs. Johnson, <u>our neighbor,</u> was taken to the hospital.
>
> **Essential:** The ship *Titanic* sank when it hit an iceberg.

If you read only, "Mrs. Johnson was taken to the hospital," you would still know which person went to the hospital. The appositive *our neighbor* is not essential. However, if you read just, "The ship sank when it hit an iceberg," you would not know <u>which</u> ship sank. The appositive *Titanic* is essential.

6. Use commas to set off a parenthetical expression such as *for example, however,* or *of course.*

> **Correct:** The contract, <u>of course,</u> must be signed in ink.

PRACTICE

Add commas where they are needed in each sentence.

1. Because new businesses are coming to this area we need new zoning laws.

2. We will handle this legally of course by going to the zoning board.

3. The Huitts will talk to the newspaper while Mr. Ortiz handles the petitions.

4. We expect to get some good coverage from WCRB the local news station.

5. The developers however will put up a good fight.

Write a sentence using each group of words.

6. (my friend) _____

    _____

7. (for example) _____

    _____

Capitalization

1. Use a capital letter for the first word in a sentence.

   Do I smell something burning?   That paper is on fire.   Help!

2. Use a capital letter for **proper nouns.** A proper noun names a certain person, place, or thing. Do not use a capital letter for common nouns.

	Proper Nouns	Common Nouns
Person:	Mark Walsh	man
Place:	Kenya	country
	Elm Street	street
	North Carolina	state
Thing:	the White House	building
	Star Wars	movie
	Microsoft	company

3. Use a capital letter for **proper adjectives.** A proper adjective is an adjective that is made from a proper noun.

   the French language   African clothing   South American food

---

PRACTICE

Use the editing mark to show where capital letters are needed (a = A).

harriet quimby was the first woman to earn a pilot's license. she was a writer in new york before she flew a plane. she fell in love with airplanes in 1910 when she saw her first flying meet. harriet became a pilot and toured in mexico with a troupe of pilots. she decided she would be the first woman to cross the english channel. she took off on april 16, 1912, sitting on a wicker basket in the cockpit. after a scary flight, she landed on a french beach.

Answer each question with a complete sentence. Use capital letters correctly.

Sample: _____ I live in Little Rock, Arkansas. _____

1. What city (or town) and state do you live in?

   _____

2. Where do you like to shop? (use names of stores)

   _____

Mechanics

4. Use a capital letter for each part of a person's name. Also use a capital letter for a title when it is used with a person's name.

   Dr. McNally   Mr. J. S. Goldfarb   Ms. Van Slyke   Miss Chen
   But: The doctor will see you now.

5. Use a capital letter for any place that can be found on a map.
   Streets: Broadway   Park Place   Main Street
   Towns and cities: Sioux Falls   Berlin   Baghdad
   States: Texas   Kansas   Georgia
   Countries: Spain   Chad   France
   Islands: Guam   Cuba   Prince Edward Island
   Bodies of water: Dead Sea   Great Salt Lake   Mississippi River
   Natural landmarks: Mt. Rainier   Grand Canyon   Everglades
   Tourist attractions: Six Flags   Yellowstone National Park
   Yankee Stadium

PRACTICE

Use the editing marks to show where capital letters are needed (a = A) or where letters should be lowercase (A̲ = a).

1. writer ed j. smith reports that people are taking cheaper trips in the Summer.

2. mr. and mrs. mott drove to orlando, florida, and went camping.

3. last year, the Motts went to sea world.

4. this year, dr. ortega and his family went hiking instead of going to mt. rushmore in south dakota.

5. ms. wills visited her friend in Wisconsin rather than flying to the Island of st. kitts.

6. miss e. k. link from new town, long island, spent two days in maine.

7. she went to lake mead last year.

8. busch gardens in tampa, florida, is still very busy, though.

9. My Doctor wants to go to israel and see the dead sea.

Complete each sentence. Use capital letters correctly.

Sample: _____ My dentist is Dr. Thomas Duffy. _____

10. My dentist is _____. (title + name)

11. I would love to go to _____. (place name)

12. I was born in _____.
(country)

6. Use a capital letter for the days of the week and months of the year. Do <u>not</u> capitalize the names of the seasons.

> My birthday is in **March**.　　It's hard to get up on **Monday** mornings.
> I've always loved summer.

7. Use a capital letter for holidays.

> Will you go to a party **New Year's Eve**?　　My friends celebrate **Kwanzaa**.

PRACTICE

Use the editing marks to show where capital letters are needed (a = A) or where letters should be lowercase (A̸ = a).

1. This year, monday, january 18, dr. martin luther king, jr. day will be a paid holiday.

2. This holiday is in the place of columbus day, which we took as a day off on october 10.

3. The plant will, of course, be closed for the usual Fall and Winter holidays—thanksgiving, christmas, and new year's.

4. If any of these holidays fall on a monday or a friday, you will have a long weekend.

5. This year the Company's independence Day picnic will be on sunday, july 7.

6. I will be back at work on Tuesday, september 6, the day after labor day.

7. Some people want to have the party on Flag day, june 14, instead.

8. There has also been talk of a halloween party for october 31, which is a thursday this year.

9. We could hold the party on friday, october 25, if that is a better time.

Answer each question with a complete sentence. Use capital letters correctly.

Sample: _My favorite holidays are Thanksgiving and New Year's Eve._

10. What are your favorite holidays?

_____

11. Which is the best day of the week for you?

_____

12. What is your favorite season of the year?

_____

Mechanics

Plurals

Plural means "more than one." For example, the singular word *cat* means one cat; the plural form *cats* means more than one cat.

1. To form the plural of most nouns, add *-s*. Add *-es* to nouns that end in *ch, sh, s, x,* or *z.*

friend/friends   box/boxes   watch/watches

2. For most nouns that end in *f* or *fe*, change the *f* or *fe* to *v* and add *-es.*

leaf/leaves   knife/knives

3. For nouns that end in a consonant followed by *y*, change the *y* to *i* and add *-es.*

city/cities   try/tries

4. For irregular plurals, look in the dictionary. Here are some common irregular plurals.

child/children   crisis/crises   deer/deer
tooth/teeth   woman/women   mouse/mice

Circle the correct plural form of each word.

1. My brothers and their (**wifes, wives**) are taking a few (**daies, days**) off in August.

2. My (**nephews, nephewes**) and young (**cousines, cousins**) are coming for a visit.

3. I like to watch the (**childrens, children**) play in the yard.

4. They like to pick (**peachs, peaches**) from the trees.

5. My nephew Sam lost his two front (**teeth, tooths**) and looks cute.

6. I always have great (**memorys, memories**) of their (**visites, visits**).

Make each word plural and use it to complete each sentence.

7. (celebrity) My two favorite

_____

8. (man) In our class, there are

_____

9. (shelf) My refrigerator has

_____

Possessives

The **possessive** form of a noun shows that something is owned, and it shows who or what the owner is.

1. Add an **apostrophe** (') and *s* to form the possessive of singular nouns and irregular plural nouns that don't end with an *s*.

> Troy drove his <u>wife's</u> car to work yesterday.
>
> I saw him yesterday at <u>Roberto's</u> house.
>
> I have already put away the <u>children's</u> toys.

2. Add only an apostrophe (') to form the possessive of plural nouns that end in *s*.

> Both of my <u>sisters'</u> houses are on the west side.
>
> We left the <u>Sanchezes'</u> house at eight o'clock last night.

3. Use an apostrophe for possessive nouns only. Do not use an apostrophe with plural nouns that are *not* possessive.

> My <u>sisters</u> and the <u>Sanchezes</u> live near each other.

PRACTICE

Circle the correct word in the story about a man named Tran.

1. (**Trans, Tran's**) workday begins very early.

2. He gets up at six o'clock to make his (**childrens', children's**) breakfast.

3. At seven o'clock, he drives by his (**friend's, friends'**) houses to take them to work.

4. By eight o'clock, Tran and his friends are at work on the (**factories, factory's**) main floor.

5. Tran enjoys his work painting car (**body's, bodies**).

Write about people's favorite foods or activities. Use the possessive form.

Sample: (My cousin) _____ My cousin's favorite sport is soccer.

6. (My friends)

_____

7. (My boss)

_____

8. (My mother)

_____

Contractions

A **contraction** is a word formed by joining two other words. An apostrophe (') shows where a letter or letters have been left out. Many people use contractions when they speak and write informal letters. Do <u>not</u> use contractions in formal writing such as business letters or your GED essay.

Common Contractions

Contraction	Words It Replaces
I'm	I am
he's, she's, it's	he is, she is, it is; he has, she has, it has
you're, we're, they're	you are, we are, they are
isn't, aren't, wasn't, weren't	is not, are not, was not, were not
he'll, she'll, you'll	he will, she will, you will
I'll, we'll, they'll	I will, we will, they will
won't	will not
doesn't, don't, didn't	does not, do not, did not
I'd	I would, I had
I've, we've, you've, they've	I have, we have, you have, they have
who's	who is, who has
there's	there is, there has
let's	let us
can't	cannot

PRACTICE

Write a contraction to replace the underlined words.

_____ 1. I know a writer <u>who is</u> writing a book about baseball.

_____ 2. <u>I have</u> read about the first pro baseball player, Al Reach.

_____ 3. He <u>was not</u> cheered when he left Brooklyn for the Phillies.

_____ 4. Fans <u>were not</u> pleased that a player wanted a salary.

_____ 5. In Reach's time, players <u>did not</u> even get paid.

Write two sentences—one about something you cannot do and one about something you will not do. Change each word to a contraction.

6. (cannot) _____

7. (will not) _____

Contraction or Possessive?

Be careful not to confuse **contractions** with **possessives.** Contractions use apostrophes. Possessive pronouns and possessive adjectives do <u>not</u>.

Pronoun	Contraction	Possessives
he	he's (he is)	his
she	she's (she is)	her, hers
it	it's (it is)	its
you	you're (you are)	your, yours
they	they're (they are)	their, theirs
we	we're (we are)	our, ours
who	who's (who is)	whose

Note: The possessive *its* and the contraction *it's* are often confused.

Possessive: The airplane lost power in one of <u>its</u> engines.

Contraction: <u>It's</u> possible to make an emergency landing.

Note: These words are misspellings: *its', his', her's, yours', theirs', whos'.* Always correct them.

PRACTICE

Circle the correct word to complete each sentence.

1. People have a lot to say about (**their, they're**) jobs.

2. "(**Its, It's**) hectic!" says a thirty-year-old nurse's aide.

3. "My patients are so ill that (**they're, their**) always asking for me."

4. "(**You're, Your**) always up and down helping someone."

5. "(**Who's, Whose**) going to do the job with as much care?"

6. "I know one thing about this job: (**it's, its**) never dull."

7. A manager said, "What I really like is helping people solve (**their, they're**) problems."

8. A cook said, "(**They're, Their**) never going to come back for seconds if I don't put in the time!"

9. "I'm happy when (**your, you're**) at the counter at 6:00 A.M.," he said.

10. "(**Who's, Whose**) job is it to clean the griddle?"

Write *their* or *they're* to complete each sentence. Use a capital letter when necessary.

Some people are always complaining about _____

jobs. _____ always talking about the things they don't

like about _____ work.

Homonyms

Homonyms are words that sound alike but are spelled differently and have different meanings. Study this list of common homonyms to help you use each word correctly.

Word	Meaning	Word	Meaning
aisle	a space between rows	forth	forward
isle	an island	fourth	number four
brake	to stop	hole	opening
break	to destroy; a short time off	whole	complete
capital	seat of government	know	to understand
capitol	building in which a legislative body meets	no	not at all
		lessen	decrease, make less
clothes	things to wear	lesson	something that is taught
close	to shut		
fair	even, just; a festival	weak	not strong
fare	money for transportation	week	seven days

Some words are not exact homonyms, but their sounds and spellings are close enough to cause problems.

I <u>accept</u> your apology.   Do not <u>lose</u> your bus pass.

We're all here <u>except</u> Jim.   Do you have any <u>loose</u> change?

PRACTICE

Circle the correct word to complete each sentence.

1. Last (**week, weak**) our state passed a new law allowing more dumps.

2. The government thinks the law is (**fair, fare**), but many people don't agree.

3. Some of us gathered to meet in the (**capital, capitol**) city.

4. The meeting was so crowded that even the (**isles, aisles**) were full.

5. I (**no, know**) we have to work out a way to deal with this problem.

6. We need to (**lessen, lesson**) our need for new dumps.

7. We should be trying to (**clothes, close**) old dumps, not open new ones.

8. We need a (**hole, whole**) new plan for taking better care of our environment.

Write a sentence using each word.

9. (accept) _____

10 (brake) _____

Spelling

One good way to improve your spelling is to study a few basic spelling rules. While some words must be memorized, many others follow these seven spelling rules.

Rule 1: *ie:* There is a rhyme to help you learn the *ie* rule: Use *i* before *e* except after *c* or when sounded as *a* as in *neighbor* and *weigh*.

i before *e:*	achieve	believe
ei after *c:*	receive	conceive
ei when sounded as *a:*	weight	reins

The following words do not fit this rule. You need to memorize them.

either	neither	heir	seize	forfeit	foreign
weird	sheik	their	height	ancient	conscience

Rule 2: *-ceed/-cede:* Only three English verbs end in *-ceed*. All the other verbs with that long *e* vowel sound end in *-cede*.

-ceed:	succeed	proceed	exceed
-cede:	secede	recede	concede

Note: There is one exception—the verb *supersede*, which ends in *-sede*.

Rule 3: *-ful:* The sound */ful/* at the end of a word is spelled with one *l*.

graceful   careful   helpful

Circle the correct spelling of each word.

1. Sitting Bull was (**chief, cheif**) of the Hunkpapa tribe of Sioux.

2. Sitting Bull felt he had to (**succede, succeed**) against efforts to (**sieze, seize**) his tribe's land.

3. After all, he was the (**hier, heir**) to a great nation.

4. (**Their, Thier**) culture reached back hundreds of years.

5. Sitting Bull was (**hopefull, hopeful**) that the Sioux would be a (**powerful, powerfull**) nation again.

6. However, the Sioux were not (**successful, successfull**) in remaining a great nation.

7. Sitting Bull and his people could not (**acheive, achieve**) their dream.

Rule 4: Adding prefixes and suffixes: In general, do not change the spelling of a word when you add a prefix or a suffix.

dis- + pleased = displeased   mis- + spell = misspell

joy + -ous = joyous   hope + -ful = hopeful

govern + -ment = government

But: lay/laid   pay/paid

Rule 5: Adding suffixes to words ending in *y* after a consonant: If a word ends in *y* after a *consonant,* change the *y* to *i* before adding the suffix. Exception: Keep the *y* before a suffix that begins with *i,* such as *-ing* and *-ish.*

hurry/hurried   happy/happier

But: apply/applying   baby/babyish

Rule 6: Adding suffixes to words ending in silent *e:* If a word ends in silent *e* and the suffix begins with a vowel, drop the final *e.* If the suffix begins with a consonant, do not drop the final *e.*

fascinate/fascinating   nice/niceness

But: true/truly

Rule 7: Doubling consonants before a suffix: If a short (one-syllable) word ends in *one* vowel and *one* consonant, double the consonant before a suffix that begins with a vowel, such as *ed, ing, er, est.* If a longer word ends in one vowel and one consonant, double the consonant *only* if the last part of the word is stressed, such as *comMIT* or *exPEL.* Never double *x, y,* or *w.*

rap/rapping   trap/trapped   big/biggest

stop/stoppable   rebel/rebelling   commit/committed

PRACTICE

Circle the correct spelling of each word.

1. I have not been (**geting, getting**) my paychecks on time.

2. My checks have been (**delayed, delaied**) by three days or more.

3. I have not been (**payed, paid**) on time for the last month.

4. That is why I am (**submiting, submitting**) this complaint in (**writing, writting**).

Add the suffix to each word. Write a sentence with the new word.

5. carry + *-ed* _____

   _____

6. begin + *-ing* _____

   _____

Words That Cause Trouble

Here are some words that are often misused.

Word	Use	Example
few, fewer, many	pieces you can count	I have very few books. I have fewer books than you do. How many books do you have?
little, less, much	amounts you can't count	I have little patience. I have less patience than you do. How much patience do you have?
good	an adjective; tells about a person, place, or thing	This is a good picture.
well	an adverb; tells about an action	You draw well.
among	three or more	The three fought among themselves.
between	two	The choice was between the two of them.
who, whom	use with people	My children, who are now grown, live close by. He is the one to whom I spoke.
which	use with things	Cigarettes, which can cause cancer, aren't cheap.

PRACTICE

Circle the correct word to complete each sentence.

1. Michael Cullen, (**who, which**) opened the first "warehouse grocery" store, did not know that he was making history back in the 1930s.

2. Times were hard then, and people were looking for (**good, well**) prices.

3. Almost at once, his store was doing (**good, well**) because it was self-service, cash-and-carry, and one-stop shopping.

4. There was a lot of competition (**among, between**) all the grocery stores.

5. Mr. Cullen's store, (**which, who**) was the first supermarket, beat all the other stores.

Complete each sentence.

6. I don't have much _____.

7. I have very few _____

Paragraph Organization

Topic Sentence

A paragraph is a group of sentences organized around one idea. The **topic sentence** states the main idea of a paragraph. It tells what the entire paragraph is about. The topic sentence is usually the first sentence in a paragraph, but sometimes it may be the last sentence.

Notice how the underlined topic sentence in the paragraph below tells the main idea. The rest of the sentences in the paragraph explain, or support, that idea.

> <u>The job requirements for a customer service agent are excellent people skills and good organization.</u> You will be working with all kinds of people. You must be able to communicate with customers and make them feel understood and respected. All of our successful agents know that the customer is always right. Good organization skills go hand in hand with people skills. A good agent knows the customer, what his or her needs are, and the best way to work with the customer. It's also important to keep accurate records of customer information, both in the agent's files and in our computer database. If you have these organization and people skills, we are interested in reviewing your application.

Each sentence that follows the topic sentence adds detail to the main idea. The topic sentence introduces them in one general statement.

PRACTICE

Underline the topic sentence in each paragraph below.

1.   The Edgebrook Neighborhood Association will meet Thursday to discuss the upcoming community awards lunch. Many details need to be worked out, including who the chairperson is, what date is appropriate, and where the event will take place. All community members who can attend are most welcome. We hope to see you there.

2.   Go to the grocery store and pick up a ready-to-bake cake mix. Usually you'll need to add water or an egg or both, but once you've done that, all that's left to do is to put the mixture into the oven or microwave. In less than 30 minutes, you'll have a delicious "homemade" dessert! These days, baking is a lot easier than you might think.

Choosing an Effective Topic Sentence

A topic sentence should state the topic of a paragraph. It should also tell the main point that the paragraph makes about that topic. If it just states the topic, it is too general. If it states a detail that supports the main point, it is too specific.

The following paragraph lacks a topic sentence. Read the paragraph. Then compare the effective topic sentence that follows with the general and specific ones.

Clean conveyor belt surfaces with plain soap and water. Then dry them thoroughly. Once the belt has been shut down for the day, oil the gears with fresh lubricants. Bag and label as trash all defective products coming off of the line. Finally, be sure to update inventory logs.

Effective: The following steps are necessary after an assembly line run.
Too general: This factory has assembly lines.
Too specific: Conveyor belts and gears need to be maintained.

The effective topic sentence states the topic—assembly lines. It also tells the main point about that topic—that steps must be followed to maintain the assembly line.

PRACTICE

Circle the letter of the most effective topic sentence for each paragraph below. Remember that an effective topic sentence should both state the topic and say what the main point about the topic is.

1.   I do not think a newspaper is the place for a photograph like this. Although your readers should be informed of the facts of the car accident, is it really necessary to print such a shocking picture on the front page? Where is your sense of decency? Give us the facts, but do not try to sell newspapers by using other people's suffering.
    a.   I am writing to express my outrage over the picture in yesterday's newspaper.
    b.   Some newspapers print shocking photographs just to sell papers.

2.   Understanding different cultures helps us learn about ourselves. In this class, we will study other religions, educational systems, and family structures. We will look at cultures in Africa, Asia, and Latin America. We will then examine our own culture and its accompanying values.
    a.   Religion and family life are part of culture.
    b.   This class will focus on cultures—both our own and others.

Check your answers on page 254.

Moving Sentences Around

The sentences that relate to the topic sentence in a paragraph are called **supporting sentences.** They contain details about the main idea. These sentences make the main idea clear to the reader. Supporting sentences need to follow a logical order. If they do not, they may confuse the reader.

In the following example, the underlined sentence is out of place. As you read the paragraph, it might confuse you for a moment. Think of where the sentence <u>should</u> be in the paragraph.

> Perseverance means sticking to the task no matter what is in the way. <u>Perseverance is the first quality we look for in an employee of Belgrade Industries.</u> We look for people who will stick to a task even when it is hard. People who persevere keep trying despite long odds. If you are a person who is not stopped by obstacles and who enjoys a challenge, we would like to talk with you about job opportunities at Belgrade.

The underlined sentence should be the first sentence in the paragraph because it states the topic of the paragraph. The first sentence defines "perseverance" and is a detail in the paragraph. It should come after the topic sentence.

In the next paragraph, notice how a sentence that needs to be moved can be marked.

> The second quality important to us at Belgrade is a commitment to teamwork. Nothing at Belgrade has ever gotten accomplished by one employee alone. Instead, people here work together to get a job done. Teamwork means listening to each other, valuing each other's point of view, and using a team approach to solving problems. Individuality is an honorable quality, but we find that teamwork is what works best at Belgrade. If you can work on a team, you can work on Belgrade's team.

When you need to move a sentence to a more logical place, circle it and draw an arrow to where it belongs. This is an editing mark that you can use when you write the first draft of any piece of writing.

Paragraph Organization

In each piece of writing below, find the sentence that should be moved. Circle the sentence and draw an arrow to where it should be placed.

1. The next meeting of the People Care Club will be held tomorrow at 7:00 P.M. The meeting will focus on holiday outreach to the homeless. The holidays can be a difficult time for people, and we want to provide as much support as we can. It is being held in the evening so that those who work during the day will be able to attend.

2. You will not find a better person for the position of shift foreman in your company than John Gordon. John has been a fine employee here at Lab Industries, and we will miss him. However, it will be tough to fill his shoes. We understand completely that John needs to move on to new challenges, so we wish him well.

3. To replace the ink cartridge in your laser printer, remove the old cartridge by pressing down on the release lever. Remove the new cartridge from the box and peel off the protective strip from the bottom of the cartridge. Align the arrow on the ink cartridge with the arrow on the printer. Finally, make sure the release lever has returned to the locked position. Press firmly on the ink cartridge until you hear it snap into place.

4. Mr. Davis, I am writing to ask how much I should help my son, Jason Wennik, with his homework. He enjoys your class, but when he sits down to do his homework, he seems to forget everything he has learned in school. Please let me know what to do. I would like to help him, but I am not sure you want parents doing their children's homework with them.

Removing Irrelevant Ideas

All the sentences in a paragraph should help support the main idea. An **irrelevant idea** is an idea that does not belong in a paragraph because it does not support the main idea. Instead, it distracts the reader from the point the writer is trying to make. Sentences that are irrelevant should be removed.

In the paragraph below, the first sentence is the topic sentence. It states the main idea. The underlined sentence is irrelevant to that main idea.

Mrs. Meadows has been a valued member of our community. It is with sincere appreciation that we acknowledge her retirement and move to the Sunbelt. Mrs. Meadows has taught kindergarten at the Heath School since 1961. She has also been a tireless supporter of the public library, and she has sung in the community chorus for over 15 years. Her daughter and son-in-law also sang in the chorus until they moved out of town several years ago. Mrs. Meadows has been generous with her time and talent. She has also been a major contributor to the Arts Endowment Fund, which is responsible for bringing much cultural enrichment to our schools and our town. Mrs. Meadows will be greatly missed.

The sentence about Mrs. Meadows' daughter and son-in-law is irrelevant because the main idea of the paragraph is Mrs. Meadows' contributions to her community. It should be marked out.

PRACTICE

Mark out the irrelevant sentence in each of the following paragraphs.

1. The most important thing we can provide our young people today is the opportunity for employment. A lack of jobs is what causes so much of the trouble in our inner cities. In the past, people had jobs and a way to get to them. Today, the few jobs available to young people are out in the suburbs. The Star Market requires a year of experience before you can be hired there. Getting and keeping a job is a major factor in establishing self-esteem, something that is missing in many youths. Jobs keep kids off the streets, let them earn money honestly, and help them feel good about themselves.

2.   I disagree that employment is the answer to the trouble that exists among young people in the city. The best thing we can give these kids is good schools. We can offer them all the jobs in the world, but without an education, young people will not be able to perform them. My co-worker's son just got a scholarship to the state university, so he will likely have a well-paid career ahead of him. Rather than providing our youth with low-skilled, low-paying jobs, let's keep them in school by offering high-quality, safe, and interesting places to learn. We are selling our kids short if we shuffle them off to dead-end jobs as a way of keeping them occupied and off the streets.

3.   The annual company picnic was an unfortunate flop. We all know that disappointment is a part of life. Several factors were involved in making it a disappointing day. First of all, it rained almost the entire day. People could not stay dry, even under the tent. Second, although 300 people had said they planned to attend, there was only enough food for 250. The caterers scrambled to get more food, but by the time it was prepared, many people had decided to go home. Finally, the activities planned were not varied enough for the group. If you were not interested in bingo, you were left sitting with nothing to do. Clearly, more planning needs to be done next year to have a picnic that all can enjoy.

4.   I am a long-term tenant in your apartment building, and I am hoping you will be able to answer some questions for me. You have been an excellent landlord over the years, but I have noticed some changes that concern me. First of all, why is there only one day of trash pick-up when there used to be two? The garbage that is left out back begins to smell after only two or three days. A week is too long to wait before it's collected. Second, I have heard rumors that rent may go up next fall. I hope that this is not true. In my experience, spreading rumors only gets you into trouble. The services here have not improved enough to justify such an increase. In fact, service is getting worse. Finally, even though you stated that you would replace the front walkway, it is still in terrible condition. My wife has trouble getting in and out of the building because of this walkway. When can we expect the repairs to be complete? I look forward to a reply on these matters as soon as possible.

5.   Here are the rules for the housesitting job. First, please perform the following tasks: bring in the mail each day, water the plants twice a week, and walk the dogs three times a day. While you are staying at the house, please be careful with all heating appliances and turn out the lights when you're not using them. We bought all of our lighting fixtures at Purple Sun, so they are quite expensive. Smoking is not allowed in the house. We would prefer that you do not have guests and that you use the telephone for local calls only.

Dividing Paragraphs

A paragraph should contain only one main idea. Sometimes, however, a paragraph may actually have two main ideas. When this is the case, it is best to divide the paragraph into two shorter ones.

The main idea of the following paragraph shifts halfway through. The first part of the paragraph is about one ballot item. The second part is about another.

> The Neighborhood City Alliance recommends that you vote YES on two of the ballot items in this Tuesday's election. The first one is the school renovation referendum. By voting yes, you will be taking a step toward building the kinds of high schools our young people need to learn skills appropriate for the twenty-first century. Briefly, the plan calls for the renovation of all existing science labs as well as the addition of new technology and media centers. A *yes* vote is a vote for the future. The second item is for more money for the city parks. This money will go toward maintaining our present parks and acquiring land for new parks. The parks department will be able to purchase land that has abandoned, dangerous buildings on it and turn this land into playgrounds and mini-parks. City residents will benefit greatly if this measure passes.

The paragraph should be divided into two paragraphs by starting a new paragraph with the sentence beginning "The second item. . . ." The main idea of the first paragraph is to vote yes on the school renovation issue. The main idea of the second paragraph is to vote yes for appropriation of park funds.

To show where a new paragraph should begin, this mark can be used: ¶. This is how to mark the division between the paragraphs.

> The Neighborhood City Alliance recommends that you vote YES on two of the ballot items in this Tuesday's election. The first one is the school renovation referendum. By voting yes, you will be taking a step toward building the kinds of high schools our young people need to learn skills appropriate for the twenty-first century. Briefly, the plan calls for the renovation of all existing science labs as well as the addition of new technology and media centers. A *yes* vote is a vote for the future.
> ¶ The second item is for more money for the city parks. This money will go toward maintaining our present parks and acquiring land for new parks. The parks department will be able to purchase land that has abandoned, dangerous buildings on it and turn this land into playgrounds and mini-parks. City residents will benefit greatly if this measure passes.

Put a paragraph mark (¶) to show where each of the following paragraphs should be divided. Two paragraphs <u>do not</u> need to be divided.

1.   We wish to express our appreciation to all those people who contributed their time, effort, talent, and money to rebuild the community center. Without your generosity, the senior citizens of this city would be without a gathering place. For three years, you have worked hard to make this dream a reality for the seniors. Now, look before you and see the fruits of your labor. We'd also like to thank the seniors themselves for their patience as the project got underway. Your input on building design and safety issues was invaluable. Thank you for taking the time to meet with our architects and consultants.

2.   Learning to draw is a developmental process. People often think one is either "born artistic" or not. However, research shows that just as one can learn to read, so too can one learn to draw. In fact, almost all children go through a well-documented process of learning to draw, starting with the scribbling phase in early toddlerhood, the symbolic stage around age 3 or 4, and then the story-telling phase by age 6. The stage a child reaches in late elementary school is of particular interest. At this stage, usually around the sixth grade, children begin to focus on adding detail to their drawing. Their drawing becomes more complex and realistic.

3.   The best way to get in and out of the building now that our new security system is in place is to carry your pass card with you at all times. This card will allow your entry into all public areas of the building, the restrooms, the employee lounge, and the cafeteria. If you forget or lose your pass card, contact Mr. Reynolds in the Security Department immediately. He will issue you a temporary card that will work for 24 hours. The other way to get into and around the building is to use the keypad to the right of each door entrance. Simply key in the 24-hour pass code, press enter, and proceed through the doorway within 25 seconds. You must go to the security office on the tenth floor to get the daily code. The downside of this method is that the code changes every day.

4.   As you requested, I am writing this summary of the events of last Thursday in order to give you my side of the story. I think you will find that I did not act inappropriately and that a three-day suspension is unfair. On May 25, I left my position at the reception desk for approximately 45 minutes in order to take care of some personal business in town. Before I did so, however, I contacted Mr. Leon Stanford and asked him to fill in for me. Mr. Stanford agreed, and I left. When I returned, I learned that Mr. Sanford never did take my place and that the reception desk was vacant the entire time I was gone.

Combining Paragraphs

You have learned that sometimes a paragraph should be divided into two paragraphs because there are two main ideas. In contrast, sometimes two paragraphs should be combined into one because they both relate to the same main idea.

Read the paragraphs below. Paragraph B should be combined with paragraph C. Both are about the underlined main idea.

(A)

Stress can be a killer. Can you manage stress in difficult situations? Understanding why a situation is difficult and knowing how to handle it can help most people reduce their stress level. The goal should not be to avoid stressful situations. Rather it should be to recognize them and have a plan to deal with them.

(B)

Knowing what "pushes your buttons" is the first step in stress management. For example, some people become anxious and irritable in crowds. Others have trouble working with people who are loud and opinionated.

(C)

Some people panic when they are running late and are stuck in traffic. Still others experience stress when they are alone and without plans. Knowing your stressors will bring you closer to managing them.

When you start to read a new paragraph, you expect to read about a new idea. If you do not, you may be confused. Both paragraph B and paragraph C give examples of what causes stress in people. They are both short paragraphs, and they would be more effective and less confusing if they were combined into one.

Knowing what "pushes your buttons" is the first step in stress management. For example, some people become anxious and irritable in crowds. Others have trouble working with people who are loud and opinionated. Some people panic when they are running late and are stuck in traffic. Still others experience stress when they are alone and without plans. Knowing your stressors will bring you closer to managing them.

PRACTICE

Read each group of paragraphs on the next page, and decide which two paragraphs in each group should be combined into one. Write the letters of the two paragraphs on the line. Remember: If two paragraphs deal with the same main idea, they should be combined.

(A)

1. I would like to apply for the position of customer service ad associate that was advertised in your paper on Monday, October 2. My skills and background meet your need for an experienced customer service associate to take ad copy over the phone.

(B)

The job of customer service ad associate requires a pleasing telephone voice, the ability to get along with the public, and attention to detail. For the past two years, I have answered the phone as a receptionist at Quest Publishing Company. I enjoy talking with both customers and vendors, and I speak Spanish as well as English.

(C)

Every day I keep a detailed log of all calls. This log must be complete, accurate, and up-to-date. I believe my skills and experience match your requirements precisely.

Combine paragraphs _____

(A)

2. Mrs. Tolland, I am sorry you are disappointed with the service you received at Ron's Restaurant last Sunday. As you know, we appreciate all of our customers and want to serve them well.

(B)

If it were not for our regular customers, we would not be in business. We want to provide our customers with the best service possible.

(C)

We have spoken directly with your waiter regarding his behavior. We have also had a refresher training session on customer service. Please accept our apology and a gift certificate for dinner at Ron's.

Combine paragraphs _____

(A)

3. Getting sick while traveling is not uncommon. In fact, illness seems to be expected during travel outside the United States. However, there are precautions travelers can take to prevent illness.

(B)

One of the most important is adapting slowly to new eating and drinking habits. If you immediately consume all the local foods and beverages, you are asking for stomach trouble.

(C)

Instead, eat and drink like you do back home for at least 24 hours. Then gradually add new foods over the next 48 hours. Going slowly helps ensure you will enjoy your whole trip—not just the first meal.

Combine paragraphs _____

Writing at Work

Horticulture: Nursery Worker

Some Careers in Horticulture

Nursery workers cultivate new trees, shrubs, and flowers, and also tend growing and mature plants and trees. Nursery workers usually learn about their profession on the job. They gain experience with fertilizing, watering, pruning, staking, and wrapping the plants and trees. They use their knowledge of the seasons, growing schedules, local climates, and customers' buying habits to grow and sell products.

Because much of the work may be physically demanding, nursery workers should be in good shape. In addition, workers should be able to follow written directions, write directions, and make notes of their own. This writing must be clear and accurate. Nursery workers are also called upon to apply basic math skills involving money and measurement. Nursery workers who work at landscaping companies may also have to interpret plans and blueprints.

Look at the box showing some careers in horticulture.

- Do any of the careers interest you? If so, which ones?

- How could you find out more about those careers? On a separate piece of paper, write some questions that you would like answered. You can find out more information about those careers in the *Occupational Outlook Handbook* at your local library and online.

Florist
sells plants, flowers and floral arrangements; arranges flowers

Garden Center Worker
tends plants in store; assists customers; stocks gardening supplies

Groundskeeper
works in private or public settings caring for flowers, grass, trees, and shrubs

Landscape Worker
plants flowers, shrubs, and trees according to design plans

Lawn Service Worker
mows lawns; tends flowers and shrubs

Read the following note. Then answer the questions.

Bev,

While I'm on vacation next week, please take care of the following items. Thank you for doing this, as the plants will not survive without your care.

1. Be sure to water all the plants located indoors every two days, except for the cacti.

2. Pay close attention to the bedding plants. You can use the sprinkling system in the greenhouses. Turn the system on for 15 minutes when you first come in.

3. Do not water in the evening, as the plants may sit in the cold, damp soil too long. This can cause root damage to some plants.

4. Apply plant food fertilizer to the flowering plants. Since we are entering our heavy selling season for these plants, we want them to look really terrific. The more blooms on each plant, the better they look. The plant food will help them produce lots of blooms.

Thanks,

Joe

1. Which plants did Joe ask Bev not to water?

_____

2. According to Joe's note, what does plant food fertilizer help plants do?

_____

3. On a separate piece of paper, write a short note asking someone to do a task for you. As the note above does, give a reason why doing the task is important. Also, include a series of steps to complete the task.

Prewrite: What is the task that you want done?
Why is it important?
What are the steps that need to be taken?

Write: Write the note.

Revise and Edit: Have your instructor or another student read the note. Ask if the instructions are clear. If they are not, find out what is not clear. Also, ask your reader if there are any grammar, spelling, capitalization, or punctuation errors. Use the feedback to revise the note.

Unit 3 Review
Language Skills

Write the correct pronoun to replace the underlined noun or nouns.

1. <u>Jeff and Melissa</u> decided to buy a new car. _____

   They   Their

2. Their bank offers <u>the bank's</u> customers low-cost auto loans. _____

   their   its

3. Jeff's parents approved of <u>Jeff and Melissa's</u> buying a new car. _____

   them   their

4. His parents depend on Melissa and <u>Jeff</u> for rides. _____

   he   him

If the group of words is a sentence, write *S*. If it is a fragment, add words to complete it.

5. The apartment on the fourth floor.

   _____

6. Pedro looked at it last week.

   _____

7. Thinking about it on the way home from work.

   _____

Use one of the connecting words listed below to create a complex sentence from each group of words.

| after | because | before | if | since | so that |
| unless | when | whenever |

8. Jen likes to walk her dog at night _____.

9. It's also pleasant in the morning _____.

10. _____ she treats her dog like a person.

Correct each run-on sentence by writing it as two complete sentences.

11. Craig has an unusual job he is a chef.

    _____

    _____

12. He used to work in a store, he was a cashier.

    _____

    _____

13. Then he went to cooking school for two years, it was a long program.

    _____

    _____

Write the correct adjective or adverb to complete each sentence.

14. Weldon Jones is a _____ worker.

    fine (adj.)   **finely** (adv.)

15. He takes his work _____ .

    serious (adj.)   **seriously** (adv.)

16. He works _____ and makes few mistakes.

    quick (adj.)   **quickly** (adv.)

17. I feel _____ that he will do an excellent job.

    confident (adj.)   **confidently** (adv.)

Write the correct form of the adjective or adverb to complete each sentence.

18. Of the three gas stations in town, Sun Gas has the _____ service.

    good   better   best

19. It is also the _____ .

    expensivest   more expensive   most expensive

20. Joe's Truck Stop is _____ from downtown than Sun Gas.

    farther   more farther   farthest

21. The owners of Diamond Gas are doing _____ this year than ever before.

    bad   more badly   worse

Write the correct verb to complete each sentence.

22. I _____ TV when the power went out.

    watched   **am watching**   **was watching**

23. Gloria _____ a haircut last week.

    got   **has gotten**   **will get**

24. Jeff _____ in the shop ever since he finished high school.

    will be working   **has been working**   **was working**

25. On January 10, I _____ here for one year.

    will have lived   **will live**   **am living**

26. When he finally got through, he said he _____ to reach me for several days.

    was trying   **had been trying**   **is trying**

Rewrite each sentence. Correct the errors in capitalization.

27. Rob went to new york in september to visit his uncle.

    _____

28. Because it was Autumn, sights like the statue of liberty weren't crowded.

    _____

29. On labor day, Rob walked through central park and up fifth avenue.

    _____

30. He ate french food and saw a game at Yankee stadium.

    _____

Add punctuation marks where they are needed in each sentence.

31. My husband and I were married on June 15 1999

32. The wedding took place in Chicago Illinois

33. His brothers Edward Hal John and Joe attended the wedding

34. You wouldn't believe the crazy toasts they made

35. The wedding was beautiful and all the guests had a good time

36. Do you know where we went on our honeymoon

37. We went to Atlantic City Niagara Falls and New York City

Write the correct verb to complete each sentence.

38. Allen had _____ the movie before it came out on video.

    saw   seen

39. Therefore, he already _____ how it ended.

    knew   known

40. The movie is about a boy who _____ his nose in a fight at school.

    broke   broken

41. He had _____ with almost everyone in the class at some time.

    fight   fought

42. Surprisingly, the principal _____ him another chance.

    gave   given

43. By the end, the boy had _____ to control his violent behavior.

    began   begun

Write the correct word to complete each sentence.

44. Those _____ don't fit you properly.

    clothes   close

45. How much is the subway _____?

    fair   fare

46. Tim's mother is finding it hard to _____ his decision to move away.

    accept   except

47. That store is open seven days a _____, twenty-four hours a day.

    weak   week

48. I've learned an important _____ from this experience.

    lessen   lesson

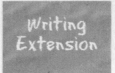

Use your language skills to edit a piece of writing done by a friend, coworker, or family member. If you find any mistakes explain to the person what each error is and how to correct it.

Mini-Test • Unit 3

This is a 15-minute practice test. After 15 minutes, mark the last number you finished. Then complete the test and check your answers. If most of your answers were correct but you did not finish, try to work faster next time.

Directions: Choose the <u>one best answer</u> to each question.

Questions 1 through 4 refer to the following instructions.

DRIVER'S EDUCATION AT VILLAGE DRIVING SCHOOL

(A)

(1) Registering for classes at Village Driving School is an easy process. (2) Lessons include thirty hours of classroom instruction six of driving, and six of road observation. (3) You must do the classroom work, but the other instruction is optional. (4) Check off option A on the form. (5) If you wish to take only the classroom portion of the course. (6) You're form must be accompanied by the full course fee of $285 at the time of enrollment.

(B)

(7) The driver's education course must be completed within twelve months. (8) At the end of the course, each student was given a certificate of completion to present to the Department of Motor Vehicles. (9) Take this certificate and an application fee of $20 with you to the driving test. (10) There are no guarantees that you will pass the exam.

1. Sentence 2: **Lessons include thirty hours of classroom instruction six of driving, and six of road observation.**

   Which correction should be made to sentence 2?

   (1) change include to includes
   (2) replace hours with ours
   (3) change classroom to Classroom
   (4) insert a comma after instruction
   (5) no correction is necessary

2. Sentences 4 and 5: **Check off option A on the form. If you wish to take only the classroom portion of the course.**

   Which is the best way to write the underlined portion of these sentences? If the original is the best way, choose option (1).

   (1) form. If you
   (2) form if you
   (3) form, if you
   (4) form, and if you
   (5) form although you

3. Sentence 6: **You're form must be accompanied by the full course fee of $285 at the time of enrollment.**

   Which correction should be made to sentence 6?

   (1) replace You're with Your
   (2) change be to have been
   (3) insert a comma after accompanied
   (4) replace by with buy
   (5) insert a comma after $285

4. Sentence 8: **At the end of the course, each student was given a certificate of completion to present to the Department of Motor Vehicles.**

   Which correction should be made to sentence 8?

   (1) remove the comma after course
   (2) change student to Student
   (3) change was given to will be given
   (4) change Department to department
   (5) no correction is necessary

Questions 5 through 8 refer to the following business document.

Recent Company Promotions

(A)

(1) In keeping with our company's goals of informing all employees of changes within the office, we'd like to make the following announcement. (2) Please join the Personnel Department and I in acknowledging the promotions of Meg Tyburk, Lisa Fay, and Winston Burns. (3) Each of these managers are a supervisor who deserves recognition.

(B)

(4) As you have learned, or as you undoubtedly know, excellent performance is recognized by this company. (5) These individuals exemplify the three qualities of our company's motto: caring, effort, and accountability. (6) All three of our promoted managers live in the suburbs. (7) Our company is proud to announce that Meg Tyburk, Lisa Fay, and Winston Burns now hold the title of Senior Manager. (8) Please take the time to congratulate them when you see them in the hall.

5. Sentence 2: **Please join the Personnel Department and I in acknowledging the promotions of Meg Tyburk, Lisa Fay, and Winston Burns.**

   Which correction should be made to sentence 2?

   (1) insert a comma after Please
   (2) change Personnel Department to personnel department
   (3) replace I with me
   (4) remove the comma after Tyburk
   (5) no correction is necessary

6. Sentence 3: **Each of these managers are a supervisor who deserves recognition.**

   Which is the best way to write the underlined portion of this sentence? If the original is the best way, choose option (1).

   (1) are
   (2) were
   (3) being
   (4) was
   (5) is

7. Sentence 4: **As you have learned, or as you undoubtedly know, excellent performance is recognized by this company.**

   The most effective revision of sentence 4 would begin with which group of words?

   (1) As you know, this company recognizes
   (2) As you have learned and know,
   (3) As excellent performance is recognized
   (4) Having learned that this company
   (5) Excellent performance, as you have learned

8. Sentence 6: **All three of our promoted managers live in the suburbs.**

   Which revision should be made to the placement of sentence 6?

   (1) move sentence 6 to the beginning of paragraph B
   (2) move sentence 6 to follow sentence 4
   (3) move sentence 6 to follow sentence 7
   (4) remove sentence 6
   (5) no revision is necessary

Revising and Editing Checklist

	YES	NO
Content		
Does the content achieve its purpose—that is, does it respond to the assignment topic?	☐	☐
Is the content right for its audience?	☐	☐
Is the main idea stated clearly?	☐	☐
Does each paragraph have a topic sentence?	☐	☐
Are topic sentences supported by details?	☐	☐
Are details written in a logical order?	☐	☐
Is the right amount of information included—that is, are any details missing? Are any details unnecessary?	☐	☐
Does the writing hold your interest?	☐	☐
Style and Word Choice		
Are thoughts and ideas expressed clearly?	☐	☐
Are any ideas repeated?	☐	☐
Are some words used too many times?	☐	☐
Are precise words and fresh language used?	☐	☐
Are slang and informal expressions used appropriately, if at all?	☐	☐
Sentence Structure		
Are all sentences complete sentences?	☐	☐
Are any sentences too long and hard to understand?	☐	☐
Are any sentences too short and choppy?	☐	☐
Usage		
Are nouns and pronouns used correctly?	☐	☐
Are verbs used correctly?	☐	☐
Are adjectives and adverbs used correctly?	☐	☐
Mechanics		
Are all words spelled correctly?	☐	☐
Is punctuation used correctly?	☐	☐
Are words capitalized correctly?	☐	☐

	YES	NO
Are new paragraphs clearly shown?	☐	☐
(Check to see if paragraphs either are indented or have an extra line space in between.)		
If handwritten, is the handwriting as neat as possible?	☐	☐
Is there enough space between words and lines?	☐	☐
If typed on a computer or word processor, are the type font and size appropriate?	☐	☐
Are the margins adequate?	☐	☐

Editing Marks

Mark	Meaning
a̿	change to a capital letter
ꓘ	change to a lowercase letter
⊙	insert period
⋀	insert comma
word⋀	insert word(s)
sp (thiir)	check spelling
¶	insert a paragraph indent
no ¶	no new paragraph
ℓ	delete a letter, word, group of words
ℐ	delete and close up space
#	add a space between words

ANSWER SHEET

Posttest
Language Arts, Writing

Name: _____ Class: _____ Date: _____

1 ① ② ③ ④ ⑤   14 ① ② ③ ④ ⑤

2 ① ② ③ ④ ⑤   15 ① ② ③ ④ ⑤

3 ① ② ③ ④ ⑤   16 ① ② ③ ④ ⑤

4 ① ② ③ ④ ⑤   17 ① ② ③ ④ ⑤

5 ① ② ③ ④ ⑤   18 ① ② ③ ④ ⑤

6 ① ② ③ ④ ⑤   19 ① ② ③ ④ ⑤

7 ① ② ③ ④ ⑤   20 ① ② ③ ④ ⑤

8 ① ② ③ ④ ⑤   21 ① ② ③ ④ ⑤

9 ① ② ③ ④ ⑤   22 ① ② ③ ④ ⑤

10 ① ② ③ ④ ⑤   23 ① ② ③ ④ ⑤

11 ① ② ③ ④ ⑤   24 ① ② ③ ④ ⑤

12 ① ② ③ ④ ⑤   25 ① ② ③ ④ ⑤

13 ① ② ③ ④ ⑤

POSTTEST

Directions

This is an 83-minute practice test. Spend no more than 38 minutes on the 25 multiple-choice questions, leaving the remaining time for the essay. After 38 minutes, mark the last number you finished. Then complete the test and check your answers. If most of your answers were correct but you did not finish, try to work faster next time.

The PreGED Writing Posttest measures your ability to use clear and effective written English. This test includes both multiple-choice questions and an essay. The following directions apply only to the multiple-choice section; a separate set of directions is given for the essay.

The multiple-choice section consists of passages with lettered paragraphs and numbered sentences. After reading the passage, answer the multiple-choice questions that follow.

Some of the sentences contain an error in sentence structure, usage, and mechanics. Some questions refer to sentences that are correct as written. The best answer for some questions is one that produces a sentence that is consistent with the verb tense and point of view used throughout the text. Some of the passages need to be revised to improve their organization.

Record your answers on the answer sheet on page 218. You may make a photocopy of this page. To record your answers, fill in the numbered circle on the answer sheet that corresponds to the answer you select for each question in the Posttest.

EXAMPLE

Sentence 1: **I was excited to receive an invitation to you're party.**

Which correction should be made to sentence 1?

(1) change was to is
(2) change was to will be
(3) change you're to your
(4) change receive to recieve
(5) no correction is necessary

(On Answer Sheet)
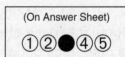

The correct answer choice is 3.

PART I

Questions 1 through 4 refer to the following business memo.

To: All Employees
From: Ruelle Fox, Benefits Office

(A)

(1) All Cardell Industries employees can now receive free services at Champlin Community Bank (CCB). (2) Free checking has been the most popular service offered at CCB, but there is other nice options as well. (3) I've enclosed a complete brochure of free CCB services. (4) If you have any questions, please stop by the Benefits Office or call me. (5) You can also ask me about the Chamber of Commerce coupon books that are available now!

(B)

(6) Noting one special highlight in the CCB brochure. (7) You'll have easy access to CCB's new branch, located only a block from our main entrance. (8) Every time you visit this branch, you can enter a drawing to win a gift certificate to a nearby shop restaurant, or movie theater.

1. Sentence 2: **Free checking has been the most popular service offered at CCB, but there is other nice options as well.**

    Which correction should be made to sentence 2?

    (1) remove the comma after CCB
    (2) replace but with since
    (3) replace there with their
    (4) change is to was
    (5) change is to are

2. Which revision would improve the effectiveness of the memo?

    (1) begin a new paragraph with sentence 5
    (2) remove sentence 5
    (3) move sentence 5 to the beginning of paragraph B
    (4) move sentence 5 to the end of paragraph B
    (5) no revision is necessary

3. Sentence 6: **Noting one special highlight in the CCB brochure.**

    Which is the best way to write the underlined portion of this sentence? If the original is the best way, choose option (1).

    (1) Noting one
    (2) Noting, one
    (3) Be sure to note one
    (4) You noted one
    (5) In noting one

4. Sentence 8: **Every time you visit this branch, you can enter a drawing to win a gift certificate to a nearby shop restaurant, or movie theater.**

    Which correction should be made to sentence 8?

    (1) remove the comma after branch
    (2) change can enter to entered
    (3) insert a comma after shop
    (4) remove the comma after restaurant
    (5) no correction is necessary

Questions 5 through 9 refer to the following article.

WHAT IS WORK-LIFE BALANCE?

(A)

(1) Nowadays companies pay more attention to workers' whole lives. (2) This trend was called "work-life balance." (3) However you have your life in balance, you are better able to meet your responsibilities in all areas of your life.

(B)

(4) You may wonder why your Company would want your life balanced. (5) Wouldn't it be better for them if you just worked all the time? (6) Actually, workers perform better when they have more balance in their lives. (7) Their healthier, so they can do more. (8) They worry less about their families, so they can focus better on their work. (9) If you feel that your life is out of balance, visit the Human Resources office at your company. (10) Ask if the staff has any programs on work-life balance. (11) You might get some help!

5. Sentence 2: **This trend was called "work-life balance."**

   Which is the best way to write the underlined portion of this sentence? If the original is the best way, choose option (1).

   (1) was
   (2) was being
   (3) were
   (4) will be
   (5) is

6. Sentence 3: **However you have your life in balance, you are better able to meet your responsibilities in all areas of your life.**

   Which correction should be made to sentence 3?

   (1) replace However with When
   (2) replace you have with they have
   (3) remove the comma after balance
   (4) replace meet your with meet you're
   (5) no correction is necessary

7. Sentence 4: **You may wonder why your Company would want your life balanced.**

   Which correction should be made to sentence 4?

   (1) change You may to You will
   (2) change may wonder to were wondering
   (3) change Company to company
   (4) replace your life with you're life
   (5) no correction is necessary

8. Sentence 7: **Their healthier, so they can do more.**

   Which correction should be made to sentence 7?

   (1) replace Their with They're
   (2) remove the comma after healthier
   (3) replace so with yet
   (4) remove so
   (5) no correction is necessary

9. Which revision would improve the effectiveness of the article?

   (1) begin a new paragraph with sentence 8
   (2) remove sentence 8
   (3) begin a new paragraph with sentence 9
   (4) remove sentence 9
   (5) no revision is necessary

Go on to the next page.

Questions 10 through 13 refer to the following information.

HOW TO PREPARE FOR
A JOB INTERVIEW

(A)

(1) Most people dread job interviews, and for good reason. (2) In a job interview, you are not in control of the situation. (3) Someone else chooses the questions you have to answer them.

(B)

(4) No matter how stressed you feel it's better to prepare for the interview in advance. (5) Make a list of the questions the interviewer might ask.

(C)

(6) Then practice answering the questions. (7) Get ready to talk about how you learn from your mistakes, solve problems, and working as part of a team.

10. Sentence 3: **Someone else chooses the questions you have to answer them.**

Which is the best way to write the underlined portion of this sentence? If the original is the best way, choose option (1).

(1)　questions you
(2)　questions, and you
(3)　questions, you
(4)　questions, or you
(5)　questions and you

11. Which revision would improve the effectiveness of the article?

(1)　remove sentence 2
(2)　move sentence 3 to follow sentence 5
(3)　combine paragraphs A and B
(4)　combine paragraphs B and C
(5)　remove sentence 6

12. Sentence 4: **No matter how stressed you feel it's better to prepare for the interview in advance.**

Which correction should be made to sentence 4?

(1)　insert a comma after feel
(2)　replace you with they
(3)　replace it's with its
(4)　insert a comma after interview
(5)　no correction is necessary

13. Sentence 7: **Get ready to talk about how you learn from your mistakes, solve problems, and working as part of a team.**

Which correction should be made to sentence 7?

(1)　remove the comma after mistakes
(2)　change solve to solving
(3)　insert a comma after and
(4)　change working to work
(5)　change team to Team

Questions 14 through 17 refer to the following information.

WHAT FACTORS INFLUENCE VOTER TURNOUT?

(A)

(1) Who wins in an election? (2) That depends on which voters show up to cast their votes in november. (3) As a result, many candidates and political organizations pay close attention to voter turnout.

(B)

(4) Some voters feel that their vote does not matter and so they are less likely to vote. (5) On the other hand, when voters feel a personal connection to a candidate, they are likely to vote. (6) Finally, many candidates would like to have more control over the factor of weather! (7) Bad weather tends to keep them away from the polls.

14. Sentence 2: **That depends on which voters show up to cast their votes in november.**

    Which correction should be made to sentence 2?

    (1) change depends to depended
    (2) change show to shows
    (3) replace their with they're
    (4) change november to November
    (5) no correction is necessary

15. Which sentence would be most effective if inserted at the beginning of paragraph B?

    (1) Voter turnout is influenced by many factors.
    (2) Weather most influences voter turnout.
    (3) Most people do not care about voting.
    (4) Candidates always want voters to turn out, no matter who they vote for.
    (5) Voters will turn out no matter who is running for office.

16. Sentence 4: **Some voters feel that their vote does not matter and so they are less likely to vote.**

    Which is the best way to write the underlined portion of this sentence? If the original is the best way, choose option (1).

    (1) matter and so they
    (2) matter, and so they
    (3) matter, so they
    (4) matter, they
    (5) matter and they

17. Sentence 7: **Bad weather tends to keep them away from the polls.**

    Which is the best way to write the underlined portion of this sentence? If the original is the best way, choose option (1).

    (1) them
    (2) they
    (3) us
    (4) candidates
    (5) voters

Questions 18 through 21 refer to the following memo.

To: Alexa Vargas, Operations Manager
From: Terence Urgan, Security Director
Re: Recommended Action Following Break-in

(A)

(1) The recent break-in at the Water Street warehouse shows our need to improve security. (2) Around a large area, our security guard must walk long distances, leaving the front entrance unattended. (3) The entrance faces a street with very little traffic during the night. (4)The doorway provides a burglar too much cover, and the front of the building was only partly lit.

(B)

(5) We can make the entrance more secure. (6) If we do this, we will not need to hire an additional guard. (7) Instead, I have asked a firm called Secure Construction to renovate the entrance and light the building front. (8) Mr. Torres Martin, an engineer in this firm, will be meeting with you and I next week.

18. Sentence 2: **Around a large area, our security guard must walk long distances, leaving the front entrance unattended.**

    Which is the best way to write the underlined portion of this sentence? If the original is the best way, choose option (1).

    (1) Around a large area, our security guard must walk long distances
    (2) Our security guard must walk long distances around a large area
    (3) Around a large area, our security guard walking long distances
    (4) Our security guard walking long distances around a large area
    (5) Around a large area, our security guard walked long distances

19. Sentence 4: **The doorway provides a burglar too much cover, and the front of the building was only partly lit.**

    Which correction should be made to sentence 4?

    (1) change provides to providing
    (2) remove the comma after cover
    (3) replace and with or
    (4) change was to were
    (5) change was to is

20. Sentences 5 and 6: **We can make the entrance more secure. If we do this, we will not need to hire an additional guard.**

    The most effective combination of sentences 5 and 6 would include which group of words?

    (1) When we need to hire an additional guard
    (2) the entrance being more secure if we
    (3) If we make the entrance more secure, we
    (4) Making the entrance more secure,
    (5) We will need to hire an additional guard

21. Sentence 8: **Mr. Torres Martin, an engineer in this firm, will be meeting with you and I next week.**

    Which correction should be made to sentence 8?

    (1) change engineer to Engineer
    (2) change firm to Firm
    (3) change will be to was
    (4) change I to me
    (5) no correction is necessary

Questions 22 through 25 refer to the following information.

HOW TO WRITE A PERFECT THANK YOU NOTE

(A)

(1) A thank you note is a simple, polite gesture that is too often forgotten. (2) A perfect thank you note shows that you truly enjoyed you're gift. (3) For example, when ten-year-old Jonah received movie coupons from his aunt, he wrote this charming note:

(B)

Dear Aunt Irene,

(4) Thank you for the movie coupons. (5) I took Jacob to the show last Sunday. (6) Him and I saw *Spiderwoman Lives.* (7) We had a blast, and we even got popcorn.

Love, Jonah

(C)

(8) Some people are embarrassed to send a thank you note if you feel too much time has slipped by. (9) However, sincere expressions of gratitude is never too late.

22. Sentence 2: **A perfect thank you note shows that you truly enjoyed you're gift.**

Which correction should be made to sentence 2?

(1) change shows to show
(2) replace you with they
(3) change enjoyed to enjoying
(4) replace you're with your
(5) no correction is necessary

23. Sentence 6: **Him and I saw *Spiderwoman Lives.***

Which correction should be made to sentence 6?

(1) change Him to He
(2) change Him and 1 to I and him
(3) change saw to seen
(4) change saw to seed
(5) change saw to sawed

24. Sentence 8: **Some people are embarrassed to send a thank you note if you feel too much time has slipped by.**

Which correction should be made to sentence 8?

(1) change are to is
(2) replace to with too
(3) replace you with they
(4) replace too with to
(5) replace by with bye

25. Sentence 9: **However, sincere expressions of gratitude is never too late.**

Which is the best way to write the underlined portion of this sentence? If the original is the best way, choose option (1).

(1) is
(2) are
(3) were
(4) was
(5) being

PART II

Essay Directions and Topic

In the box below, you will find a topic. Read the topic carefully; then write an essay based on it. Use the writing skills you have practiced throughout this book.

1. Begin with prewriting. Brainstorm, ask yourself questions, or use any other technique that helps you generate ideas.

2. Organize your ideas with an outline, idea map, or any other technique that works for you.

3. Write a draft of your essay on a separate piece of paper. Use every other line of your paper so that you will have room to revise and edit.

4. Review your essay to see how you can improve its organization and support. Then read it carefully for correct sentence structure, usage, spelling, capitalization, and punctuation. Use editing marks to revise and correct your essay. (Because this is a test essay, you won't have the time to write a final version.)

TOPIC

What is a problem in your community that you would like to solve?

In your essay, explain the problem and your solution. Use your personal observations, knowledge, and experience to support your answer.

Essay Evaluation

When you have finished writing your essay, review it based on the following questions. If possible, ask your instructor or another person to help you evaluate your writing.

☐ Does your essay address the topic completely? Did you stick to the topic throughout your essay?

☐ Is your essay organized into paragraphs, including an introduction, body paragraphs, and a conclusion?

☐ Does your essay contain interesting and relevant details, based on your personal observations, knowledge, and experiences?

☐ Is your essay generally correct, with few errors in sentence structure, usage, spelling, capitalization, and punctuation?

☐ Did you choose precise words that convey your meaning, avoiding slang and other informal expressions?

Posttest Evaluation Chart

The chart below will help you determine your strengths and weaknesses in writing skills.

Directions

Check your answers on pages 256–257. On the chart below, circle the number of each question you answered correctly on the Posttest. Count the number of questions you answered correctly in each row. Write the number in the Total Correct space in each row. (For example, in the Usage row, write the number correct in the blank before *out of 8*.) Complete this process for the remaining rows. Then add the four totals to get your total correct for the Posttest.

Skill Area	Questions	Total Correct	Pages
Usage	1, 5, 17, 19, 21, 23, 24, 25	_____ out of 8	20, 64–65, 152–156, 161–167
Sentence Structure	3, 6, 10, 13, 16, 18, 20	_____ out of 7	19, 32–35, 49, 138–139, 168–180, 182–183
Mechanics	4, 7, 8, 12, 14, 22	_____ out of 6	97–99, 125–127, 154, 185–189, 191–194
Paragraph Organization	2, 9, 11, 15	_____ out of 4	198–199, 200–201, 202–207

Total Correct for Posttest _____ out of 25

• If you answered fewer than 20 questions correctly, determine which of the skill areas you need to study further. Page numbers to refer to for practice are given in the right-hand column above.

• If you answered 20 or more questions correctly and wrote an effective essay, your teacher may decide that you are ready to go on to Steck-Vaughn's *GED Writing* book.

PRETEST

1. **E** <u>days?</u>
Use a question mark at the end of a question.

2. **E** <u>actors, athletes, or singers</u>
Use commas to separate items in a list.

3. **C**

4. **E** <u>National Football League</u>
Capitalize all elements in a proper noun.

5. **E** <u>October 27, 2002</u>
Use a comma between the day and year in a date.

6. **E** <u>heroes, but</u>
Use a comma in a compound sentence.

7. **C**

8. **E** <u>day and</u>
Do not use a comma between verbs in a compound predicate.

9. **E** <u>March</u>
Capitalize months.

10. **C**

11. **E** <u>aunt</u>
Do not capitalize a family title when it is used without a name.

12. **E** <u>Smith and</u>
Do not use a comma between subjects in a compound subject.

13. **parents**
Use the plural form of the noun.

14. **expert's**
Use an apostrophe to show ownership (the advice of one expert).

15. **children**
Use the plural form of the noun.

16. **lives**
Use the plural form of the noun. Drop the *fe* and add *ves* when a word ends in *fe*.

17. **family's**
Use an apostrophe to show ownership (the rules of one family).

18. **friend's**
Use an apostrophe to show ownership (the house of a friend).

19. **know**
Know means to have knowledge of; *no* is a negative.

20. **break**
Break means to split apart; *brake* means to stop.

21. **pieces**
Pieces means little bits; *peace* means a time without conflict.

22. **weight**
Weight means a heaviness; *wait* means to remain in a place.

23. **hole**
Hole means a space or cavity; *whole* means the complete thing.

24. **they're**
They're is the contraction for *they are*; *their* is the possessive pronoun meaning *belonging to them*.

25. **it's**
It's is the contraction for *it is*; *its* is the possessive pronoun meaning *belonging to it*.

26. **can't**
Can't is the correct spelling of the contraction for *cannot*.

27. **through**
Through means going in and out of; *threw* is the past tense of *throw*.

28. **your**
Use a possessive pronoun before a gerund (a verb form ending in -*ing* that acts as a noun).

29. **me**
Use the object pronoun *me* after the preposition *to*.

30. **C**

31. **her**
Use a singular feminine pronoun to match the antecedent *woman*.

32. **he**
Use a subject pronoun as the subject of a sentence.

33. **them** or **Jean** or **Paula**
Use a plural pronoun to match the two antecedents connected with *and,* or pick one of the antecedents and use it in place of the pronoun.

34. **well**
Use an adverb to describe the verb *live.*

35. **worse**
Use the comparative form to compare two things.

36. **slowly**
Use an adverb to describe the verb *recover.* Do not use both *more* and the comparative *-er* form of a word together.

37. **sooner**
Use the comparative form to compare two things.

38. **most difficult**
Use the superlative form to compare three or more things. Use *most,* not *-est,* with long words.

PAGE 6

39. **was**
Use the past tense to show that the action happened in the past.

40. **went**
Use the correct irregular past tense form of the verb *go.*

41. **brought**
Use the correct irregular past tense form of the verb *bring.*

42. **learn**
Use the present tense to show that the action is happening today.

43. **will not be**
Use the future tense to show that the action will happen in the future.

44. **agree**
Use the verb form that agrees with the plural subject *supervisors.*

45. **are**
Use the verb form that agrees with the plural subject *reasons.*

46. **have**
Use the verb form that agrees with the compound subject *Ms. Gomez and her staff.*

47. **believes**
Use the verb form that agrees with the singular subject *each.*

PAGE 7

48. **F** The verb is missing.
49. **S** The thought is complete.
50. **RO** Two complete thoughts run together without correct punctuation or a connecting word.
51. **F** The subject is missing.
52. **RO** Two complete thoughts run together without correct punctuation or a connecting word.
53. **F** The thought is incomplete.
54. The sun dries out your skin, **and** it affects the growth of skin cells.
55. The sun feels good, **but** it's not good for you.
56. You should see your doctor **if** a mole changes shape or color.
57. **Because** moles can be cancerous, it is a good idea to pay attention to changes.

PAGE 8

58. **to understand**
Use a verb phrase beginning with *to* in order to have parallel structure with *to cut back* and *to have.*

59. **you can more easily**
Supply the subject *you* that is being modified by the phrase at the beginning.

60. **today's world**
Use a few, concise words to express a thought; avoid repetition of ideas.

61. **(2) after sentence 2**
The idea of thinking about world affairs logically follows the idea of thinking about domestic issues.

62. **(1) Once you have developed your own opinions, it's time to identify a candidate who most closely represents your point of view.** This sentence is a good topic sentence for the paragraph because it states the main point of the paragraph.

63. **(1) sentence 6** This idea is irrelevant; it does not support the main idea.

UNIT 1: CREATIVE AND ESSAY WRITING

LESSON 1

PAGE 15, PRACTICE

1. a. 3
   b. 4
   c. 5
   d. 1
   e. 2
2. a. 5
   b. 1
   c. 4
   d. 3
   e. 2

PAGE 15, WRITE

Revise and edit your paragraph. Use the checklist on page 216. Be sure that the order of events makes sense. Write a final draft. Share your paragraph with a partner.

PAGE 16, PRACTICE

1. c
2. e
3. a
4. d
5. b

PAGE 17, WRITE A

1. Sample paragraph:

   Carlos came to the United States to improve his life, but he never dreamed he would become such a success. He immigrated to New York City in 1995. He was 25 years old. After working for two years as a chef's assistant, he decided to go to school to learn to become a chef. When he got his degree, he found a great job in New Orleans, Louisiana. Now he is a chef at a five-star restaurant!

2. Sample paragraph:

   Patricia has learned that hard times can make you stronger. Last year, she lost her job because her company went bankrupt. Then her husband, Jon, had a stroke. Patricia had to get a new job and take care of Jon and the children. The stress was almost too much. But now Patricia realizes that the stress had one benefit. She has learned that she can do much more than she ever imagined she could.

PAGE 17, WRITE B

Revise and edit your personal narrative. Use the checklist on page 216. Be sure you support your topic sentence with details that answer questions such as *What happened?* and *Where?* Write a final draft. Share your paragraph with a partner.

PAGE 18, LANGUAGE EXERCISE

1. My niece Alicia plans to be a track star.
2. She runs and exercises every day.
3. Her father trains and coaches her for track meets.
4. My sister and I attend and give our support.
5. Alicia runs for the high school track team.
6. The team won a meet against the state champs last week.
7. My niece completed in three events.
8. She got first place in two events.

PAGE 19, LANGUAGE EXERCISE A

1. **S**
2. **F** The sentence needs a subject.
3. **F** The sentence needs a completed thought.
4. **F** The sentence needs a subject and a predicate.
5. **S**

PAGE 19, LANGUAGE EXERCISE B

1. subject and predicate
2. predicate
3. predicate
4. subject

Sample answers:

2. The host and hostess asked us to hide from Li Ling in the living room.
3. At seven o'clock, Li Ling surprised the guests by coming in the back door.
4. The look on the host's face was the funniest thing ever.

PAGE 20, LANGUAGE EXERCISE A

1. **he, her** (*Sam* is the subject; *Alice* is the object.)
2. **He, their** (*Paolo* is the subject; *Sam* and *Alice's* are possessive nouns.)
3. **them** (*Sally, Keisha,* and *Corinne* are objects of the preposition *to*.)
4. **him** (*Diego* is the object of the preposition *to*.)
5. **They** (*Sam* and *Alice* are subjects.)

PAGE 20, LANGUAGE EXERCISE B

1. **me** (*Me* is the object of the preposition to.)
2. **We** (*We* is the subject.)
3. **mine** (*Mine* is a possessive pronoun telling whose bedroom.)
4. **us** (*Us* is the object of the preposition *to*.)
5. **I** (*I* is the subject.)
6. **we** (*We* is the subject.)
7. **Our** (*Our* is a possessive pronoun telling whose goal.)

PAGE 21, PRACTICE A

1. **I** (*I* is the subject.)
2. **my** (*My* is a possessive pronoun.)
3. **my** (*My* is a possessive pronoun.)
4. **me** (*Me* is the object of *telling*.)
5. **I** (*I* tells who the proud father is.)

PAGE 21, PRACTICE B

Ray left in September for overseas duty knowing that **his** wife was going to have twins. Imagine **his** surprise when the telegram came telling **him** that **he** was the proud father of triplets!

PAGE 21, WRITE

Revise and edit your paragraph. Use the checklist on page 216. Be sure that your pronouns show the correct point of view. Write a final draft. Share your paragraph with a partner.

LESSON 2

PAGE 27, PRACTICE A

Sample answers:

2. My birthday cake had pink icing.
3. The old oak tree was over sixty feet tall.
4. A stooped-over man wobbled down the street with a cane in his hand.

PAGE 27, PRACTICE B

1. d
2. b
3. c
4. a
5. f
6. e

PAGE 27, WRITE

Revise and edit your paragraph. Use the checklist on page 216. Be sure you include descriptive details and precise words. Write a final draft. Share your paragraph with a partner.

PAGE 28, PRACTICE A

1. sight
2. touch
3. hearing
4. smell
5. taste

PAGE 28, PRACTICE B

Sample answers:

1. The blazing red sun sunk slowly behind the jagged trees.
2. The rhythms of beating drums came from the open window at the factory.
3. The smell of my newly powdered baby is like perfume to me.
4. My hamburgers are always spicy because I add extra onions and hot mustard.
5. Her handshake was sweaty and cold.

PAGE 28, WRITE

Revise and edit your descriptive paragraph. Use the checklist on page 216. Be sure you include sensory details. Write a final draft. Share your paragraph with a partner.

PAGE 29, PRACTICE

Sample answers:

2. Scott has hair that is softer than a kitten's fur.
3. The wind howled like a mad dog all night long.
4. The ice cold lemonade was the perfect drink for a hot summer day.
5. The smell of her perfume came through the door ten minutes before she did.

PAGE 29, WRITE

Revise and edit your descriptive paragraph. Use the checklist on page 216. Be sure you include sensory details and figurative language. Write a final draft. Share your paragraph with a partner.

PAGE 30, LANGUAGE EXERCISE

1. fine

2. fresh
3. brightly
4. beautifully
5. regularly

PAGE 31, LANGUAGE EXERCISE

1. hottest
2. new *or* newest
3. more quickly
4. most important
5. easy

PAGE 33, LANGUAGE EXERCISE A

1. The skies opened up, **and** lightning streaked across the clouds.
2. Last year we had floods, **but** this year was not as bad.
3. The storm caused severe damage, **and** several people were injured.
4. Windows were shattered by the wind, **so** we went into the basement.
5. We read books, **or** sometimes we played cards.

PAGE 33, LANGUAGE EXERCISE B

Sample answers:

2. The street was deserted, **and** the stores were closed.
3. The couch was new, **so** we tried not to get it dirty.
4. The soldiers marched bravely, **but** their mission failed.
5. The sky looked threatening, **so** we left the beach early.
6. The fruit was ripe, **so** we picked as much as we could.
7. I should get gas soon, **or** I will run out.
8. We could see this movie, **or** we could see a different one.

PAGE 34, LANGUAGE EXERCISE

Sample answers:

2. **When** you drive on the Blue Ridge Parkway, you can stop at many overlooks.

3. Most people stop at Mt. Mitchell **because** that's the most spectacular view of all.
4. **Although** you'll want to take pictures**,** it's hard to get those mountain ranges on film.
5. Stay on the parkway **until** you reach the city of Asheville.

PAGE 35, LANGUAGE EXERCISE

1. The bus driver signaled, turned into the traffic, and slowly made her way along the street.
2. Jose's car has a sun roof, bucket seats, and chrome trim.
3. The sofa cushions were old, plaid, and worn-out.

LESSON 3

PAGE 41, PRACTICE

Sample answers:
2. Then; Later,
3. As a result
4. In addition; Also
5. However
6. Therefore
7. As a result

PAGE 42, PRACTICE

There are many ways to make this paragraph flow more smoothly. Here is one example:

People who win big prizes in the lottery often find that the money does not make them happy. First, they have to deal with many people trying to get a piece of the pie. In addition, winners find that their friends expect them to hand over some of the winnings. Therefore, they have to be on guard all the time. After a while, lottery winners find that they cannot trust anyone. All this pressure takes the fun out of winning. They can no longer relax and enjoy life. Still, I am willing to give it a try!

PAGE 42, WRITE

Revise and edit your expository paragraph. Use the checklist on page 216. Be sure you use connecting words and phrases to link your ideas. Write a final draft. Share your paragraph with a partner.

PAGE 43, PRACTICE

Sample answers:
1. maroon, scarlet, wine, ruby, crimson, cherry, rose, flame, communist
2. succeed, master, conquer, overcome, earn, gain, attain
3. stroll, amble, trek, march, hike, saunter
4. cash, funds, coins, bucks, riches, income, bills

PAGE 43, WRITE

Revise and edit your expository paragraph. Use the checklist on page 216. Be sure you use synonyms for the word *money*. Write a final draft. Share your paragraph with a partner.

PAGE 44, PRACTICE A

1. neat
2. racket
3. mansion
4. decrease
5. gentle
6. scorn

PAGE 44, PRACTICE B

1. (A)
2. (C)
3. (B)
4. (A)
5. (C)

PAGE 44, WRITE

Revise and edit your expository paragraph. Use the checklist on page 216. Be sure you use synonyms for the word *laugh* and include details to help a reader picture and hear someone laugh in various ways. Write a final draft. Share your paragraph with a partner.

PAGE 45, PRACTICE

Sample answers:

1. I like to read forecasts of the future, but **I** have to wonder if any of them are true.
2. When people are treated with respect at work, **they** feel better about their work.
3. Correct.
4. When **you** look for a loan, you find who has the best rate. *or* When one looks for a loan, **one** finds who has the best rate.

PAGE 45, WRITE

Revise and edit your expository paragraph. Use the checklist on page 216. Be sure you give examples of happiness and use the same point of view throughout the paragraph. Write a final draft. Share your paragraph with a partner.

PAGE 46, PRACTICE

1. **(1)** The word *backgrounds* was misspelled without the letter *g*.
2. **(3)** The word *they*, the first word in the sentence, was not capitalized.
3. **(3)** The word *language* was misspelled; the letters *a* and *u* were switched.

PAGE 47, LANGUAGE EXERCISE A

1. **passive** (action done to the subject, *pill*)
2. **active** (action done by the subject, *We*)
3. **active** (action done by the subject, *I*)
4. **passive** (action done to the subject, *New York*)

PAGE 47, LANGUAGE EXERCISE B

1. 1
2. 3
3. 2
4. 3

PAGE 48, LANGUAGE EXERCISE A

1. With great force, the thief broke the lock. (The subject, *thief*, did the action, *broke*.)
2. The crew of *Apollo 11* landed on the moon. (The subject, *crew*, did the action, *landed*.)
3. They left a plaque on the moon. (The subject, *they*, did the action, *left*.)

PAGE 48, LANGUAGE EXERCISE B

1. (B)
2. (A)
3. (A)

PAGE 49, LANGUAGE EXERCISE

Sample answers:

1. He drove a taxi and also worked as a gardener.
2. Today, many people do not vote.
3. The large dog growled at anyone who walked by the yard.
4. Sam quit his job because it took too long to get to work.
5. In the distance, we could see the small ships.
6. Modern cars can be driven faster than older cars.
7. I asked the speaker to repeat what he had said.

PAGE 50, LANGUAGE EXERCISE

1. **Because** the subway is more crowded, I prefer the bus.
2. You **may be able to** get a ticket if you are willing to wait in line.
3. The reason I am late is **that** my car broke down.
4. The **minister says** that new families are always welcome.
5. This boy's parents are **getting ready** to take him to the doctor.
6. We **shouldn't** lose these insurance papers.

PAGE 51, LANGUAGE EXERCISE A

Sample answers:

1. out of money
2. made little progress
3. enthusiastic about
4. insulted

PAGE 51, LANGUAGE EXERCISE B

Sample answer:

You **made me angry** when you accused me of taking the **stolen** tools. I'm not the one who **took** them. **Alvin says** they disappeared **at the same** time Annette quit. You've been treating me **badly** all week, and the reason is **that** you don't trust me. Try to believe what I tell you, or **I will resign from this job.**

LESSON 4

PAGE 57, PRACTICE

1. Therefore
2. so
3. For example
4. In addition
5. so

PAGE 57, WRITE

Revise and edit your persuasive letter. Use the checklist on page 216. Be sure you use connecting words to make your points easier to follow. Write a final draft. Share your letter with a partner.

PAGE 58, PRACTICE A

1. **contrast** (shows the difference between people who walk and people who drive to work)
2. **compare** (shows one way that peanuts and ice cream are the same)
3. **contrast** (tells one way Japan is different from France)
4. **contrast** (tells one way Lake Superior is different from the other Great Lakes)

PAGE 58, PRACTICE B

Sample answers:

2. The movie told the ending in the first scene, in contrast to the movie I saw last week.
3. I like his acting as much as his singing.

PAGE 59, WRITE

Sample answers:

1. compare: Marie is like Helen because they both enjoy watching movies, dancing, and bowling.
   contrast: Unlike Helen, Marie does not like jogging.
2. compare: My apartment and my sister's apartment are both cold in the winter and hot in the summer.
   contrast: My apartment is much smaller than my sister's, and I can clean it in one hour.

PAGE 60, PRACTICE

Sample answers:

2. My leg was broken in the crash.
3. Mr. Mori drives a moving van from 4:00 P.M. until 8:00 P.M.
4. The shop steward stormed to the boss' office for an answer.
5. They were gobbling candy in the next row and grunting like pigs.

PAGE 61, PRACTICE A

1. through thick and thin
2. as American as Mom's apple pie
3. selling like hotcakes
4. tried and true
5. raining cats and dogs
6. sick and tired
7. as hard as nails
8. take the bull by the horns

PAGE 61, PRACTICE B

Sample answers:

1. I've had both good and bad experiences today.
2. "Now it's time to suffer the results of our actions," the congressman said.
3. If you eat well, get enough rest, and have a good outlook, you will live a long life.
4. A summer cold is horrible.

Answers and Explanations

PAGE 61, WRITE

Revise and edit your persuasive paragraph. Use the checklist on page 216. Be sure you support your belief with reasons and examples. Also be sure you use specific and fresh language. Write a final draft. Share your paragraph with a partner.

PAGE 62, PRACTICE

1. F
2. O
3. O
4. O
5. F
6. F

PAGE 63, PRACTICE

1. (A)
2. (B)
3. (C)
4. (C)

PAGE 64, LANGUAGE EXERCISE A

1. hope
2. take
3. has
4. works

PAGE 64, LANGUAGE EXERCISE B

1. A salad ~~with extra carrots~~ (is) my usual lunch.
2. The people ~~at the back of the crowd~~ (need) to be heard.
3. Ned, ~~with his three dogs,~~ (runs) around the block after work.
4. The leader ~~of the union~~ (says) dues will go up.

PAGE 65, LANGUAGE EXERCISE A

1. **leak** (plural subject with *and*)
2. **gives** (singular subject with *or*)
3. **bring** (plural subject with *and*)

PAGE 65, LANGUAGE EXERCISE B

1. C
2. C
3. loves
4. takes

LESSON 5

PAGE 71, PRACTICE

Sample answers:
1. Sports Topic 1: How to Play Soccer; Topic 2: Keeping Score in Bowling
2. Jobs Topic 1: My Dream Job; Topic 2: Good Bosses and Bad Bosses
3. Movies Topic 1: My Favorite Movie of All Time; Topic 2: My Favorite Movie Character
4. Animals Topic 1: Adopt an Animal; Topic 2: Hunting Should Be Outlawed

PAGE 72, PRACTICE

Advantages of a Large Family: never lonely, learn to get along with others, support one another
Sample outline:
Topic: Advantages of a Large Family
  I. Never lonely
    A. When young you have someone to play with
    B. When older you have someone to go out with
  II. Learn to get along with others
    A. Learn to share
    B. Learn to solve arguments
    C. Learn to compromise
  III. Support one another
    A. Have people to call on when you need help
    B. Have people to borrow money from
    C. Have people to talk to about your problems

236
ANSWERS AND EXPLANATIONS

Sample idea map:

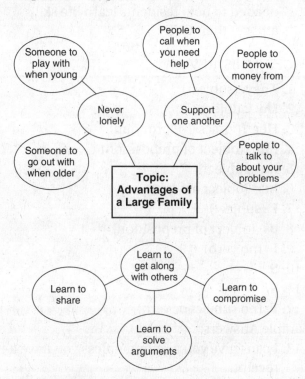

PAGE 74, PRACTICE

1. **A**
   Sentence A is the best opening statement. Sentence B is not clear about which view the writer is taking. Sentence C is too general.
2. **A**
   Sentence A is the best opening statement. It makes a strong statement about the main idea. Both Sentences B and C are vague statements that do not clearly support the topic.
3. **B**
   Sentence B is the best opening statement. It clearly introduces the author's topic. Sentence A does not clearly support the topic. Sentence C is a supporting detail.

PAGE 75, PRACTICE

You should have checked 1, 3, 4, and 6.

PAGE 75, WRITE

Revise and edit your paragraph. Use the checklist on page 216. Be sure you write a topic sentence that states the main idea of your paragraph. Also be sure to include details that support your topic sentence. Write a final draft. Share your paragraph with a partner.

PAGE 76 PRACTICE A

Paragraph 1: 2, 1, 4, 3, 5
Paragraph 2: 4, 5, 1, 3, 2 *or* 3, 2, 1, 5, 4

PAGE 76, PRACTICE B

Paragraph 1: time order
Paragraph 2: facts/reasons, cause/effect

PAGE 76, WRITE

Sample paragraphs:
1.   Morning people and night people are very different. Morning people wake up with the sun, smile, and start talking. When night people have to get up early, they grumble and refuse to talk. Night people come alive at the end of the day. They are ready to party just as morning people are about to turn in for the night. **(organization: compare/contrast)**
2.   Learning to organize your time will change your life. You can begin by writing down how you spend every hour of the day. Do this for one week and you will begin to see where your time is going. Next, make a list of the time wasters you can avoid. Then figure out how much time you have left for the things you have been putting off. **(organization: time order)**
3.   Friendship is one of the most important things in life. If you know how to be a good friend, then you know how to be loyal. Friendship also teaches you how to keep secrets and how to make sacrifices for someone else. Friendship is supposed to be a two-way street. If this is true, then all the good you give will come back to you. **(organization: facts/reasons)**

PAGE 79, PRACTICE A

Here are some changes that would improve this paragraph. Did you make at least three changes?

1. Revise the first sentence, which is too broad. A good revision could read, "Kingston Heritage Chorus goes on a rehearsal retreat every spring."
2. Delete the fifth sentence. The concert outfits are not related to the topic here.
3. Begin a new paragraph with the sentence "Organizing the retreat is a big job."
4. Move the sentence "The Retreat Coordinator needs a committee of at least six people" to follow the sentence "Organizing the retreat is a big job."

PAGE 79, WRITE

Did you use the Revising Checklist on page 78 to improve your essay? Read your essay again and decide whether it is improved.

PAGE 80, PRACTICE A

I can achieve success and improve my reading by making some easy changes in my daily life. Reading is essential to success. At first, I thought it might be hard to become a better reader, but after careful thought, I realized it doesn't have to be.

PAGE 83, WRITING AT WORK

1. (3)
2. (2)
3. Explanation:
   Both Paragraphs 1 and 3 offer specific examples. Paragraph 1 talks about shelter, food, and clothing. Paragraph 3 talks about specific items that donations were used to purchase: toys; cribs; transportation services; washer and dryer. While Paragraph 2 talks about two specific programs Judy's House would like to start, it does not offer any specific supporting details to describe the programs.

Sample sentences:

Sentence 1: A counseling program is needed to help residents understand and deal with chemical dependency and mental health.

Sentence 2: An educational program is needed to help residents learn life skills and get their GEDs.

PAGES 84–85, REVIEW

1. **They** (subject)
2. **He** (subject)
3. **Her** (possessive pronoun)
4. **him** (object of preposition)
5. **he** (subject)
6. **her** (object of verb)
7. **I** (subject)
8. **us** (object of preposition)
9. **F** (no verb)
10. **S**
11. **S**
12. **F** (no subject or verb)

Sample Answers:

13. I can't give you a refund **unless** you have a receipt.
14. **Although** they had never been friends, Rudy and Ana went on a date.
15. **When** he was finished with the application, Carlos gave the file to Ms. Webb.
16. You are ready for this test **because** you have studied so hard.
17. She read his resume and liked it. It was neat and well organized.
18. Ms. Golov offered George a job, **but** he would have to work Saturdays.
19. The job pays well, **and** the company also offers good benefits.
20. He likes the company, **so** he'll probably take the job.
21. **fastest** (compares three or more)
22. **well** (no comparison; adverb describes the verb)
23. **harder** (compares two people)
24. **help** (compound subject connected by *and*)
25. **is** (singular subject)
26. **cost** (plural subject); costs (singular subject)

Revise and edit your essay. Use the checklist on page 216. Be sure you use connecting words to make your points easier to follow. Write your final draft. Share your essay with a partner.

PAGES 86–87, MINITEST

1. **(5) are** *(Revision: Usage: Subject-Verb Agreement)* The plural pronoun *We* is the subject, so the verb must agree with it. Since the entire letter is in the present, the verb must be in the present tense.
2. **(3) insert <u>and</u> before <u>we</u>** *(Correction: Sentence Structure: Comma Splice)* By adding a coordinating conjunction, you correct the comma splice.
3. **(2) meal, Hammond's** *(Revision: Sentence Structure: Fragment)* Sentence 4 is a fragment. It needs to be attached to Sentence 5.
4. **(1) replace <u>They</u> with <u>We</u>** *(Correction: Usage: Pronouns)* The letter is written with the first-person plural pronouns, *we* and *us*.
5. **(3) store, and you** *(Revision: Sentence Structure: Run-on Sentence)* This run-on can be made into a correct compound sentence with a comma and coordinating conjunction.
6. **(3) insert a comma after <u>frame</u>** *(Correction: Mechanics: Punctuation)* This compound sentence begins with a dependent clause, so a comma is needed after it.
7. **(1) Now a medical research study has found a surprising new use for duct tape.** *(Construction Shift: Organization: Topic Sentence)* This topic sentence helps the reader understand what the new paragraph is about. It states the topic and the main point about the topic.
8. **(3) remove sentence 7** *(Construction Shift: Organization: Irrelevant Detail)* This sentence does not relate to the overall topic of the paragraph.

UNIT 2: PERSONAL AND WORKPLACE WRITING

LESSON 6

PAGE 90, WRITE
Sample answer:

> 111 West Street
> Chicago, IL 60606
> February 1, 2003

Dear Aaron,

How are you? I've been thinking about you lately and wondering when you might be able to come for a visit. It's only a two-hour ride by train, and I could meet you at the station. I'm free almost every weekend. Just let me know in advance so I can plan some interesting things for us to do.

I hope to hear from you soon.

> Sincerely,
>
> Sandra

PAGE 91, WRITE
Sample answer:

> 201 Lowell Avenue
> Overland Park, MA 02110
> October 10, 2003

Ms. Joyce Hawkins
Overland Medical Center
39000 South Oak Drive
Overland Park, MA 02115

Dear Ms. Hawkins:

I received your letter and description about the winter training program at Overland Medical Center. Thank you for getting in touch with me.

A copy of my resume is enclosed. As you can see, I worked as a clerk/typist at the Lenox Hill Hospital for the past two summers. Working at the hospital helped me decide that I want to pursue a career in the health field. I believe your program offers the kind of training I need to achieve my goal of becoming a medical professional.

I am pleased that you are considering me for entry into the program. If there is anything else I can do, please let me know.

> Sincerely,
>
> *Antonio Torres*
>
> Antonio Torres

PAGE 92, PRACTICE

Sample answers:

1. Dear Kareem,

I've been calling you but haven't gotten an answer. Do you think you could help me move my grandmother's sofa this weekend? She's willing to pay us. Give me a call when you get the chance.

2. Dear Ms. Bowman:

I belong to a community group that is holding a jobfest for young people on Saturday, August 21. We are seeking the help of local business people who are willing to share their expert knowledge and experience. We would be extremely pleased if you could find time in your busy schedule to speak to the group on the topic of "Success in Your Career."

PAGE 93, PRACTICE

> P. O. Box 32
> Eden Prairie, MN 55344
> October 20, 2003

Dear Aunt Frances,

Thanks for the beautiful sweaters! It gets really cold up here this time of year, so your timing was perfect. After living in Florida for so long, I had forgotten what cold weather feels like.

Give my love to Uncle Harold. Tell him I'll visit soon.

> Your nephew,
> Danny

PAGE 94, PRACTICE

> 222 East 24th St.
> Philadelphia, PA 19135
> June 14, 2003

Mr. Bernard Adams
Travelworld
901 Harrison Avenue
Philadelphia, PA 19139

Dear Mr. Adams:

Thank you for talking to me about the position in your word processing unit. I know my skills would fit your needs. Our meeting made me eager to work at Travelworld.

I look forward to hearing from you about the job.

> Sincerely,
> *Elaine Evans*

PAGE 96, WRITE

Sample answer:

It was a pleasure meeting you during my interview at the day care center last week. Thank you for considering me for the position of administrative assistant.

Below are the names, addresses, and telephone numbers of two people you can contact for references:

1. Mr. Henry Banks, 1800 Doheny Drive, Los Angeles, CA 90003 (212-555-7390)
2. Mrs. Mary Kirby, 1600 Maple Avenue, Long Beach, CA 90821 (212-555-0079)

Mr. Banks was my basketball coach, and Mrs. Kirby is a family friend.

I look forward to hearing from you, and I hope your decision will be positive.

PAGE 98, LANGUAGE EXERCISE A

1. Last year I worked on **Senator Smith's** campaign.
2. The campaign office was on **Fifth Avenue** in the **Chrysler Building**.
3. A debate was sponsored by a group called **Independent Voters of America** at their building on the **Hudson River**.

4. Laura Washington, vice president of the organization, made a speech.

PAGE 98, LANGUAGE EXERCISE B

may 20, 2003

supreme computer, inc.
958 alexander street
river tower
Columbus, oh 43221

dear mr. Potter:

my supervisor, doris healy, director of sales here at bradley associates, asked me to send you the enclosed brochure detailing the services our company provides to computer stores like yours. If interested, you can take advantage of our free trial offer by calling before may 31. We are closed next Monday because of memorial day.

Sincerely,

James Hobson

james hobson
sales assistant

PAGE 99, LANGUAGE EXERCISE C

1670 Evergreen Road
Houston, TX 77023
January 25, 2003

Ms. Vanessa Lewis
Lewis and Evans Assoc.
Houston, TX 77025

Dear Ms. Lewis:

I attended your career planning workshop at the Valley College Library on December 15, 2002. Your presentation was just what I needed to organize myself. Would it be possible for you to send me copies of your resume-writing guidelines, the worksheet, and the sample?

Unfortunately, you ran out of these three handouts before you got to me.

Sincerely,

Joseph Wallach

Joseph Wallach

LESSON 7

PAGE 104, PRACTICE

Objective, Work Experience, Education, Skills, References

PAGES 107–109, WRITE

Your personal data sheet should include the information requested. Share it with your instructor or a friend who can review it with you.

PAGE 111, LANGUAGE EXERCISE A

1. Typed
2. Handled
3. Completed
4. Operated

PAGE 112, LANGUAGE EXERCISE B

Sample answers:
2. Created signs for window displays
3. Scheduled coverage for reception desk
4. Managed newsstand in owner's absence
5. Won awards for running track

PAGE 112, LANGUAGE EXERCISE C

Share your lists with your instructor or a partner who can evaluate your use of action verbs and phrases.

LESSON 8

PAGE 118, WRITE

Forms like the W-4 should be filled out completely and accurately because incorrect information can cause errors in an employee's records. Such errors can cost both time and money.

PAGE 119, PRACTICE

2. 111 E. Main St., Jonesville, IL 60623
3. 12 imprinted binders
4. October 1, 2003
5. No, he put it on his account.
6. $38.00

PAGE 120, WRITE

INVOICE	**TAYLOR HARDWARE**		INVOICE NO. 7602

SOLD TO	Anne Johnson	SHIP TO	same
ADDRESS	21 Ford Avenue	ADDRESS	same
CITY, STATE, ZIP	Detroit, MI 48011	CITY, STATE, ZIP	same

ORDER NO. 6626	SOLD BY M. Jones	TERMS 30 days	DATE 10-3-03

ORDERED	SHIPPED	DESCRIPTION	PRICE	UNITS	AMOUNT
10-3	10-8	wood paneling, pine	30.00	8	240.00
10-3	10-8	3" wood nails, pkg.	5.00	1	5.00
10-3	10-8	decorative mirror	75.00	1	75.00
				TAX	16.00
				TOTAL	336.00

PAGE 121, PRACTICE

1. a letter
2. Ben Martinez of Martinez, Inc.
3. Glenn Bono, 21 N. Main St., Austin, TX 78755
4. Sender

PAGE 122, PRACTICE

1. when Jim Cowens called, why he won't be in, and what his telephone number is
2. First, Terry should explain that Jim won't be in. Then it makes sense to say "Call Jim Cowens."

PAGE 123, WRITE A

FAX TRANSMITTAL SHEET			
TO: Abdel Tahiri		FROM: John Mandel	
COMPANY: Tahiri Retail		DATE: 12-5-03	
FAX NUMBER: 847-555-1212		PHONE NUMBER: 847-555-3311	
CONTENTS: Parts information		TOTAL NUMBER OF PAGES INCLUDING COVER: 5	
NOTE: The items you ordered last week are now in stock. Please call to tell us when you would like them delivered.			

PAGE 123, WRITE B

Sample email message:

TO: Mcox   SUBJECT: Meeting

Dear Marty:
Alicia Stoppen is holding a meeting on Monday, October 1 from 9–10 a.m. She would like you and your team to attend. We'll meet in the conference room. If anyone has any questions, please call me at ext. 7224.
Thanks,
(your name here)

PAGE 124, PRACTICE

1. vacation requests
2. Beverly Smith
3. all employees
4. A more thorough message would have included how to request vacation time.

PAGE 124, WRITE

Sample answer:
Date: 09/22/02
To: Art Balsam, Supervisor
From: (your name)
Subject: Time Off Request

I would like to leave work at 4:00 P.M. on September 27 for a doctor's appointment. I can work an extra hour any day this week to make up the lost time. Please let me know if this is OK. Thank you.

PAGE 125, LANGUAGE EXERCISE

2. wharves
3. men
4. attorneys

5. secretaries
6. women
7. teeth

PAGE 126, LANGUAGE EXERCISE

2. children's
3. friends'
4. company's
5. boss'
6. Amos'
7. everyone's
8. workers'
9. players'
10. Women's
11. Jacksons'
12. machines'

PAGE 127, LANGUAGE EXERCISE

1. I've
2. didn't
3. There's
4. wasn't
5. weren't
6. won't
7. Let's
8. didn't

PAGES 128–129, COMPLETE A FORM

Part 1.   (the date)   584-906-792
    (your name)   313-555-0795
    ABC Supplies
    100 Hudson St.
    Detroit   MI 48255

Part 2.   AC-34

Part 3.   Mary Money   216-555-4875
    Adams Company
    1421 Wilson
    Cleveland   OH 44101

Part 4a.   [X] FedEx Priority Overnight

Part 5.   [X] FedEx Letter

Part 6.   [X] No

Part 7.   [X] Sender
    ___1___ Total Packages
    _8 oz_ Total Weight

PAGES 130–131, WRITE A MEMO

Sample memo:

Date: (today's date)
To: All Cashiers
From: (your name)
Subject: Customer Service Workshop

I have been noticing that some of our cashiers are not following basic store policies about how to act with customers. For example, some cashiers don't smile and greet the customer. Others don't count back change. Some even make the customers bag their own food.

Customer service is essential to our store's success. For that reason, a refresher workshop in customer service will be held in the staff break room on Wednesday, May 9, at 8:00 A.M. before the store opens. All checkout cashiers are required to attend. If you cannot, please let me know, and we will schedule a second workshop. Thank you.

LESSON 9

PAGE 133, PRACTICE

First, go north to the corner. **Second,** turn right at the food store. Look for the sign for Smith Street. **When** you see the sign, walk a block more. **Then** turn left. **Last,** stop at the dress shop. Our apartment is on the second floor.

PAGE 133, WRITE

Sample answer:

First, walk one block to Price Street. When you pass the gas station, turn left. Next, turn right at the train tracks. After you see the post office, pass the bank and walk four more blocks. The grocery store will be on the northwest corner.

Answers and Explanations

PAGE 134, PRACTICE

Did you ever wonder how peanut butter is made? **First,** the peanuts are shelled. **Second,** they are sorted for size and value. **Next** (or **Then**), they are roasted. **After** they are cooked, the red outer skin is removed. **Then** (or **Next,**) the nut is split, and the small piece called the "heart" is taken off. The heart makes the peanut butter sour. **Last,** the nuts are mashed. **During** the last step of mashing, workers add honey, sugar, and salt.

PAGE 134, WRITE

Revise and edit your explanation. Use the checklist on page 216. Be sure that the steps are in the correct order and that you have used transition words. Write a final draft. Share your explanation with a partner.

PAGE 135, PRACTICE

Sample answers:
1. You can relax at night by listening to soft jazz and taking a warm bath.
2. You can protect yourself from crime by not walking alone after dark and learning some simple self-defense.
3. I can make my lifestyle healthier by eating low-fat foods and exercising 30 minutes, three times a week.

PAGE 136, PRACTICE

1. how long to soak it
2. It might catch on fire if you don't soak it long enough.

PAGE 136, WRITE

Revise and edit your explanation. Use the checklist on page 216. Be sure that you used precise words and specific details. Write a final draft. Share your explanation with a partner.

PAGE 137, LANGUAGE EXERCISE A

1. future   2. present
3. past   4. past

PAGE 137, LANGUAGE EXERCISE B

1. (1)
2. (1)
3. (2)
4. (4)

PAGE 138, LANGUAGE EXERCISE A

1. Save a room with a bath for the couple.
2. I found a letter that is not mine in the mailbox.
3. **Correct**
4. We bought a cat we call Fluff for my son.

PAGE 138, LANGUAGE EXERCISE B

1. (3)
2. (1)

PAGE 139, LANGUAGE EXERCISE A

1. **Parallel**
2. **Not parallel** Hard workers are intense, motivated, and **careful.**
3. **Parallel**
4. **Not parallel** They like watching football, playing baseball, and **bowling.**

PAGE 139, LANGUAGE EXERCISE B

1. It is good for people to run, swim, and **jog.**
2. Running, for example, helps you stay fit and **healthy.**
3. Swimming can help in toning your muscles and **lowering** your blood pressure.
4. You can start by walking a block a day and **eating** good food.
5. Exercise can help you look better, be stronger, and **become more alert.**

PAGE 143, WRITING AT WORK

1. (4)
2. (2)
3. (5)

1. Handled
2. Operated
3. communities
4. knives
5. taxes
6. workers'
7. people's
8. Charles'
9. I've
10. I wouldn't
11. past
12. future
13. present
14. had been cooking
15. has been
16. written
17. began
18. cost
19. Her uncle was a well-known mexican doctor.
20. He went to work for a texas company called lonestar.
21. Is Mrs. May serving hot dogs, potato salad, and baked beans?
22. Sheila B. Cohn was born on May 25, 1965.
23. Juan saw his motorcycle, broken beyond repair, in the front yard.
24. When I was watching my son, he ran into the street.
25. The meal was cheap, tasty, and **healthy.**
26. I should walk, jog, or **swim** to stay in shape.

Write the first draft of your business letter. Then, revise and edit it using the checklists on pages 216–17. Be sure to state your request clearly. Share your business letter with your instructor or a partner.

PAGES 146–147, MINITEST

1. **(1) change thanksgiving to Thanksgiving** *(Correction: Mechanics: Capitalization)* The names of holidays are capitalized.

2. **(2) If cost is on your mind** *(Revision: Sentence Structure: Modification)* "Keeping cost in mind" is a dangling modifier. The "two tips" can't keep cost in mind.

3. **(1) change Grandmother to grandmother** *(Correction: Mechanics: Capitalization)* Do not capitalize family roles unless they are used along with or in place of a name.

4. **(3) change were to are** *(Correction: Usage: Verb Tense)* The passage as a whole is written in present tense.

5. **(1) insert a comma after home address** *(Correction: Mechanics: Punctuation)* This series has three items, which should be set off with commas.

6. **(5) purchase tickets to attractions** *(Revision: Sentence Structure: Parallelism)* This phrase should start with a verb in order to be parallel with "reserve your accommodations."

7. **(1) move Along your route to the end of the sentence** *(Correction: Sentence Structure: Modification)* This phrase is a misplaced modifier. It should be moved closer to what it modifies, "a campground or motel room."

8. **(3) sentence 8** *(Construction Shift Organization: Dividing Paragraphs)* At this point, the topic of the paragraph changes from making reservations and buying tickets, to information about the Roadside Reference Book. Each paragraph should contain only one main idea. Therefore, you should separate the two ideas into two paragraphs.

UNIT 3: LANGUAGE

LESSON 10

PAGE 150, PRACTICE

1. The meeting between the lawyers of Martello Company and our client will take place on Tuesday, November 1.
2. The client has asked Ms. Robinson to be present at the meeting as well.
3. The first item on the agenda will be to discuss the accusations against Martello Company.
4. *Business Times* magazine has been reporting on the situation for several months now.
5. Our client plans to be at the Hartford Street office by nine o'clock.
6. Many businesses in the United States are interested in this investigation.

PAGE 151, PRACTICE

1. is (collective noun: company)
2. cheers (collective noun: crowd)
3. is (mass noun: water)
4. waits (collective noun: family)
5. seems (mass noun: speed)
6. has (collective noun: group)
7. is (mass noun: time)

Sample answers:

8. My favorite team is the New England Patriots.
9. During a game, the crowd usually gets excited and loud.

PAGE 152, PRACTICE

1. We
2. He
3. We
4. She
5. They

Sample answers:
6. They are nice.
7. We have a lot in common.

PAGE 153, PRACTICE

1. me
2. him
3. us
4. her
5. them

Sample answers:

6. Please listen to me.
7. I don't want the tickets, so I am giving them to you.
8. Our boss gave the tickets to us.

PAGE 154, PRACTICE

1. his
2. His
3. your
4. mine, yours
5. our

Sample answers:

6. Mine is neat. *or* My home is neat.
7. Mine is small. *or* My hometown is small.

PAGE 155, PRACTICE

Circled words:

1. Cities
2. snowstorms
3. newspaper
4. mayor
5. police chief
6. brother

Sample answers:

7. My car had been sitting in the snow for three days, and it was dead.
8. Although he was already late for work, Joe offered to jump-start the car.

PAGE 156, PRACTICE

1. our
2. they
3. she

4. their

5. his

Sample answers:

6. That <u>actress</u> was good in <u>her</u> first movie role.

7. Take the <u>beef or chicken</u> out of the freezer and thaw <u>it</u>.

PAGE 157, PRACTICE

Underlined words:

1. long-ago, skilled

2. Irish, Russian, some, early

3. strong, intelligent

4. German, English, this

5. good, sharp

Sample answers:

6. Cats are independent.

7. Birds can be beautiful but messy.

8. Horses are fast and powerful animals.

9. Rats can be wonderful, clean pets.

10. Elephants have long trunks and curved tusks.

PAGE 158, PRACTICE

Are people <u>ever</u> <u>really</u> happy with their appearance? They must not be, judging by <u>how warmly</u> they greet each new diet. They must want to lose weight <u>very</u> <u>badly</u>. Some people <u>hardly</u> finish one diet before they begin another. My friend had <u>just</u> finished his powdered-drink diet when he <u>quickly</u> started a new diet.

Sample answers:

1. I take care of my children well.

2. I sing badly.

3. I drive carefully.

PAGE 159, PRACTICE

1. harder

2. most crowded

3. more slowly

4. best

PAGE 160, PRACTICE

1. worse

2. carefully

3. best

4. more

Sample answers:

5. My new apartment is far from the laundromat, but my old apartment was farther.

6. My dream last night seemed so real.

PAGE 161, PRACTICE

1. collected

2. collect

3. will collect

Sample answers:

4. As I child, I liked to play checkers.

5. Now I like to play bingo.

6. Next year I hope I will like my new school.

PAGE 162, PRACTICE

1. has suffered

2. had been

3. has gotten

4. will have been

5. has not shown

Sample answers:

6. By next month, I will have lived in this state for ten years.

7. My life has been fairly happy so far.

8. Until last year, I had wanted to get a new job.

9. I have seen that movie three times.

10. When I finish, I will have written a twenty-page report.

PAGE 163, PRACTICE

1. Your application (is being reviewed) <u>currently</u>.

2. The documents (were mailed) at the end of <u>last month</u>.

3. Most people (mailed) their requests <u>last week</u>.

4. Next Monday, the committee (will make) its final decisions.
5. Your task right <u>now</u> (is) to wait patiently for the information.

Sample sentences:

6. My son will be twenty years old in 2008.
7. The minister gave his last sermon in 1990.
8. My grandfather lives in a retirement home now.

PAGE 164, PRACTICE

1. left
2. lost
3. was
4. gone, begun

Sample answers:

5. I have always known that I would go back to school.
6. During the last year, I have done some things to change my life.
7. We ate at the new restaurant last night.

PAGE 165, PRACTICE

1. appears
2. are
3. glow
4. shines
5. is
6. are

Sample answers:

7. Cars clog the roads in my town.
8. The city buses or the train is a better way to go to work.
9. The locks on the door are broken.

PAGE 166, PRACTICE

1. **is** (singular subject: family)
2. **wants** (singular subject: group)
3. **are** (plural subject: decorations)
4. **are** (plural subject: cups)
5. **seem** (plural subject: crumbs)

Sample sentences:

6. Here is the money you asked for.
7. The jury has not reached a verdict yet.

PAGE 167, PRACTICE

1. are
2. has
3. take
4. gives
5. are
6. have

Sample answers:

7. Everyone in my family is going to the reunion.
8. No one in my family has a van.
9. All of my friends are wonderful people.
10. Several of my coworkers have the flu.

LESSON 11

PAGE 168, PRACTICE

1. C
2. F
3. F
4. F
5. F
6. C
7. C

Sample sentences:

8. The minimum driving age in this state is 16.
9. Many drivers simply drive too fast.

PAGE 169, PRACTICE

1. the verb is missing
2. the subject is missing
3. the verb is missing
4. the subject is missing

Sample sentences:

5. My older sister is still living with our parents.
6. She enjoys spending time with them in the evenings.

PAGE 170, PRACTICE

1. RO
2. RO

3. RO
4. RO
5. C
6. RO
7. C
8. C

PAGE 171, PRACTICE

Sample answers:

1. The Special Olympics was started more than 30 years ago; it is a sports competition for people with disabilities. *or* The Special Olympics was started more than 30 years ago. It is a sports competition for people with disabilities.
2. More than 7,000 athletes attend, **and** they come from 150 nations.
3. Each nation competes in nineteen sporting events, **but** athletes do not have to enter every event.
4. Everyone is a winner, **for** each athlete gets a ribbon or a medal.
5. Many people come to watch, **and** they are impressed by the athletes.

Sample answers:

6. I enjoy watching the Olympic Games, and I'm looking forward to seeing the next games on TV.
7. Winning a gold medal must be a thrill. The athletes work so hard for it.

PAGE 172, PRACTICE

1. CS
2. CS
3. S
4. CS
5. S
6. CS

Sample answers:

7. James watches soap operas every day, but his roommate only watches the news.
8. Some soap stars have been on the air for many years, yet others have just started their careers.

PAGE 173, PRACTICE

Sample answers:

1. My first week on the job was a disaster, **and** my boss told me so.
2. I was really upset, **yet** I knew things had to get better. *or* I was really upset, **but** I knew things had to get better.
3. I tried as hard as I could, **for** I really wanted to keep the job.
4. My coworker gave me good advice, **so** I felt more confident.
5. Next week has to be better, **or** I'll think about quitting!

PAGE 174, PRACTICE

1. NP
2. P
3. NP
4. P
5. P
6. NP
7. NP

Sample answers:

8. Three places you can buy food are a grocery store, a snack shop, and a restaurant.
9. When you are sick, you should stay home, drink fluids, and rest.

PAGE 175, PRACTICE

1. Writing helps people think, speak, and **learn.**
2. Those who can write well will be leaders in the community, state, and **nation** in years to come.
3. By writing frequently, reading often, and **seeking** feedback, writers can improve.
4. Learning to write clearly, correctly, and **effectively** is a goal.

Sample answers:

5. I can write letters, messages, and lists.
6. Three qualities of good writing are precise words, vivid details, and correct grammar.

Answers and Explanations

PAGE 176, PRACTICE

Underlined clauses:

1. <u>Although I have a car</u>, I usually take the bus.
2. I prefer the bus <u>because I care about the environment</u>.
3. <u>If we don't help to reduce pollution</u>, the problem will only get worse.
4. Let's act <u>before it's too late</u>.

Sample answer:

Walk one block south on Andrews until you get to Anchor Lane. Turn right on Anchor. Continue west on Anchor, crossing Hyridge and Mesa. Keep walking until you get to Washington. Turn right and walk one block to the community swimming pool. If you keep going straight on Anchor, there is an easy shortcut. If you cut through the first parking lot on your right, you'll see the pool. You can't miss it!

PAGE 177, PRACTICE

Sample answers:

1. **After** I went to bed, I heard a loud crash in the kitchen.
2. **Because** I was afraid, I pulled the blankets over my head.
3. **After** I heard the cat's meow, I finally got up.
4. **Once** I saw the cat sitting by the broken plate, I knew what had happened.

Sample answers:

5. I went to get a broom so that I could clean up the mess.
6. I didn't get very much sleep that night because my nerves were still on edge.

PAGE 178, PRACTICE

1. M
2. C
3. M
4. C
5. C
6. M
7. M
8. C
9. M

Sample answer:

One night a tremendous windstorm ripped through our town. All night long the wind howled around our house. At one point I heard a crunching sound, followed by a loud snap. The next morning we found our small pussy willow tree uprooted, lying across our garden.

PAGE 179, PRACTICE

Sample answers:

1. While I was passing a large rock, a clap of thunder made me scream.
2. Sailing up the harbor, we saw the boat. *or* We saw the boat sailing up the harbor.
3. As we flew over the town, the cars and houses looked like toys.
4. While I was putting the chair together, I lost the screw.
5. When I opened the jar, the sauce spilled all over the floor.
6. As he was walking up the steps, the packages fell.

Sample answers:

7. Going to my class, I met an old friend.
8. Angry at her husband, the woman stormed out of the house.
9. Already hungry, the dog sat by his empty food bowl.
10. Without thinking, I left the garage door up.

PAGE 180, PRACTICE

Sample answers:

1. The baseball game took place on Saturday at 3 P.M.
2. When the game started, the players relaxed.
3. The pitcher did not know who to throw the ball to. *or, more formal language,* The pitcher did not know to whom to throw the ball.
4. After each inning, they repeated their signals.

5. The game ended with a home run with the bases loaded. *or* The game ended with a grand slam home run.

6. No one knows where the next game will be held.

Sample answer:

Solitaire is a card game I can happily spend hours playing. This game has two advantages over the other games I play. First, solitaire is played by one person, so I don't need partners to play. Also solitaire has many versions. Some are simple games using only one deck of cards. Other versions are complicated and require two decks. The more complex games can continue for a long time. Maybe that's why solitaire is also called "Patience."

PAGE 181, PRACTICE

1. W
2. C
3. W
4. C
5. W
6. W
7. C
8. W

PAGE 182, PRACTICE

1. b
   Some people rely on garage sales to buy the things they need inexpensively.

2. a
   People enjoy going to garage sales to browse and haggle.

3. Sample reconstruction: You can probably find in your own home things you don't need or just don't want anymore.

PAGE 183, PRACTICE

1. a
   I make an award-winning bread using a special recipe handed down by my great-grandmother.

2. b
   I'd like my request to be considered with care and respect.

3. Sample combination: The witness said last Sunday's accident involved a red sports car and a bike.

LESSON 12

PAGE 184, PRACTICE

1. ?
2. .
3. .
4. !
5. .
6. ?
7. .
8. ! *or* .

Sample sentences:

9. My boyfriend never watches soap operas.
10. Have you ever watched the soap opera *All My Children?*
11. I just love it!

PAGE 185, PRACTICE

1. My aunt was born on January 13, 1960.
2. She grew up in Toledo, but she and her family moved to Los Angeles in 1975.
3. She is a store manager, a swimmer, and a mother of two.

Sample answers:

4. My son was born on June 15, 1998.
5. My son's eyes are dark brown, and his hair is shiny black.

PAGE 186, PRACTICE

1. Because new businesses are coming to this area, we need new zoning laws.
2. We will handle this legally, of course, by going to the zoning board.
3. The Huitts will talk to the newspaper, while Mr. Ortiz handles the petitions.
4. We expect to get some good coverage from WCRB, the local news station.

5. The developers, however, will put up a good fight.

Sample sentences

6. My friend Gloria, my exercise partner, is visiting family in Mexico.

7. I like, for example, seafood or pasta.

PAGE 187, PRACTICE

harriet quimby was the first woman to earn a pilot's license. she was a writer in new york before she flew a plane. she fell in love with airplanes in 1910 when she saw her first flying meet. harriet became a pilot and toured in mexico with a troupe of pilots. she decided she would be the first woman to cross the english channel. she took off on april 16, 1912, sitting on a wicker basket in the cockpit. after a scary flight, she landed on a french beach.

Sample answers:

1. I live in (name of city capitalized), (name of state capitalized).

2. I like to shop at (store name capitalized), (store name capitalized), and (store name capitalized).

PAGE 188, PRACTICE

1. writer ed j. smith reports that people are taking cheaper trips in the Summer.

2. mr. and mrs. mott drove to orlando, florida, and went camping.

3. last year, the Motts went to sea world.

4. this year, dr. ortega and his family went hiking instead of going to mt. rushmore in south dakota.

5. ms. wills visited her friend in Wisconsin rather than flying to the Island of st. kitts.

6. miss e. k. link from new town, long island, spent two days in maine.

7. she went to lake mead last year.

8. busch gardens in tampa, florida, is still very busy, though.

9. My Doctor wants to go to israel and see the dead sea.

Sample answers:

10. My dentist is Dr. Lou Graham.

11. I would love to go to Jamaica.

12. I was born in Mexico.

PAGE 189, PRACTICE

1. This year, monday, january 18, dr. martin luther king, jr. day will be a paid holiday.

2. This holiday is in the place of columbus day, which we took as a day off on october 10.

3. The plant will, of course, be closed for the usual Fall and Winter holidays— thanksgiving, christmas, and new year's.

4. If any of these holidays fall on a monday or a friday, you will have a long weekend.

5. This year the Company's independence Day picnic will be on sunday, july 7.

6. I will be back at work on Tuesday, september 6, the day after labor day.

7. Some people want to have the party on Flag day, june 14, instead.

8. There has also been talk of a halloween party for october 31, which is a thursday this year.

9. We could hold the party on friday, october 25, if that is a better time.

Sample answers:

10. My favorite holidays are Thanksgiving and Valentine's Day.

11. The best day of the week for me is Sunday.

12. My favorite season is spring.

PAGE 190, PRACTICE

1. wives, days
2. nephews, cousins
3. children
4. peaches
5. teeth
6. memories, visits

Sample answers (compare your spelling of the plurals with the underlined words):

7. My two favorite **celebrities** are (names of two famous people).
8. In our class, there are seven **men.**
9. My refrigerator has three **shelves.**

PAGE 191, PRACTICE

1. Tran's
2. children's
3. friends'
4. factory's
5. bodies

Sample answers:

6. My friends' favorite activity is bowling on their league team.
7. My boss' favorite activity is working!
8. My mother's favorite activity is reading.

PAGE 192, PRACTICE

1. who's
2. I've
3. wasn't
4. weren't
5. didn't

Sample answers:

6. I **can't** dance the tango.
7. I **won't** answer the phone at night.

PAGE 193, PRACTICE

1. their
2. It's
3. they're
4. You're
5. Who's
6. it's
7. their
8. They're
9. you're
10. Whose

Some people are always complaining about **their** jobs. **They're** always talking about the things they don't like about **their** work.

PAGE 194, PRACTICE

1. week
2. fair
3. capital
4. aisles
5. know
6. lessen
7. close
8. whole

Sample answers:

9. I accept your apology.
10. He tried to brake the car in time, but couldn't.

PAGE 195, PRACTICE

1. chief
2. succeed, seize
3. heir
4. Their
5. hopeful, powerful
6. successful
7. achieve

PAGE 196, PRACTICE

1. getting
2. delayed
3. paid
4. submitting, writing

Sample answers:

5. My husband **carried** the groceries into the house.
6. I am just **beginning** to study for the GED test.

PAGE 197, PRACTICE

1. who
2. good

3. well
4. among
5. which

Sample answers:

6. I don't have much money.
7. I have very few pictures of myself.

LESSON 13

PAGE 198, PRACTICE

1. The Edgebrook Neighborhood Association will meet Thursday to discuss the upcoming community awards lunch.
2. These days, baking is a lot easier than you might think.

PAGE 199, PRACTICE

1. **a**
   I am writing to express my outrage over the picture in yesterday's newspaper.
2. **b**
   This class will focus on cultures—both our own and others.

PAGE 201, PRACTICE

1. The sentence *It is being held in the evening so that those who work during the day will also be able to attend* should be the second sentence in the paragraph.
2. The sentence *However, it will be tough to fill his shoes* should be the last sentence in the paragraph.
3. The sentence *Finally, make sure the release lever has returned to the locked position* should be the last sentence of the paragraph.
4. The sentence *Please let me know what to do* should be the last sentence in the paragraph.

PAGES 202–203, PRACTICE

The following irrelevant sentences should be crossed out:

1. The Star Market requires a year of experience before you can be hired there.

2. My co-worker's son just got a scholarship to the state university, so he will likely have a well-paid career ahead of him.
3. We all know that disappointment is a part of life.
4. In my experience, spreading rumors only gets you into trouble.
5. We bought all of our lighting fixtures at Purple Sun, so they are quite expensive.

PAGE 205, PRACTICE

1. Begin a new paragraph with the sentence *We'd also like to thank the seniors themselves for their patience as the project got underway.*
2. This paragraph should not be divided because it is about one main idea.
3. Begin a new paragraph with the sentence *The other way to get into and around the building is to use the keypad to the right of each door entrance.*
4. This paragraph should not be divided because it is about one main idea.

PAGES 206–207, PRACTICE

1. B and C
2. A and B
3. B and C

PAGE 209, WRITING AT WORK

1. Joe asked Bev not to water the cacti.
2. Plant food fertilizer helps plants produce more flowers.
3. Sample answer:

Kevin,

I need you to take the car to Sam's Garage before you go to work. Since we are going on our family vacation next week, I want to be sure that the car is in good shape for the drive.

1. Get the oil changed.
2. Get the tires' pressure and tread checked. If Sam says we need to replace one or more tires, go ahead and have him do it.

3. Check the radiator fluid. If it is low, have Sam put more in.

Thanks,

Dad

PAGES 210–213, UNIT 3 REVIEW

1. They
2. its
3. their
4. him

Sample answers:

5. The apartment on the fourth floor is vacant.
6. S
7. Thinking about it on the way home from work, he decided to take it.

Sample sentences:

8. Jen likes to walk her dog at night **after** she gets home from work.
9. It's also pleasant in the morning **before** it gets too hot.
10. Her husband thinks she's a little silly **because** she treats her dog like a person.
11. Craig has an unusual job. He is a chef.
12. He used to work in a store. He was a cashier.
13. Then he went to cooking school for two years. It was a long program.
14. fine
15. seriously
16. quickly
17. confident
18. best
19. most expensive
20. farther
21. worse
22. was watching
23. got
24. has been working
25. will have lived
26. had been trying
27. Rob went to New York in September to visit his uncle.
28. Because it was autumn, sights like the Statue of Liberty weren't crowded.
29. On Labor Day, Rob walked through Central Park and up Fifth Avenue.
30. He ate French food and saw a game at Yankee Stadium.
31. My husband and I were married on June 15, 1999.
32. The wedding took place in Chicago, Illinois.
33. His brothers Edward, Hal, John, and Joe attended the wedding.
34. You wouldn't believe the crazy toasts they made!
35. The wedding was beautiful, and all the guests had a good time.
36. Do you know where we went on our honeymoon?
37. We went to Atlantic City, Niagara Falls, and New York City.
38. seen
39. knew
40. broke
41. fought
42. gave
43. begun
44. clothes
45. fare
46. accept
47. week
48. lesson

PAGES 214-215, MINITEST

1. (4) **insert a comma after instruction** *(Correction: Mechanics: Punctuation)* Commas should separate the three items in a series.
2. (2) **form if you** *(Revision: Sentence Structure: Fragment)* Fix the fragment by joining it to the sentence that comes before it. In the new sentence, the dependent clause comes after the independent clause, so no comma is necessary.

3. **(1) replace You're with Your** *(Correction: Mechanics: Spelling)* The contraction *You're* means *You are* and does not make sense in this sentence. The possessive pronoun is correct.

4. **(3) change was given to will be given** *(Correction: Usage: Verb Tense)* The entire passage is about something that could be done in the future. Also, the clue phrase *at the end of the course* tells you that the future tense is needed here.

5. **(3) replace I with me** *(Correction: Usage: Pronouns)* The object pronoun *me* is correct, not the subject pronoun *I*.

6. **(5) is** *(Revision: Usage: Subject-Verb Agreement)* The subject of the sentence is *each*, a singular noun. Therefore, *is* is the correct verb. Since the entire passage is in the present, the verb must be in the present tense.

7. **(1) As you know, this company recognizes** *(Construction Shift: Sentence Structure: Wordiness)* Improve this sentence by taking out the wordiness and using the active voice.

8. **(4) remove sentence 6** *(Construction Shift: Organization: Irrelevant Detail)* A sentence about where the managers live is not relevant to this document and should be removed.

POSTTEST

PAGE 220

1. **(5) change is to are** *(Correction: Usage: Subject-Verb Agreement)* The verb must agree with the subject *options*, which is plural.

2. **(2) remove sentence 5** *(Construction Shift: Organization: Irrelevant Detail)* This sentence does not relate to the overall topic of the memo, so it should be removed.

3. **(3) Be sure to note one** *(Revision: Sentence Structure: Fragment)* The

original sentence is a fragment. The revision supplies a subject (the understood *you*) and a complete verb.

4. **(3) insert a comma after shop** *(Correction: Mechanics: Punctuation)* A comma is needed after each item in a series.

PAGE 221

5. **(5) is** *(Revision: Usage: Verb Tense)* The paragraph as a whole is in the present tense, so the verb in this sentence should be too.

6. **(1) replace However with When** *(Correction: Sentence Structure: Subordination)* *However* is not the appropriate connecting word to use here. The subordinating conjunction *When* makes the meaning of the sentence clearer.

7. **(3) change Company to company** *(Correction: Mechanics: Capitalization)* Because the specific name of the company is not used here, the word should not be capitalized.

8. **(1) replace Their with They're** *(Correction: Mechanics: Spelling)* If you substitute *They are* in the sentence, it makes sense, so the contraction is correct.

9. **(3) begin a new paragraph with sentence 9** *(Construction Shift: Organization: Dividing Paragraphs)* There is a shift in the main idea, beginning with sentence 9, so a new paragraph is needed here.

PAGE 222

10. **(2) questions, and you** *(Revision: Sentence Structure: Run-on)* These two independent clauses should be separated by a comma and a coordinating conjunction.

11. **(4) combine paragraphs B and C** *(Construction Shift: Organization: Combining Paragraphs)* Sentence 6 clearly continues the same thought as

sentence 5, so there should not be a paragraph break between them.

12. **(1) insert a comma after feel** *(Correction: Mechanics: Punctuation)* A comma is needed after the introductory dependent clause.

13. **(4) change working to work** *(Correction: Sentence Structure: Parallelism)* The list of actions should be in parallel structure: *learn, solve,* and *work*.

PAGE 223

14. **(4) change november to November** *(Correction: Mechanics: Capitalization)* The names of months are always capitalized.

15. **(1) Voter turnout is influenced by many factors.** *(Construction Shift: Organization: Topic Sentence)* Paragraph B needs a topic sentence. Option (1) is broad enough to introduce the whole paragraph.

16. **(3) matter, so they** *(Revision: Sentence Structure: Coordination)* The sentence contains two independent clauses. The most meaningful conjunction to join these clauses is *so,* and a comma is needed as well. The conjunction *and* is not needed.

17. **(5) voters** *(Revision: Usage: Pronouns)* It's not clear enough what the pronoun *them* refers to in this sentence. In the context of the passage, *voters* makes the most sense.

PAGE 224

18. **(2) Our security guard must walk long distances around a large area** *(Revision: Sentence Structure: Modification)* The phrase *Around a large area* is misplaced. It needs to follow the word it modifies, *distances*.

19. **(5) change was to is** *(Correction: Usage: Verb Tense)* This paragraph is written in the present tense, as is the first part of the sentence. It describes the current situation with building security.

20. **(3) If we make the entrance more secure, we** *(Construction Shift: Sentence Structure: Subordination)* The complete new sentence would read, *If we make the entrance more secure, we will not need to hire an additional guard.*

21. **(4) change I to me** *(Correction: Usage: Pronouns)* Read the sentence without *you and* to test which pronoun is correct: *Mr. Torres Martin, an engineer in this firm, will be meeting with me next week.*

PAGE 225

22. **(4) replace you're with your** *(Correction: Mechanics: Spelling)* Try reading the sentence with *you are* instead of *you're*. It doesn't make sense, so the contraction must be incorrect.

23. **(1) change Him to He** *(Correction: Usage: Pronouns)* Read the sentence without *and I* to test which pronoun is correct: *He saw Spiderwoman Lives.*

24. **(3) replace you with they** *(Correction: Usage: Pronouns)* The pronoun refers to *people*.

25. **(2) are** *(Revision: Usage: Subject-Verb Agreement)* The verb must agree with the subject *expressions,* which is plural.

active voice a style of writing in which the subject of the sentence performs the action

adjective a word that modifies, or helps describe, a noun or a pronoun. A **proper adjective** is made from a proper noun.

adverb a word that modifies a verb, an adjective, or another adverb

antecedent the noun to which a pronoun refers

antonym a word that has the opposite meaning of another word

apostrophe a mark of punctuation (') used to show possession or a contraction

audience the person or persons for whom you are writing

body the middle paragraphs of an essay, which develop and support the main idea; the contents or message of a letter

brainstorm to generate ideas about a topic by listing everything you can think of about it

business letter a formal letter written to a company, an organization, or a person who works for a company or organization

cause and effect a way of organizing details showing how one thing (the **cause**) makes another thing (the **effect**) happen

clause a group of words with its own subject and predicate. An **independent clause** can stand alone as a sentence; it is a complete thought. A **dependent clause** cannot stand alone as a sentence because it is not a complete thought.

closing a parting phrase in a letter

comparative form the form of an adjective or adverb when comparing two things

compare to show how things are the same

complex sentence a sentence with an independent clause and a dependent clause

compound sentence a sentence with two or more independent clauses, or complete thoughts

compound subject the subject of a sentence consisting of two or more nouns or pronouns joined by *and, or,* or *nor*

conclusion the last paragraph of an essay, which signals the end and highlights the points the reader should remember

construction shift GED-style questions that test your ability to change sentences or paragraphs to make writing clearer and more organized

contraction a word formed by joining two other words, using an apostrophe (') to show where a letter or letters have been left out

contrast to show how things are not the same

coordinating conjunction a connecting word that may be used with a comma to join two independent clauses, or complete thoughts, in a compound sentence

descriptive writing writing that describes a person, place, or thing

direct object the noun or pronoun that receives the action of the verb in a sentence

edit to check the content, style, and grammar of a piece of writing

explanatory writing writing that explains or instructs, such as how to do something

expository writing writing that informs or explains a complicated idea to make it easier to understand

fact a statement that can be proved true

figurative language words that describe one thing by comparing it to something very different; language that is not meant to be literal

final draft the final version of a piece of writing, prepared after editing and revising

first draft the first version of a piece of writing

form a printed document with spaces for filling in information. Common forms are **order forms, invoices, shipping forms,** and **job application forms.**

format the way the parts of a letter or any type of written material are set up on the page

gerund an *-ing* form of a verb that acts like a noun

homonym a word that sounds like another word but is spelled differently and has a different meaning

idea map a way of organizing ideas by putting them in groups that are related

indirect object the noun or pronoun that tells to whom or for whom an action is done in a sentence

inside address the name and address of the company being written to, written near the top of a letter

irrelevant idea an idea that does not support the main idea of a paragraph

letterhead stationery, or writing paper, that has a company name and address printed at the top

literal language words that describe exactly how something looks, tastes, feels, smells, and sounds

main idea the main point of a piece of writing

memo a memorandum; a short, written workplace message

modifier a descriptive word or phrase. A **misplaced modifier** is one that is in the wrong place in a sentence. A **dangling modifier** is one that does not modify a word in the sentence.

narrative writing a form of writing in which you tell a story about yourself or someone else

noun a word that names a person, place, or thing. A **common noun** names a person, place, or thing. A **proper noun** names a specific person, place, or thing. A **collective noun** refers to a group of people or things as a single unit. A **mass noun** names a quality or thing that cannot be counted.

object of a preposition the noun or pronoun that follows a preposition such as *in* or *from* in a sentence

opinion a belief that cannot always be proved

order of importance a way of organizing ideas from the most important to the least important or from the least important to the most important

outline a way of organizing ideas by putting them in numbered and lettered lists

parallel structure words or phrases that are in the same form

passive voice a style of writing in which the action of the sentence is performed upon the subject

personal data sheet a listing of personal information that is useful in job-search writing

personal letter an informal letter written to someone you know well

personal narrative narrative writing about yourself

persuasive writing writing that shows readers why they should agree with a certain side of an issue or why they should take a certain action

plural a form of a word that shows more than one

point of view the perspective from which a piece of writing is written. The point of view may be **first person, second person, or third person.**

possessive the form of a noun or pronoun that shows something is owned and to whom it belongs

predicate the part of a sentence that tells what the subject does or is, or what is being done to the subject. The **complete predicate** may be one or more words.

prewriting planning before you begin to write. It includes defining your topic, generating ideas about it, and organizing those ideas.

pronoun a word that can take the place of a noun in a sentence. A **subject pronoun** can act as the subject of a sentence. An **object pronoun** is used as the object of a verb or preposition.

publishing sharing your final draft with your audience

punctuation the set of symbols used in writing to guide the reader

purpose your reason for writing—for example, to tell a story, to describe, to explain, or to persuade

resume a written summary of your qualifications for work

return address the writer's address, written at the top of a letter

revise to change writing in order to improve or correct it

run-on sentence two or more independent clauses, or complete thoughts, that are not correctly separated by punctuation

salutation an opening greeting in a letter

sensory detail words that help the reader see, hear, smell, taste, or feel

sentence a group of words that expresses a complete thought

sentence fragment a group of words that does not express a complete thought

subject the person or thing that a sentence is about. The **complete subject** may be one or more words.

subordinating conjunction a connecting word used before a dependent clause to connect it to an independent clause

superlative form the form of an adjective or adverb when comparing three or more things

supporting detail a sentence in a paragraph or essay that tells something about the main idea. Also called **supporting sentence.**

synonym a word that has nearly the same meaning as another word

tense the form of a verb that shows time, or when an action takes place. **Simple tenses** show past, present, and future actions. **Perfect tenses** show actions that have ended or that will end soon.

time order a way of organizing events in the order in which they happened; sequence

topic sentence a statement of the main idea that will be developed in a paragraph

transition word a connecting word that signals the way ideas are related

verb a word that shows action or state of being. Verbs have four basic forms, or **principal parts.** A **regular verb** forms the past and past participle by adding *-ed*. An **irregular verb** does not follow this pattern. A **helping verb** is a form of the verb *be* or *have* that is used with another verb to form its present or past participle.

voice the form of a verb that helps show how an action happens. With the **active voice,** the subject of the sentence does the action. With the **passive voice,** the subject of the sentence is acted upon.

writing portfolio a special folder or notebook that contains your best pieces of writing

writing style the way you choose words and sentences to express yourself. You may use a formal or informal style depending on your purpose and audience.